Vizzini: *The Secret Lives of America's Most Successful Undercover Agent*

Vizzini: *The Secret Lives of America's Most Successful Undercover Agent*

by Sal Vizzini
with OSCAR FRALEY
and MARSHALL SMITH

ARBOR HOUSE
NEW YORK

Library of Congress Catalog Card Number: 77-184886

ISBN: 0-87795-050-4

Manufactured in the United States of America

To my mother, whose memory
still inspires me

Contents

Foreword

I KNOW Sal Vizzini both as a friend and one of the most effective undercover agents the Bureau ever had. If it meant making a case, he would grow a tail and dance with the devil. In fact, he did it many times in suppressing the flow of narcotics in the United States and abroad. At his job, he was an ingenious, no-limit professional. His undercover exploits would fill two volumes.

—HARRY J. ANSLINGER
former Commissioner of Narcotics

Author's Note

I COULD end up dead by writing this book.

I'm not being melodramatic.

Against all the rules of undercover work, I'm "putting myself in the window." I'm putting myself on display. I'm revealing my true identity.

Many agents have been killed because their identity was revealed. They died by knife, gun and garrotte. One was thrown out of a window in Mexico. There's a long roster of underworld characters out there, in prison and wandering loose, who accepted me as one of their own.

For thirteen years as an undercover agent for the Federal Bureau of Narcotics, and sometimes for other government agencies and on loan to various foreign governments, all that kept me alive was the anonymity of assumed names and fabricated covers.

I was an infiltrator.

I joined the criminals, in one guise or another, to obtain the information that would put them out of business. Blow your cover and you risk becoming an instant corpse.

11

These were the years in which I became an intimate of Charlie "Lucky" Luciano (real name Salvatore Lucania), tracing his continuing connection with the narcotics racket and gangland activities in the United States. I infiltrated a heroin factory in Sicily, became the prison cellmate of a mobster dealing in stolen stocks and bonds, made countless "buys" as a pseudo pusher in searching out the kingpins of the international narcotics trade and set up a hit on one of the world's most artful counterfeiters.

It was a masquerade that took me from New York to Cuba, Puerto Rico, Turkey, Lebanon, France, Sicily, Italy, Thailand and to a tiny southeast Asian country, bordering on Thailand, I'll call "Mongo" in a real place called Shan Province. Many of the names of the hoods, mobsters, pushers, counterfeiters, killers and thieves in this book are real, taken from my official reports in government files stamped "Secret." Some have been changed. The people are real.

"Mongo" is necessary, from my viewpoint. The reason is that I blew up the largest single concentration of hard drugs ever assembled under one roof—a heroin factory containing some forty tons of opium and heroin. Some people may have gone up in that blast. I can't be sure because I didn't wait around to watch. The diplomatic situation being what it is, I still could become a sacrificial goat for that one. The fact that I did it under orders might not be enough to keep someone there from demanding my arrest and extradition and, in the interests of international politics, might not prevent someone here from going along with the deal.

Possibly you recoil from such an act. Not I. They deserved it; they were preparing the living death that would be sold right on the corner of the block you live in, maybe to your kid or your neighbor's child. Rules mean nothing in cases like that, and to me it was a personal as well as a professional vendetta.

I played a lot of roles during those years. I posed as a Turkish engineer, an Italian assistant consul, a U.S. Air Force major, a New York gangster, a pool hustler, a convicted bank robber, a commercial pilot flying dynamite and a croupier in a San Juan gambling casino.

I switched identities so often that sometimes I needed a score card to figure out who I really was and was supposed to be.

I lived under a dozen names in cities stretching from Istanbul to Bangkok, and from Marseilles to Miami. I became quite attached to some of them. The one I liked most was Pasquale Lombardi. He got to be almost my other self—I put a few people out of circulation in Palermo, Havana and New York City posing as Pasquale Lombardi. I was also known as James Patrick Larkin, Vincent Vento, Ismet Kural, Theodore Warner, Tony Tivoli and Michael Anthony Cerra.

I was well prepared for the work I did. I am of Sicilian descent, and that gave me an edge dealing with Sicilian members of the Mafia. It also made me realize the hard way, once I got into the business, that the world is quick to paint all Sicilians with the same dirty brush. So by striking at the Mafia, I felt that I was striking at a few bad apples who gave millions of decent, law-abiding people a bad name.

They say Turks are tough. But Sicilians are tougher. And I guess I was tougher than most. I grew up over a pool room in Pittsburgh's rough East Liberty section and cut my teeth on a pool cue. I later moved to the North Broadway section of Chicago, another neighborhood where it is more blessed to give than to receive —to give it to the other guy before he gives it to you. A baseball bat against a guy's head earned instant respect.

I used my fists, too. As a kid, when other guys were talking about owning a car and knocking off the corner candy store to finance it, I was working out in CYO gyms. My idol was Tippy Larkin, the welterweight, and I actually sparred with him one day. Got my head knocked off.

At seventeen I joined the Marines and became expert in karate, knife-fighting and marksmanship. They not only came in handy during World War II on those South Pacific islands and later in running down Japanese war criminals, but also in the undercover years that lay ahead. My I.D. card said I stood six-feet-two, weighed 190 pounds, had blue eyes, brown hair.

More important, probably, was my ear for languages. Sicilian and Italian were my natural heritage. At the Marine Corps Language School at Camp LeJeune I also became fluent in Japanese. Later, I picked up two Chinese dialects—Mandarin and Cantonese —while serving in China, and had no trouble mastering Spanish. While working undercover in Turkey, I made Turkish my sixth language.

Those early years ingrained in me an irresistible taste for action. A post-war period as an investigator for the Air Force Provost Marshal temporarily satisfied this craving, until the time I worked on a case involving forged government checks with a Secret Service agent named Rufus Youngblood. This is the agent who later threw himself protectively across then Vice President Lyndon B. Johnson during the Kennedy assassination in Dallas. Youngblood influenced me to take the Treasury Department examination, and then I was sent to the Treasury Department School in Washington for several months.

But you don't sit in a classroom and read books and then go out in a jungle and expect to survive. Dope peddlers in the hills of Turkey, and in New York City, don't read books. They're predators, and they learned by doing. When you go undercover you become one of them. You think like they do. You talk like they do. You give the professional responses. And you stay cool.

If you want to stay cool, or give the impression of staying cool, the less you say the better. You don't over-explain. When they try to put you on the defense, you turn it around and put them on defense. This is what keeps you alive and makes cases for you. More important, it keeps you from getting lumps.

I've taken some. Give some guy a story and boom—he decks you. You don't get up and say, "Don't hit me again. I'm a federal agent." You make an on the spot decision that might take the Supreme Court a year. If the case is important enough, maybe you stay on the deck and say, "Listen, fellow, maybe you're not so smart. I'm here to do business and I represent an organization. You'll probably be hearing about this one way or another. That's not for me to decide."

At least you might get him thinking. Who the hell did I hit? Did I hit Frank Costello's son, or his nephew? It worked that way for me once down in Little Italy on New York's lower East Side. The guy turned right around, we did business, I put him in jail.

I joined the Bureau of Narcotics in 1953 and left in 1966. Sometimes I wonder why I stayed so long. It wasn't for the $3,100 a year I made as a junior agent or the $16,000 I received as a Grade-12 senior. I earn more than that now as Police Chief for the City of South Miami, Florida, and with far less danger.

You're always aware of imminent danger as an undercover agent. It's part of the job, routine as a morning cup of coffee. But you don't think about it. You never worry as much about getting killed as not getting the job done. It's like one of the big race drivers once said, "You're afraid of losing, not dying."

It keeps you going. I've been scared. Anybody who hasn't been scared on this job is either a damned fool or hasn't been around long, and won't be. Fortunately, I get the chills after it's all over. Like the time a Turkish opium peddler put a gun in my stomach and pulled the trigger—and it misfired. I wasn't scared at the moment. I chopped him in the throat and put him down. But later back in my room I was terrified. I broke out with a skin rash and a cold sweat. I couldn't get off the bed for twelve hours.

I guess one of the most important things that kept me going was pride, starting with this thing I had about being a Sicilian. I was proud of my badge. I was proud of the Special Service awards from the Bureau and the commendations I got from Secret Service and several foreign governments. And there was the knowledge that I was combating the greatest evil in the world today, a nightmare horrible beyond all comprehension. I'm speaking of drugs —mainly heroin, and the opium and morphine-base that it comes from. The big guys I was after would nail to the cross anyone who even suggested that their kids smoked marijuana. Yet they kept peddling "living death" to addicts around the world, and especially in the United States.

I thought the figures were bad when I was with the Bureau. Ten years ago there were 60,000 known addicts in the United States. Now the figure has soared to more than a quarter of a million. And that's hardly all of it. Consider the fact that the strung-out addict needs from $75 to $100 a day to keep the habit going. Where do they get the money? They get it by turning to prostitution, mugging, armed robbery and stripping private dwellings, apartments, and offices. You don't have to be rich to be a mark. Just vulnerable.

Somewhere addicts have to get about $4½ billion a year. And because stolen goods are fenced at a fraction of real value, about $12 billion worth of goods must be and is stolen annually.

The drug habit is at the root of perhaps 85 percent of all the serious crimes committed in this country today. Many of the killings, especially of police officers, are attributable to drugs. And the sharp rise in crime is reflected by the rise in the number of addicts.

You don't have to be a boy scout—and God knows I'm not—to want to go to war against it. There are many agents out there doing just that. They're taking their chances and many will be seriously hurt, if not killed. In my years as an agent I was shot three times, knifed twice, beaten nearly to death and had several contracts put out on me.

This book is meant to give some insight into the world of under-cover.

It puts nobody in the window but myself.

—Sal Vizzini

Vizzini: *The Secret Lives of America's Most Successful Undercover Agent*

A Vendetta Begins...

HEROIN HAS many easily detected effects on the user. One of the most obvious is that the drug contracts the pupils of the eyes almost to a pinpoint. As a result of using the drug, addicts experience very little need for food, the habit killing off their hunger, but they do have a continual craving for sweets. They also do a great deal of yawning, which is called "yapping."

These are some of the tip-offs a narcotics agent looks for when he is hitting pads and breaking down doors in his search for sources, informants or addicts.

He looks for other things, also, which are signposts in his business. If a house is habitually cluttered and there is no solid food around except for fruit, it is cause for suspicion. Addicts go for anything which loosens the bowels because the drug constipates them.

You learn to keep your eyes open for a bent spoon with a burnt mark on the bottom, or the innocent-seeming cap from a soda bottle which has that same burned mark, or an eye-dropper with a needle attached, or a nipple from a baby's nursing bottle. These are all standard items of equipment for the strung-out junkie.

But if you are serious about your job, it is necessary to go beyond these tangible bits or ordinary evidence. To function properly, you have to know every move a junkie makes from the time he gets out his "works" until the moment he goes "on the nod." You've got to know everything a junkie knows, and everything a junkie feels, without getting on the stuff yourself.

Sometimes, when you're working undercover, you have to act the part of a junkie—and you don't learn to be convincing sitting in a classroom listening to lectures. You learn out in the savage precincts of the concrete jungle and there's no better teacher than a strung-out junkie. It's actually the only valid way to really know what it's all about.

I got my first lesson sitting eyeball-to-eyeball with one in a second-rate motel in Andalusia, Alabama.

Technically I was breaking the law. The Bureau has rules against an agent helping or watching an addict shoot up. There are some moralists who would contend, I suppose, that I was putting myself in the same category with a voyeur or a Peeping Tom. But this was an occasion when I was given the opportunity, and I had a compelling need to know, to arm myself with knowledge that would help me become more effective in my job—at the time this happened I was a relatively inexperienced agent.

My opportunity came when I was put in charge of a man named Arthur Bee, a strung-out junkie who had turned stoolie. Unless I gave him money for a fix, he would quickly sink into his own private hell. He needed a quarter-grain of morphine every four hours to stay well enough to work. He depended on me. I could cut off his supply.

The reason I owned Arthur Bee was that the supervisor at the Bureau had given him to me. Just like that. The Bureau had him under the hammer. He was "working off heat," which is another way of saying that he had been arrested on a narcotics charge and had turned informant to keep himself out of jail. Most junkies will do that if they have a choice. The mere thought of being locked up away from their source of supply is too much for them to handle.

This had happened some years before to Waxey Gordon, a big man in the mob who had gotten on junk and needed a quarter ounce of heroin a day. The day they arrested him, he got down on his hands and knees and begged agent Joe Ferro to shoot him right then and there.

I met Arthur Bee at headquarters in Atlanta after he had agreed to introduce an undercover agent to his sources. He wasn't the sort of traveling companion you'd pick even if you had maybe only two choices. He had watery eyes and a pasty complexion. He was small and skinny, about forty, and had a habit of constantly combing his hair with a dirty, dime-store comb which only had about six teeth left in it.

Arthur Bee was about as worn-out as his comb. He knew me only as Jimmy Patrick, an undercover agent playing the role of a pool hustler. That was all he needed to know, except for the details of his job.

We had it set up that, with Arthur Bee in tow, I would go on a tour of small towns in Georgia and Alabama where we had learned there was a network of pushers. It would be Arthur's job to set up buys at every stop on our itinerary and then introduce me to his sources. It had promised to be a productive trip and, as it developed, we were far from disappointed. I made arrests in Columbus, Georgia, and in Phoenix City and Anniston, Alabama.

After cleaning up those areas, at least for the time being, we went in our two-toned 1952 Chevy to Andalusia, Alabama. There we checked into the Andalusia Motor Court.

According to our information the boss supplier for the whole area was a local doctor who was selling morphine illegally. The doctor's name was Mot Morris, and he was working with a local hoodlum named Dink Henderson.

They were my targets.

Arthur Bee was in bad shape when we pulled into Andalusia. His eyes were watering more than usual and his nose was beginning to run, causing him to sniffle constantly, two signs of an addict in a bad way for a fix. He had used his last pill the night before and his complaints about how sick he felt became ever louder and more frequent. He wouldn't have had to tell me. There was little question about how much the poor devil was suffering.

Looking at him, I thought about the parting advice given to me by one of the older agents back in Atlanta, a big, easy-moving man who didn't seem to talk much but still managed to say a hell of a lot.

"He's your junkie," the veteran agent had told me. "You've got him on a leash. Just remember, he's no good to you if he's screaming and shaking. But you already know that, so good luck. Just bear in mind that sometimes we go by the book and sometimes we write the book as we go along."

So I decided I'd write at least a chapter.

We always took separate rooms, Arthur Bee and I. He wasn't my idea of a perfect roommate. I called him into my room. "Here, Arthur," I said, handing some bills to him. "Go out and cop yourself a fix." Not very admirable, I admit, but unless he got himself a fix he wasn't going to be able to work. Besides, I rationalized, he had to make a connection on his own before I could come into the picture.

While Arthur was gone I paced the room, barely aware of the noise of big trailer rigs as they roared past on the highway outside and a snorting bulldozer biting into an embankment of red clay across the highway. Inside the room the air conditioner was wheezing and the radio had come down with another screaming fit of hillbilly music.

None of it drowned out the relentless question that kept at my mind.

Should I do it?

"Hell yes!" I said aloud, talking to my own reflection in the mirror. "So quit stalling."

I didn't want to do it, but I might never have another chance like this. I had been having a go-round with ethics, but now I made up my mind I was going to learn the reactions of a strung-out junkie by making a strung-out junkie perform for me. It was one of the most difficult decisions I'd ever had to make, one that was utterly distasteful. Yet, as I said, I felt a desperate need to know. The watchmaker has to learn what makes the clock tick.

I went next door to Arthur Bee's room and picked the lock. His few belongings were scattered about and the top drawer of the dresser was partly open. In the drawer I found the standard works of the junkie—the needle, the eye-dropper, the bent spoon—and about half a dozen balls of soiled cotton.

Balls of cotton are used to strain the pill or powder after it is dissolved in a spoon or bottle cap over a flame. Out of habit, a junkie will save the old cotton. One day he can't cop a fix, and he's going to get sick, and he might be able to squeeze a little something out of that old cotton.

I left the cotton but took the works. Then I went back to my room and waited for Arthur Bee to get back from town. I heard the car drive up and park. The door to his room opened and through the thin walls I could hear dresser drawers being opened and slammed shut.

Silence.

It didn't last long. There were scurrying footsteps, the sound of a door slamming and a quick, sharp rapping on my door. Panic was in that knock.

"C'mon in, Arthur," I called. "It's open."

He came in, shaking like a dog with a chill.

"Jimmy, I can't find my works. Did you take my works, Jimmy?" His voice rose, high-pitched.

I nodded.

"I got your works. Now, tell me, where's your fix?"

His face looked more haggard than ever and his eyes were rolling.

"You're not going to take it away from me?"

"What's the matter with you?" I said, sounding tougher than I felt. "I could keep you standing there. I could handcuff you. I could take you downtown and lock you up. Now give me your fix."

He handed me an envelope containing six quarter-grain tabs of dialudid. Dialudid is a derivative of opium about four times stronger than morphine, but less than half as potent as heroin.

I told him to strip. My reasons? For one, a man loses some of his dignity and his will to resist when he is standing naked, and I didn't want any resistance from Arthur Bee. For another, I wanted to make sure he wasn't holding out any pills on me. I searched his clothes and told him to put his shorts back on.

"I'll explain this once," I said, putting one pill on the dresser and giving him his works. "Every time you shoot up, you'll shoot up in front of me. I'll ask you questions. You'll answer every one. If you play games with me, I'll spill your junk. That's all. Got it?"

"Sure, Jimmy, sure."

Arthur Bee didn't seem to care. He wasn't embarrassed. He had sunk too low for that. The only thing in the world that mattered to him was getting that fix. In his need and greed he'd have done it in the buff in Macy's window before the ladies of the D.A.R.

He clutched at the one pill I put on the dresser, scooped up his works and went into the bathroom to prepare for his awful ritual.

Outside, traffic continued to roar by in the sunshine and I could hear the laughter of kids playing on the swings in the motel playground. Inside, I felt like a two-headed ghoul as I watched Arthur Bee make ready for his four-hour stall against terror.

He cleaned his implements hurriedly. He didn't use a regular injection syringe with the hypodermic needle because the regular syringe has too much pressure. Instead he used an eye-dropper and a nipple off a baby's bottle, to make a lower-pressure bulb. The gripping fear of the junkie is that he might "lose the shot" with too much pressure.

I learned fast enough not to ask my questions before the shot. Anyway, he was usually incoherent with fear and need. But he always followed the same procedure. Quickly, he put the nipple over the end of the eye-dropper and secured it with a rubber band. Everything about this strung-out junkie was shaking except his hands. They were steady—the steel of necessity. I marveled at this phenomenon. Arthur Bee's eyes were darting and sweat stood out on his face. But his hands moved with the deft precision of a surgeon's.

He attached the needle to the other end of the eye-dropper. The needle and the dropper weren't an exact fit, so he used a washer made from a little strip torn from a dollar bill. That way it would stay on tight. U.S. currency is fairly moisture-proof and the washer, or collar, lasts a long time.

Bee looked over at me now with those watery eyes.

"Go ahead," I said, feeling sick.

He put the pill in the standard bent spoon and began to work it up. He dissolved the pill with a match, diluting it with a little water to make it a soluble liquid. Then he sucked up the solution in the dropper, straining it once through a cotton ball.

I sat fascinated, watching this shaky man perform his murderous procedures with the artistry of a watchmaker.

The tie-down was made with a handkerchief, a makeshift tourniquet that made the vein stand up. This was an intricate operation in itself, performed one-handed while operating the needle with the other hand. He inserted the needle and pumped a little, then sucked it back. A strange look came onto his face.

"What are you doing?"

He didn't answer. The look on his face became even spookier.

I got up and walked over to him.

"Answer me, dammit," I said, putting an edge in my voice. I felt I had to sound tough to get through to him. "Answer me every time I ask you a question."

"Testing, just testing."

But it was more than that, far more. He brought the blood up in the tube and pressured it back, and did it again and again. The blissful, demented look on his face was more than I had bargained for.

"What do you feel now?"

"Nothing, nothing." I learned later that he was teasing himself, pumping a little into the vein and sucking it back. It was the climax before the climax and while he did it he made little moaning sounds.

"I want some answers or I'll spill your junk."

Eight or nine seconds went by, then he said, "The pins and needles are getting sharper . . . sharper. I feel pins and needles up in the top of my head. Ohh . . . I can't stand it any more."

Then he emptied the rest of the eye-dropper into his arm.

He stiffened. Then, very slowly, his body relaxed. He didn't even bother to pull out the needle that first time. Sometimes he would pull it out and sometimes he would leave it in. If the puncture wound bled he merely put his thumb over it.

Arthur Bee was in his own junk world now. He was "on the nod," a euphoric stupor that only the junkie knows. His body stopped its shaking and twitching. He smiled at me. I was his friend.

"What do you feel? Answer me. I want to know everything you feel."

He grinned emptily at me.

"I wouldn't give you trouble, Jimmy. You made it so I can feel so good."

"What about Dink Henderson? Did you see him?"

"Yeah . . . yeah . . . I did, Jimmy."

"Did you see the doctor? Don't lie to me."

"Yeah, I did, Jimmy. I saw the doctor. I wouldn't lie to you. You're my friend. You make me able to feel so good."

Being on the nod was the highest point in the short, blissful life of Arthur Bee. In another four hours he would start dying again. . . .

Education. Training. Sure, I'd had it all. But until I sat there in that motel room watching Arthur Bee tease himself and go on the nod, it had all been just words and theory.

Now it was real. And frightening.

This poor doomed man, sniveling minutes before, had escaped to a phoney, short-lived heaven. The nod never lasts very long, and the longer you're addicted the more stuff it takes to put you there.

Right then I learned to use his nod to good advantage, because then he would tell me everything. But I had to keep him out of sight in the room until he came down off it. I didn't want him goofing around with the pupils of his eyes as narrow as pinpoints and that silly expression on his face. It might bring the local police down on us or attract attention some other way.

About an hour later Arthur Bee began yawning, or yapping—the signal that he was coming down off his high. Everything would be downhill until his next fix three or four hours later.

There were only about two hours between fixes when I could get any work out of Arthur Bee. He was my bird-dog, the necessary evil that would lead me to the pushers and suppliers who peddled the stuff. I relied on him to set me up for a buy. I couldn't very well afford to let them get a free look at me until I was ready to take possession and make the pinch.

We got Dink Henderson that way. We also got the doctor who was the main source of illegal morphine in the area.

Meanwhile, Arthur Bee was blowing his sources of supply, day by day and town by town, but he didn't really have much choice. We had the hammer on him.

The day we left Andalusia I watched him shoot up for the last time and asked him how the pins and needles were going. The pins and needles always came before the high and lasted for about eight to ten seconds.

"See the little cotton ball, Jimmy," he said with that blissful look on his face. "I feel like I'm all wrapped in cotton, all wrapped in a great big cotton ball."

Watching him depressed me, and I could feel myself getting edgy. I promised myself, right there in that little motor court in Andalusia, that those who peddled this slow death would never get one drop of mercy from me.

Arthur Bee and I finished my assignment shortly thereafter and I never say him again once we had returned to Atlanta. Somebody else took over the ownership of my strung-out junkie. For somebody would always own the Arthur Bees, every second of what was left of their wasted, pitiful lives.

My own vendetta had begun.

CHAPTER **1**

The Big Guy

THE STREAMLINED Rome-to-Naples Express skimmed across the Italian countryside, gold under a warm April sun. Tiny villages, looking much as they had when the Roman legions marched this way, flashed past the oversized glass windows. A curly-haired youngster with round eyes stared unblinkingly over the back of the seat in front of me. He was attracted, I suppose, by the Air Force uniform I wore, the pilot's wings on my chest and the major's insignia on my shoulders.

I gave him a solemn wink and he slid down out of sight. I had the fleeting thought, as I watched him disappear, that this time I could sink out of sight too. Permanently.

At that moment I quit being Sal Vizzini, undercover narcotics agent, and became the man my cover credentials said I was—Major Michael A. Cerra, U.S. Air Force, Serial Number 52220A. I had established and tried on for size the Major Cerra cover even before I'd learned who my target was. It had better fit now. I was en route to Naples to manage a planned "accidental" meeting with Luciano and hopefully to make friends with him. Good friends.

Lucky Luciano, real name Salvatore Lucania, long-time Mafia

boss, had been deported from the United States to Italy in 1946. He went to Cuba a year later, but the Cubans were pressured by the U.S., so they rerouted him back to his native Italy. Technically, he was in exile. But that didn't mean a thing.

He was the big guy of organized crime, so big that when he was deported they didn't even put his name on the International List of known criminals. He was too big for the list; it was just naturally assumed that he was No. 1. And being away from his New York territory didn't stop him from operating much as in the old days.

His tentacles were long and his influence powerful. The Narcotics Bureau, and the Justice Department, knew he was still making decisions for the mob, that he was receiving large shipments of money from the States, and that he was still engaged in directing much of the world's narcotics traffic. They wanted a Trojan horse in the enemy camp. I was the horse.

The Bureau was counting on my experience, plus my Sicilian background, to pull me through. The plan was to masquerade as a lonely Air Force pilot, maybe not fussy about turning a fast buck on the side; a man who in the line of duty would travel extensively on Air Force business ferrying military planes between the U.S. and Europe, and be accepted by Luciano, who was well known for his longing for the States and things American.

Even before the Naples Express had pulled out of Rome I knew this was a no-limit game—and that the bets were already down.

I'd known it, in fact, before that. . . .

It had started a few months before when The Man "invited" me to dinner in Miami. In District Six of the Bureau, where I was stationed, The Man was John T. Cusack. He was the district supervisor and his invitation to dinner was stronger than most people's command.

He'd heard I had been offered a job with Customs and was

thinking about accepting. In fact, the transfer had already been arranged. They wanted to give me a promotion and more money and send me to La Paz, Bolivia. They also wanted me to crack a cocaine ring there.

Cusack heard about it and got down to Miami right away. He took me to dinner at the Singapore over on The Beach, à la carte from soup to Drambuie. Cusack wasn't exactly a big spender. This had to be a special occasion. He got right to it.

"What's this crap about you leaving the Bureau and going to Customs?"

I started to tell him but he ran right over me. He had a blacksmith's jaw and hard blue eyes. His completely shaved head had a soft shine, like Yul Brynner's.

"I'm moving to Rome to take charge in Europe and you're to come with me. There's a job we've had scheduled for some time that we believe you're uniquely qualified to take on. By the way, if you think I'm giving you a hand job, the original documents were dated long before you started talking to Customs. I'll show them to you if you want."

"You know that's not necessary."

He settled back more comfortably in his chair. "All I can tell you now is work up a good cover, a military one would probably be best."

"How about the Air Force?"

"Fine. Work out the details and get back to me."

He knew I'd pick the Air Force over the other services, but he let me suggest it. Before joining the Bureau I'd worked as an investigator for the Air Force Provost Marshal and had some good contacts at Robins Air Force Base in Georgia.

So I went up to Robins, saw the Provost Marshal, my old boss, and told him I was on a confidential mission for the Bureau of Narcotics.

No questions. I picked the name Michael Anthony Cerra because it sounded Italian and decided on the rank of major. It was all cleared with the base commander, and probably with the Pentagon. Every detail of my new identity was valid—except that I didn't know how to fly an airplane.

I was photographed and fingerprinted. I received a flight card, an instrument rating card, a Geneva Convention card in case I got "shot down" over enemy territory, dog tags and an Officer's Club card. I was put on the official roster at Robins, complete with a form for "notification of next of kin" and got a San Francisco APO address.

Next I saw Charlie Parkerson, the Provost Marshal's assistant, and he fitted me out with a flight suit and flight bag, all properly stenciled. I got insignia from the PX and uniforms from the base tailor. I would even receive mail at Robins, to be immediately forwarded to a confidential Bureau drop in New York.

The dinner in Miami happened late in 1958, and I sailed for Naples aboard the S.S. *Independence* on New Year's Eve. After I'd worked a few routine cases in Paris and Rome, I received orders to report to John Cusack in Rome. Arriving there, I made my way to the Bureau's offices on the second floor of the Annex, across the Via Veneto from the American Embassy.

"You're going to meet Lucky Luciano," Cusack said.

Lucky Luciano . . . As a kid he was my idol on the wrong side of the tracks. When we'd play gangsters and G-men on the block everybody wanted to be Lucky—or his two trigger-happy enforcers, Dutch Schultz and Legs Diamond. And we'd lag bottle caps to a line for the privilege, unless there was some bigger and tougher kid who'd preempted that honor.

Lucky Luciano. A shocker, but I didn't say a word. I sat down and listened.

"We've been putting this thing together for more than a year, de-

veloping an S.E. with the background and ability to introduce you
to Luciano. He's ready. Now we need the right agent with the right
cover. You're it."

I nodded. S.E. means special employee. Also other things, such
as button man and stool pigeon, which you don't call him in an
official report.

Cusack ran a hand over his shaved head and hunched forward
in his chair. "Sal, through this investigation we hope to develop
accurate first-hand information about Luciano's legitimate and underworld interests in Italy and the U.S., his criminal and legitimate
associates in both countries, how deeply he's involved in the international narcotics traffic and other Mafia activities. We want to
know everything about Luciano, including how many times a day he
goes to the bathroom. We want to know who he sees, where he gets
his money and how often, who his couriers are, how much real
control he has back in New York."

He paused and went on. "This will have top priority. We don't
want arrests. We want information that connects Luciano with the
narcotics traffic between Italy and the U.S. We'll sacrifice cases, and
even individuals, to learn everything there is to know about Luciano.

"We realize Luciano's prominence and power will make all this
very difficult and our prospects not very promising. However, we
think it's important enough to commit at least a full year to it."

Not to mention, if necessary, "Major Michael Cerra."

"What we'll try for is to have you make periodic visits to Naples,
staggered so as not to crowd Luciano and at the same time allow
you to be away from Naples for extended periods in the develop-
ment of other investigations, probably in Turkey."

"How much time do I have before we get started with Luciano?"

"Not very much, I hope," Cusack said. "We're waiting for the
S.E., Sam Cook, to come in from Germany. Cook is an Italian

who's been working as a cook for the U.S. Army, which is how he comes by his code name. Our lever on him is that he wants to become a U.S. citizen and get back to the States. He wants out of Germany and out of the Army. We've told him if he can pull this off for us we'll do what we can for him. Hank Manfredi—you know him—is with the CIA here in Rome and will be your backup man in Naples. He'll also meet with Cook in Rome before you see him. We want to be damned sure Cook is secure. We'll be in touch."

Three days later the call came. In Cusack's office I found Manfredi and a short, paunchy Italian, about thirty-five, with curly black hair.

The S.E. had known Luciano a long time as a waiter in one of those Italian restaurants the mob owned and frequented on New York's Lower East Side, around Elizabeth and Mott. One thing about Luciano, he paid attention to little people, and somewhere along the way Sam Cook had been one of them.

When the Bureau found out about it they began to feel him out. Would he be willing to introduce somebody to Luciano? What did he want? How would he like to be sprung from the Army, be a citizen with the best connections? The leverage was applied slowly, over a period of months, until finally he'd agreed.

We sat down. Cusack looked at me and nodded. "He's going to introduce you to Lucky." I shook hands with a roly-poly whose nose came about even with my pilot wings. He smiled nervously but shook my hand with a grip like a bench vise. I liked his grip but his nervousness worried me.

I looked at Cusack.

"Sam's O.K. He knows what he has to do."

The script was fairly simple. Cook would be in the San Francisco Bar and Grill in Naples, owned by Luciano, talking to Luciano when I happened to drop in. He would recognize me as a pilot he'd known when he was a cook back at an air base in Kentucky (which he was). I was a guy who shot crap with enlisted men on pay day—or anybody else at any time who had money to lose—and wasn't too fussy altogether about rules and regulations. A swinger.

It would be a brief but obvious reunion. He would call me Mike and maybe remember I'd once swiped a bottle of Chianti from the Officer's Club for him. All this would be for the benefit of Lucky and whoever happened to be with him. One of his lines would be: "Hey, Major, you've come up in the world." Then he'd turn to Luciano and say something like, "He was a lousy lieutenant but a helluva guy when I knew him in the States . . . meet my friend, Major Mike Cerra."

That was the scenario and that was all the S.E. had to do. He didn't have to be Dustin Hoffman, but he did have to be a guy who wanted out of the Army pretty bad. He also had to make it look absolutely legitimate. Once he'd introduced me, exit Sam Cook. From then on it would be my ball game.

After Cook and I had gone over our story several times and were cross-examined by Manfredi, I asked Cook, "Do you think you can do it?"

"Yeah, I think so."

"You'd better know it," I said.

It was also agreed that Cook and I would proceed separately to Naples. Otherwise a man as jungle smart as Luciano might suspect a setup. And, of course, it would be disaster if he or someone known to him saw us together before our "chance" meeting in the San Francisco Bar and Grill.

We went back to the agent's part of the office and talked about the exact time of the meeting in the San Francisco Bar and Grill and an alternate time in case Luciano wasn't there. I finally put my hand in the S.E.'s vise and said I'd see him around.

And so Cook proceeded alone by automobile to Naples.

And on the next day, a sunny April day in 1959, I was on the streamlined Rome-to-Naples express, wondering if our staged re-union would convince its star audience once the train pulled into Naples.

CHAPTER 2

Rendezvous in Naples

I STOOD in front of Naple's Mediterraneo Hotel and looked at the city Lucky Luciano called home. Even in the bright sunlight it was a dirty, teeming place that still showed the scars of World War II, especially in the still heavily populated areas around the old waterfront that had been pounded by preinvasion shelling.

I walked to a sidewalk *pasticceria* where I ordered a cup of coffee while I waited for the time of my rendezvous at the San Francisco Bar and Grill.

Naples, I suspected, was even grimmer underside than topside. After all, this was a city that openly hosted the infamous Lucky Luciano. New York didn't want him, Rome wouldn't have him as an exile, Havana had thrown him out after a brief stopover, but sunny Naples not only accepted him but welcomed him as a celebrity. You never knew who might be on speaking terms with Luciano —bus boy, doorman, manicurist—as well as some of the town's best and most respected citizens. Lucky covered himself with friends wherever he went (that's how he knew our S.E., Cook), which meant somebody like myself had to be especially careful whom he talked to or confided in. Nobody was safe for Major Mike Cerra. I'd better believe it, and remember it. In Lucky's territory I was cut off, alone.

I knew from advance briefing that Luciano owned a restaurant called the California Restaurant, a night club called the San Francisco Bar and Grill where I'd soon be going, and even an art gallery run by a fellow ex-con. He probably owned a few police officials too, but that would be my least worry. It was the unofficial friends of the big man that could be the worst threats to me— friends that I couldn't know or identify.

At two P.M., after my second cup of coffee, I walked over toward the San Francisco Bar and Grill. As I approached, I saw a car with Cook's license plates (I'd been given the plate numbers in Rome) parked at the curb almost in front of the rendezvous point. We were on schedule. I took a deep breath and walked inside.

I immediately spotted the S.E., Cook, sitting alone at a table. He didn't show any recognition, or even look at me. I walked to the bar, ordered a beer and sipped it—I really wanted another coffee but a U.S. Army major who was also a teetotaler might attract special attention. Still no move from Cook to approach and recognize me. I wondered for a minute whether something had gone wrong with our plan, and then decided as I failed to spot Luciano that the man simply wasn't there, and for Cook to recognize me now would be pointless and defeat the plan, which was to stage the reunion for Luciano's benefit.

I decided to look around a bit more and then casually leave. The bar I stood at was about twenty feet long, and good mahogany. There were about twenty tables in a nearly spotlessly clean room. In the rear was a kitchen, and on the left side of the bar were stairs that led up to a balcony with a few additional tables and a railing. On the right of the bar was another flight of stairs going down to a section I was to learn they called the Snake Pit, a sort of mini-nightclub where the available women of the evening, "snakes" and "broads" to Luciano and his friends, gathered for the nighttime action.

After a few more minutes I finished my beer, left the bar, crossed the street and walked to the far corner from the San Francisco Bar and Grill. Glancing back, I saw Cook leave the Bar and start in my direction. I turned the corner to be out sight of the restaurant, waited until I heard him approaching and then bent over to retie my shoelace. Cook didn't stop but as he passed close behind me, he said in a low, almost whispered voice, "Luciano left, be back in about two hours. See you then."

As he walked on up the block I retraced my steps in the opposite direction and then spent the next two hours walking around the city before returning to the San Francisco Bar and Grill.

This time Cook was sitting at a table having a beer with two other men. I made my way to a table near the bar and took a seat directly facing Cook. I'd been there only a few minutes when a waiter approached me and I ordered another beer. While I was waiting for it, and for the moment when Cook would decide to "recognize" me, I looked casually around the place. There were people at a half dozen tables, and when I looked up at the balcony, I felt my pulse leap. Sitting at a table up there, flanked by two young women, was Lucky Luciano. I recognized him immediately from memory and his photos in our files.

Without letting myself look directly at him, I could see that he was neither very big nor very small. He had on a gray suit and tie, and wore silver-rimmed glasses. He looked more like a well-to-do wine merchant than a killer who'd bragged he'd buried a hundred people.

I turned a little in my chair so that I now faced Sam Cook across the room. I saw him give a start, stare at me a moment and then wave his hand my way. The act had started.

He got up and came over. "Hey, Mike," he said, leaning down to give me a closer look, "what the hell are *you* doing here?"

His voice could be heard all around the bar as he grabbed my hand and shook it hard. "You remember me? I was the cook when we were stationed back in Kentucky."

I pretended not to remember.

"Hey, it's your old buddy. Remember my lasagna and all those crap games?"

I let recognition come slow.

"Sure . . . sure," I said. "Well, I'll be damned! Sure I remember. But what are *you* doing over here?"

By now everybody in the place was looking and grinning at the fat little guy coming on with the U.S. Air Force major. And Lucky Luciano was taking it all in casually from the balcony.

"Just visiting some old buddies," he said.

I slapped him on the shoulder. "Well, it's lucky for me I bumped into you. I'm all alone over here waiting for reassignment."

The little guy went for an Oscar, back slapping and tugging at me. "Hell, Major, your problems are over. Just come on over here and let me introduce you to a couple of my friends." I let myself be led over and introduced.

Cook's friends had solid credentials, and long dossiers. One was Vincenzo Facchini, alias Joe the Wop, middle-aged but still wiry, once a bookie in New York, now deported. The other was Onofrio Raimondo, also known as "Cockeyed Johnny." He'd been deported from New York ten years earlier for, among other things, dealing in counterfeit money. As it developed, he now ran the Royal Art Studio in Naples that was owned by Luciano.

"Can you imagine," Cook told them, "I haven't seen Mike Cerra since I cooked poison at the Officer's Club back at Fort Knox couple of years ago. He's one of the hottest pilots in the Air Force but a regular guy."

The others seemed to accept me as Cook and I reminisced about happy days at Fort Knox and caught up with what had happened to us since we left there.

Within a few minutes Joe the Wop was pounding my back and saying he'd bet I was Sicilian. I told him he'd win his bet. From the corner of my eye it seemed to me that Luciano was watching and listening. I worried, though, that Cook would haul me up those steps for an introduction that would look as phoney as the counterfeit $20 bills Raimondo used to pass back in the States. When you're a candidate for a splash in the Bay of Naples, I guess you got a right to be a drama critic.

As it worked out, I didn't need to worry. Maybe Luciano was curious what his friends were doing with a U.S. Air Force officer. Anyway, in a few minutes he got up from his table on the balcony, made his way down the stairs and headed in our direction, followed by a large bodyguard.

Seeing him come our way, Cook jumped to his feet and took a step in Luciano's direction. "Hey, Charlie, I'd like you to meet an old friend of mine, haven't seen him since we were at the same Air Force base in Kentucky couple years ago."

Turning in my direction, Cook said over his shoulder to Lucky, "This is Lieutenant Mike Cerra—oh, pardon me, it's Major now. Hey, Major, you've come up in the world. . . ."

I was face-to-face with the man, one of the most feared mobsters of all time, kingpin of the Mafia, a killer who by his own words had sent more than a hundred men to their deaths, a man we believed was still the power behind the action, still the syndicate's boss of operations over the narcotics flow into the United States.

The man was something of a surprise to me. This was not the flashy, arrogant, bombastic type I might have expected. On close inspection Luciano looked even more conservatively immaculate in his quiet gray suit and sedate figured tie. He had dark bushy eyebrows and hair sprinkled with just enough gray to give him a proper, almost distinguished look. The only flashiness about him was a large diamond in the center of a pearl stickpin, and another diamond that he wore on the little finger of his left hand.

He put a thumb to the tip of his nose and pushed it over to one side, a mannerism, I was to learn, that usually went with Luciano's making up his mind about something. I hoped I didn't seem to be staring at him, but meeting this man *was* an event, and I couldn't stop looking him over. Up close he still wasn't large, about six feet, but he moved with an air of natural authority—long since acquired and now a second skin. A successful business man, sixty-two years old and in charge.

Sam Cook jumped in. "The guy walks in and the last time I see him was two years ago at Fort Knox. Hey, Mike, I want you to meet Charlie."

Taking my hand in a firm grip, Luciano said in a low, quiet voice, "Hi, Mike."

I noticed that Cook kept calling him Charlie, and later learned nobody close to him ever called him Lucky. He liked being called Charlie.

I'd been so focused on Luciano that I'd almost missed the big meaty guy who'd walked down the stairs behind him and hung in the background away from our table, apparently waiting for the boss to leave. I figured him at about six-two, 220 pounds, and dangerous in the clinches.

Luciano spoke briefly to him and then turned to me and asked how long I'd be in town. I told him just a few days, that I'd be taking in some sights before reporting back for duty.

"He likes the races," Cook broke in.

"Fine. Bring him along tomorrow." Luciano said this quietly

but it was an order, not a suggestion. Then to me, "I've got to leave now for an appointment, Major. See you tomorrow."

Luciano started for the door, stopped a moment to talk to some other people at another table, then went out of the place, trailed by his huge shadow. Everybody watched him leave. He attracted all eyes—coming or going.

"Look," I said, turning to Facchini, "I didn't want to ask, but what's Charlie's last name?"

Facchini laughed and said to Sam Cook, "Hey, *pizan,* you want to tell your buddy who that was?"

Cook leaned across the table. "Mike, you just met Charlie Lucky. That was Lucky Luciano."

"The hell you say! My God, never expected to meet him! And who was the big bird with him?"

"That's Momo," Facchini said proudly, a big man proud to know all about *the* big man, Lucky Luciano. "Momo's sort of Charlie's bodyguard. Charlie doesn't really need one around here but Momo comes in handy to keep away the moochers and drunks and sightseers."

Playing out my role I told them it was, damn straight, a thrill to meet Luciano.

"Well," Facchini told me, "You'll have a chance to know him even better when we go to Ippodromo Agnano track tomorrow. You heard Charlie say to bring you along. Be here, noon sharp."

I finished my beer and got up. "See you tomorrow," I said, and left with my buddy, the S.E. He had done his job well. I guess he went back to Germany to wait for his pay-off. Anyway, I never saw him again in my life.

I arrived promptly at noon the next day and found Luciano holding court at his balcony table. I started toward the balcony stairs and two waiters seemed to sprout from the floor, blocking my way.

"Glad you could make it, Mike," Luciano called from the balcony in a low voice that carried strong. The waiters went back into the floor and I went upstairs.

Cockeyed Johnny Raimondo and Joe the Wop Vincenzo Facchini were there. The rest I didn't know. Luciano began introducing me in an offhand way, using only first names.

"This is Luigi," he said as I shook hands. I found out later that this was a Naples harbor pilot, and his full name was Luigi Pappagallo.

"And meet Skeets," Luciano said, nodding toward a tall, thin man in his fifties. "Skeets runs this place for me. He won't let you buy a drink while you're here. You need anything, he'll take care of you. Right, Skeets?"

"Sure thing, Charlie." Skeets turned out to be Frankie, alias Skeets, Culla, a mob guy with too much heat in New York.

"This is Joe," Luciano went on, pointing to a young guy who was movie-idol handsome. He seemed freshly shaved but still had a heavy blue five o'clock shadow. "Joe works for the government, too, Major. In a way."

"In a way?" I asked. I smiled and shook hands with Joe.

"Yes," Luciano said. "He's a purser on the *Dutton,* a U.S. government cargo ship. He travels a lot slower than you do, Major."

Almost as an afterthought Lucky turned to his oversized shadow. "And this is Momo. He keeps the girls from bothering me."

I didn't like Momo on sight and he didn't like me.

Joe, the purser, would later be identified as Joe Scozzi. The Bureau was very anxious to know exactly who carried Charlie Lucky's orders to the States and brought back his pay-offs. We knew he worked through hoodlums, seamen, criminal lawyers, friends and even travel agencies—but we could never specifically identify them. Joe Scozzi, purser of the USS *Dutton*, could be a real breakthrough in setting the links in Luciano's chain of communications.

I managed to sit next to Scozzi on the way to the race track, two carloads of us. Luciano was in the other car.

"This is my first trip to Naples," I said to Scozzi as we began the drive to the racetrack. "I sure was lucky to bump into Sam Cook and meet you people. It would have been pretty lonely."

Luigi Pappagallo, the harbor pilot, laughed as he turned halfway around in the front seat. "You won't have a chance to be lonesome if you hang out with Charlie Lucky. He's got more broads around than your whole Air Force could handle, Major."

"Well, I'm damn glad I had the chance to meet him," I said, and then, turning back to Joe Scozzi, asked him casually whether like myself this was his first trip to Naples.

Scozzi and Pappagallo thought that was pretty funny.

"Hell no," Scozzi said. "The *Dutton* makes regular runs between New York and Naples about every six weeks, and I'm here between trips for a week or so. The captain knows I'm a good friend of Charlie and every time I come here he asks me if I'm gonna see my friend, 'the big crook.' But I put up with it because now and then I can do Charlie a little favor."

It would have been stupid to press him about the "little favor," but I was now sure I had uncovered one of Luciano's links with the underworld in New York. Scozzi was a man marked for extra special attention, once I got a chance to pass the word to Rome.

We got to Ippodromo Agnano in time for the first race. The horses pulled sulkies instead of carrying jockeys—where I came from they called trotters "jugheads"—but I wasn't about to complain, and you certainly couldn't knock the service we got.

We had a table right on the finish line, with waiters falling over themselves trying to be helpful to Charlie Lucky and his friends. Besides having a big reputation, he was also big with the tips, which didn't hurt. I sat next to Luciano because that was the way he wanted it.

His arrival created a good deal of commotion in the area, and shortly after we'd taken our seats a newspaper reporter came up to our table and asked Luciano if he could take his picture.

"No." He added in a voice that once again was a command, not a request, "Leave us alone, please."

The reporter was trailed by a photographer with a Speed Graphic, and Luciano hardly had the words out of his mouth when the photographer's flash bulb went off.

"I said 'No,' " Luciano said without raising his voice but in a tone that sounded like razors being honed against each other. The look he gave the photographer was full of tombstones. The two men took off in a hurry.

"God damn them," he muttered, turning to me and resuming his normal level tone of conversation. "They're always taking my picture, Major, and now they've taken one of you with me."

"Well, Charlie, *I* certainly didn't mind, but I can understand how you feel." I shrugged and hoped that I didn't show how I really felt. When I'd seen the photographer raise his camera I'd tried to turn my face away without being too obvious. I hoped he'd only gotten the back of my head, because the last thing you want in my line of work is to be photographed and risk somebody recognizing you—Luciano, for example, who someday might match me up with a face out of uniform.

He bet 200,000 lire on the first race—about $320. I bet two dollars and Momo bought the tickets. Lucky's horse finished sixth and mine was further back. It didn't seem to bother him.

He seemed much more interested in airplanes. "What kind of planes do you fly?" he asked.

"Mostly F-100s and F-101s," I lied.

He seemed impressed. "How fast do they go?"

"Up to 1,100 miles per hour if you really push."

"That's damned fast. How about normal?"

"Between 700 and 900." I'd made it a point to pick up the latest information about fighters before I left Robins.

"What if your engines crap out over the ocean?"

"Then you get wet," I said.

He laughed at that, not a thigh slapper, more a low inner chuckle.

"You're kind of young to be a major," he said, and a danger light went on in my head. "You go into the Air Force right out of college?"

I laughed. "Yeah, right out of college. I majored in hustling pool and made straight A's in street fighting. I never went to college, Charlie."

He liked that.

Every so often, Facchini would come up and whisper something in his ear.

"You pick yours, I'll pick mine," Luciano said, an edge coming into his voice. "I'll lose my money on my own hunches." His standard bet was 200,000 lire to win, and he would tuck the marker the runner brought him from the bookmaker into his vest pocket, watch a losing race without any show of emotion, and then calmly tear up the stub, He didn't have a single horse in the money.

"Don't you ever win, Charlie?" I asked.

"Not often."

He obviously didn't care about winning. Maybe the races were fixed—most other things are in Italy. Anyway, Facchini and the others kept winning steadily. They must have had a pipeline to somewhere, but Lucky wanted to be his own man and just didn't give a damn like ordinary mortals. He was above them.

"Losing all the time can get pretty expensive," I said. "On a major's income I couldn't afford this very often."

Luciano smiled, almost to himself. "I guess you could say, Major, that I can afford it."

Joe Scozzi, sitting across from us next to Pappagallo, leaned forward and asked me if I had a cigarette.

"I don't smoke, but I'd have brought some for you guys if I'd known I was going to see you," I said. "I'm flying special courier duty between Italy and the States and expect to be back next month. I'll bring some then if you're going to be here."

I hoped Luciano would get the message that I might be persuaded to carry information, or anything else, back and forth for him.

"Bring some for me," Pappagallo interrupted, "I can always use more cigarettes."

"All they let me take off the ship is two packs," young Scozzi said. "You can probably bring all you want, can't you?"

"Well," I hesitated, "it's a little risky but so far nobody has checked me out or asked what I've got on me."

"Fine," Pappagallo said, "why don't you bring me about twenty cartons, Major?"

Laughing a little at his eagerness, I told Luigi that that might be pushing my luck, that all I could safely handle was what I could get into my pockets.

The bait was dangling for Luciano. All I could do was wait and see whether he would take it, if not now at least later when, as I hoped, we might get to know each other better. Just the idea of him eventually asking me to bring him a packet from the States or deliver some messages stateside made my mouth water.

Our conversation, however, was interrupted by a nattily dressed Italian with a small black mustache who came up to the table and pulled out a chair on the other side of Luciano from where I was sitting.

"Charlie's lawyer," Facçhini told me.

I bent down to my program, as if figuring out my bets in the next race, and tried to catch a little of what was going on between Luciano and his attorney.

I managed to hear something about the conviction in New York of the fifteen defendants involved in the Vito Genovese conspiracy.

"I just read about it in the paper," the lawyer told Luciano.

"I knew it," he answered tersely. "I had a feeling they'd be convicted. Me and a lot of other people would like to know exactly how they got caught."

It was that graveyard tone again. Whoever blew the whistle would be a dead man if they ever caught up with him. As dead, say, as Sal Vizzini if it ever got out among these gentlemen that Major Mike Cerra was a phoney.

"Well, aside from that," the attorney was saying to Luciano, "you know, Charlie, we only have two weeks to come up with the two and a half million lire for the income tax on that money from the States."

That would be about four thousand dollars, I calculated, an interesting item since Luciano must have used regular banking channels to receive these funds—otherwise how could the Italians have known about and taxed them. And maybe there was a lead here to his financial sources in the United States. Figuring up later that he'd casually lost approximately two thousand dollars this one afternoon, it was obvious Luciano had a very comfortable income for a man with no visible means of support.

"Don't worry about the money," Luciano told the lawyer. "I just got a little present. Everything is all right."

It seemed that, like the Marines, young Joe Scozzi had arrived in the nick of time with money from the "boys" back in New York.

I missed the rest of their conversation before the lawyer left because Facchini insisted on being friendly. "Try the sixth horse in the next race," he said. "You won't be sorry."

He was talking about what a big man he was around Naples and had been in New York when Lucky interrupted to ask, "Mike, who did you bet on in this race?"

I gave him the name of the horse I'd gotten from Facchini.

"Momo," he said, pulling out a roll of money, "Get this down for me."

Momo gave me a look and lumbered away. It was even money I'd have trouble with this big guy before I got through.

When the horse came in at six-to-one, Charlie Lucky laid a hand on my arm and said, "You know, Mike, I think you've broken my losing streak. What can I do for you?"

"You've already done it," I told him. "Just meeting you was a pleasure."

"That goes double," he said. "Look me up when you get back to Naples. Now I hate to break this up but I have an appointment at seven o'clock and I don't want to keep the lady waiting. I've enjoyed it, Major, and I meant it when I said come back soon and we can get to know each other a little better."

"That'll suit me just fine, Charlie," I said. "I'm expecting to be back in a month or so and I'll certainly look you up."

He could have bet on that and it would have been the second time he'd have won that day. The introduction had, as far as I could tell, gone very well. My fish, I had reason to believe, was hooked.

I rode back to town in Lucky's car, a gray Alfa Romeo. Lucky was driving and he drove like a madman.

"You're not in an airplane," I said to him. I remembered to smile.

"I've got to get where I'm going fast."

Momo, who was sitting between us, pulled out a 9mm. Browning automatic and began playing with it. "Put that damned thing away," Luciano said. Momo put his toy away.

When he dropped me off at the Mediterraneo, Luciano shook my hand warmly and said, "You're O.K., Mike. Remember now, give me a call the next time you're in town."

"I promise," I said. "You can bet on that."

I got my flight bag, which contained one dirty shirt and some shaving gear, and checked out of the hotel. Now I had to learn whether my instincts were right or whether I was being tailed. It's routine in a case like this where the quarry is a man of some substance and considerable smarts.

Well, I thought, we'll find out.

I hailed a cab and told the driver to take me up the hill to the American Naval Base. It was also NATO headquarters in Italy. As an Air Force major, my credentials gave me access to the Officer's Club and the PX.

I went into the PX, resupplied myself with cigarettes and bought a bottle of bourbon. After a steak and some friendly conversation in the Officer's Club, I checked for possible tails, found none, slipped out and caught the streamliner back to Rome.

It was almost eleven o'clock when I checked into Bureau headquarters but John T. Cusack was still there. I'd never seen him so worked up. He wanted to know everything that had happened. Never mind the official report, that could come later.

"If I didn't know you so well, I might almost think you'd been worried about me," I said.

"Not about you. About the case," sentimental Cusack said.

He had kept around Monica Atwill, the Bureau's prettiest and most efficient secretary, hoping that I would show, but he wanted to get it directly from me before Monica got out her steno pad.

"Looks like we're off to a good start," he said after he'd heard most of it. "But we can't push it. You can't show again in Naples for about a month without raising suspicions. And meanwhile I've got something else for you."

"Which way and how far?"

"Palermo. To meet Mancuso."

"Which one?"

There were three Mancusos on the International List. Salvatore Mancuso was a fugitive out of New York with a narcotics record. Stefano Mancuso had been deported from the States several years before. Whereabouts unknown. Giuseppe was the third Mancuso.

"Giuseppe," he said. "Pick a new cover and hit the files."

I did. But not before taking Monica Atwill out to dinner and getting a good night's sleep.

CHAPTER 3

The Lonely Chemist
of Palermo

ONE OF the first things I did with Giuseppe Mancuso was pick his pocket and lift that knife he liked so much. A big, wicked clasp knife it was, with a hook on the end of it like a banana knife. He was always cleaning his fingernails with it. He loved that knife. But the damned thing preyed on my mind.

Giuseppe Mancuso was an old-style Sicilian mustache. He could slit your throat and finish his macaroni without a change of expression. No qualms. No regrets. He operated a big-volume heroin lab somewhere near Palermo.

My job was to get next to him and locate his lab.

So far, so good. He liked me and trusted me, I thought, as we bounced along in a donkey cart on a country road outside Palermo. Mancuso was talking a blue streak, which was unusual for a man who didn't talk at all to most people. But if something should come between us, I'd feel a lot better if he didn't have that damned knife. My hand went slowly toward the right-hand pocket of his baggy pants. I don't have a professional pickpocket's diploma, but any journeyman dip would have passed my work that day. My hand barely touched the pocket opening.

"Pasquale," Giuseppe said suddenly, and my hand froze. "Pasquale, when you do it right, like I do it, you actually get more heroin from the base than the amount of base you started with."

Shop talk. I breathed again.

I was Pasquale Lombardi to Giuseppe Mancuso. I had stopped being Sal Vizzini about ten days before, back in Rome, and by now had taken on the feeling and personality of my cover.

"Beautiful country, eh, Giuseppe?" I said, leaning forward a little to get a better view through the olive trees. The knife slid easily from his pocket, and into mine.

"Ah, yes it is, Pasquale," he said.

We stopped for a moment to admire the sea. Later, on the way back to town, he reached for the knife to indulge that nervous habit he had of cleaning his nails. He slapped all his pockets. He turned them inside out.

"I lost it," he said sadly.

I expressed deep concern over his loss. We looked for it on the floor of the cart and under the seat.

"Look, Giuseppe," I said, "do me a favor and don't worry about it. I know where I can get you one just like it."

"You don't have to do that," he said, but his tone showed his appreciation.

I raised my hand in the Sicilian say-no-more gesture. "No, I want to do it."

Giuseppe was pleased. "Pasquale, that's one of the things I like about you." He damn near smiled.

It seemed that there were a lot of things he liked about me. That was one of the breaks I got. If your target likes you—and you can always tell—you're part way home. The rest of the breaks you make as you go. Another thing I had going for me was my Sicilian blood. A Sicilian is always a Sicilian, even if like me he's Pittsburgh-born and raised in a Chicago slum. My grandfather came from Cefalu, a small fishing village on the north coast of Sicily. Actually I still had family there—and that was enough for Giuseppe.

Most Sicilians are very affectionate among their own and distant as hell with anyone who isn't Sicilian. An outsider can't crack that family sense, and you can't fake being a Sicilian. Al Capone tried it and got a scar on his face.

The best con artist in the business would stand out like an albino Watusi if he tried. Put me in a pitch-dark room with twenty men who have no accent and after a few minutes of conversation I can tell you who is Sicilian. Or put me in a lighted room with no conversation, and if the men are moving around, I'll do the same thing. Any true Sicilian can.

If they accept you, you're one of them. It was all part of why Giuseppe accepted me so completely. I didn't want to think about what would happen if I goofed my lines and got caught. Anyone as high in the local Mafia as Giuseppe Mancuso would order your death with no more emotion than your neighborhood druggist filling a prescription. In my case he would probably do the job himself.

This was the kind of man I had to get to, and it reached the point—knife point—where his own relatives couldn't have been closer to him. He finally took me into that big lab—the one nobody else could find—and taught me the art of making heroin.

I'll never forget standing in that lab with Giuseppe late at night as we poured bags of morphine base into the tubs, masks over our faces to keep from gagging on the fumes, fighting off nausea as we stirred and cooked the stuff, and I would think, Pasquale, how in the hell did you ever get yourself in a bind like this? (I not only spoke as Pasquale Lombardi, I thought as Pasquale Lombardi. You develop habits like this if you want to make cases. It also keeps you alive.)

"This is Giuseppe Mancuso," Cusack had said when he handed me some pictures to look at. "He's all yours."

We were in the Bureau office in the annex across from the Embassy in Rome. The ceiling fans turned ever so slowly as I looked at the pictures. A severe, thin-faced man looked back. He wore a half-smile, half-smirk.

Mancuso, the files showed me, was in his early 50s, about 160 pounds, black wavy hair. (My own Sicilian grandaunt had coal-black, waist-length hair in her 80s . . . they said it was the olive oil in the food.) The file said his eyes were brown, but nothing in the pictures prepared me for those one-way eyes that seemed to take everything in, I decided later, and give damn little back. . . .

The file they'd built on Giuseppe showed that he was no small-time dope peddler. He was big, big—big enough to be among the ten most wanted on the International List. And he had imagination. Before my time, I could see he had been one of the principals in the famous "Green Trunk Case" that involved smuggling heroin into the States in coffins carrying back the dead for burial.

Back in those relatively innocent days I guess a dead body was considered to be sacred. Anyhow, while the boys from Customs were standing around with their hats over their hearts, large shipments were going by them in secret compartments under the bodies. And most of it was from Giuseppe's lab.

They put Giuseppe Mancuso in jail but they didn't keep him there for long. He bribed an official—not an unheard-of thing in Sicily or even in supposedly more law-abiding places—and got back in the old business bigger than ever.

"The Italian police have been trying to locate him," Cusack said. "This will be a joint operation. You'll be working with the Rome Carabinieri. They'll back you up on the job, provide surveillance and make the arrest. I don't have to tell you what you're supposed to do. So work up a good cover."

If you're going to catch a dope peddler, you've got to masquerade as somebody who has a legitimate reason for trying to locate a dope peddler—say like a New York hood setting up on his own and looking for a new source of supply.

And so I became Pasquale Lombardi. I had all the real Pasquale Lombardi's credentials in the bottom drawer of my desk—wallet, prison I.D. card from a previous conviction, parole papers, pictures of a girl friend, the works. I had used the cover before. It almost felt comfortable and familiar.

We were old acquaintances, Lombardi and I. He was a mob guy back in the States who fitted my general description. Just before lifting his credentials we had done some business together and I knew he wouldn't be showing up to embarrass me.

He was doing time in Dannemora.

I had put him there.

As Pasquale Lombardi from the States, I was supposed to flash a big roll and start grabbing checks at bars. I did both. I also moved into a fancy penthouse suite overlooking the Tiber and the Castel Sant' Angelo and got around in a flashy Cadillac coupe de ville, government owned but with false registration.

When the phone rang in my penthouse suite it also rang on a private extension at Bureau headquarters. If nobody answered after five rings, a sleepy sexy female voice would come on and say, *"Pronto* . . . No, Pasquale isn't here . . . I don't know when he'll be back." (The voice belonged to Monica Atwill, the pretty girl at the Bureau.) I was supposed to be very big with the ladies and she was part of my cover.

Before leaving town, I secretly checked in with the Rome Carabinieri and met the informant who would duke me to my target. The informant went on ahead to Palermo so he was on hand when I arrived. I'll call him Rocco because he may still be walking around somewhere.

The police had Rocco over a barrel, which meant he had the historic choice of the stoolie—go along or go to jail, or worse. No wonder that Rocco readily agreed to duke me to Giuseppe Mancuso.

Everything, as in the case of Luciano, would start—or end—with the introduction. The guy that vouches for you is what counts, especially with a Sicilian. Never try a self-introduction. The go-between does it. He dukes you, builds you up, he brags on you. Hell, you can't very well do it yourself. So I rehearsed Rocco one more time in my room about the sterling qualities that would recommend me to the likes of Giuseppe Mancuso and sent him off to do his stuff.

Which meant Rocco would be saying to Mancuso something like: "Giuseppe, I have a man who is worth doing business with. I have known him for years. He's a friend of ours." (A friend of "ours" translates Mafia. A friend of "mine" might mean he's probably O.K. but only "a friend of ours" means Mafia.) And Rocco should also be saying, "He was brought to me by blood. I vouch for him with my life."

I hoped he was convincing. Otherwise, both of us might come up dead.

All I could do was check into a hotel and sweat it out, which wasn't altogether a hardship. I mean, the Hotel Jolly in Palermo was sort of a swinging joint. It had an open-air bar downstairs and a dining room. Bankers and local bigwigs could bring a friend there without being seen by their wives. The wine list was good.

On the second day, Rocco was smiling when he came up to my room. "He wants to meet you," he said.

"When?"

"Downstairs in front of the hotel. At three. He'll pick you up."

"Me alone?"

Rocco looked at the floor. "He don't really like me much. He trusts me and he uses me, but he don't really like me."

Well, I thought, Giuseppe and I have one thing in common already. To Rocco I said, "So get lost," which he did.

I was waiting downstairs at three. Mancuso showed like I did, right on time. I recognized him from his pictures and he knew me because I was the only American there. He nodded curtly and looked through me with those saffron eyes.

I got the impression that he was looking at somebody behind me, that I was transparent. Then I thought the hell with him. I'm Pasquale Lombardi, and he needs me. . . .

"We will take a ride," he told me. It was neither question nor statement. I shrugged. The right shrug, I hoped.

Sicilians have a shrug for everything.

And I'll be damned if we didn't go for a ride in a donkey cart.

I sized him up sideways as we walked toward the cart whose driver waited near the hotel. Giuseppe had on an expensive suit and obviously thought he looked pretty sharp. Actually, he was baggy. Everything always seemed three sizes too big for him. The full-pleated trousers seemed as if he would have to take two steps before the pants started moving. Hey, don't make jokes, Pasquale, I told myself, don't even *think* jokes.

The reason for the cart developed later. It was simply that Giuseppe didn't trust the local taxi drivers. He knew they sometimes passed information along to the police. Donkey drivers were different. They were part of the Palermo scene—uniquely Sicilian. And the gaudy carts they drove were heirlooms, painted and repainted with love and care and handed down from generation to generation.

Taking a seat in the cart, Giuseppe got out that big knife with the hook on it and started cleaning his nails. We both kept silent, except I was thinking how corny can you get with the knife and nails routine. Like an old B-grade gangster movie. And once again Pasquale Lombardi had to remind himself not to take this man lightly—and above all to shut up.

One of the hardest cons is saying nothing at all. It works best with the tough cases, cases like Giuseppe Mancuso. Besides, not volunteering information is an old Sicilian tradition. So I stayed traditional.

The cart creaked slowly along for a good ten minutes, and finally Giuseppe turned and looked at me. "Do you wish to discuss business?"

"That's possible."

He started talking but about everything else—the weather, the olive crop, his grandfather, and some other things that didn't mean a damn thing.

It seemed like forever before we were back at the hotel. "I will see you again," Giuseppe said.

"I'll be here," I said, turned and went into the hotel.

My second floor room had been searched while I was gone. No drawers were left pulled out. No clothes were scattered around. That's for bad TV shows. But someone had been there for Giuseppe. And they found exactly what I wanted them to find—a couple of letters postmarked "New York, N.Y." and addressed to Pasquale Lombardi in Rome; a photograph of a big-chested girl inscribed "To Pasquale, With Love"; and a pair of cuff links with the initial L.

In fact, if two things hadn't been moved I couldn't have been sure anybody'd been there. But the registration for my Cadillac hadn't been put back exactly, with one tiny corner under the drawer edge. And in the same drawer, a slip of paper with my phone number in Rome had been moved ever so slightly.

Whoever called that number would get an earful of a female voice saying, "No, he's away on business in Paris for several days.

No, I don't know how to reach him. Would you leave a message, please?" Monica was extremely capable.

I walked down the hall to another second floor room and knocked three times. I was checking in with three members of the Carabinieri who had come down from Rome to work with me. One of them named Gentile cracked the door and squinted out. He was a police brigadier, which is the equivalent of sergeant. The room was heavy with cigarette smoke and the beds hadn't been made. The two others looked up from a table where they were slapping down cards in their everlasting game of Scoba. They were coatless but wore their shoulder harnesses each with a gun under the left armpit. They slept with those guns. I didn't have one. It was too dangerous a giveaway in my line of work.

"Well, I met him," I said. "I think he went for me."

The card game stopped. After all, they had been on Mancuso's tail for years, and now I might be a pipeline right to him.

"Break out a new deck," I told them. "This thing might take time."

When my telephone rang the next morning it was Giuseppe Mancuso and he was downstairs. We met in the bar. I had *caffè latte*. He had espresso. I also felt it was time to take the offensive, and his telephone call gave me a good excuse.

"Giuseppe, the telephone. It goes through the switchboard, right? People could listen, right? This could be a bad business."

He looked at me with those plate glass eyes and then nodded. "You are right, Pasquale." He seemed pleased that I had given him the right lines.

We went for another ride in a donkey cart, and that was when I stole his knife.

I don't remember how many donkey rides we took in the days

that followed, but it was just about every day. Always it was the same driver, and for all I know the same donkey. Each time, Giuseppe became a little bit friendlier and a little bit more talkative. His greetings became warmer—from a nod to a handshake.

He liked me and, more surprising, I sort of liked him even though my job was to put him away. He was an intriguing guy. He took great pride in his work, such as it was. If he was going to make heroin, as his father had before him, he was damn well going to make the best heroin. A pro with a pro's pride. . . .

And he wasn't about to worry over the misery the output of his lab caused people all over the world. There was no heroin-addiction problem in Sicily and the local Mafia meant to keep it that way. It was a well-known fact they would bury anybody responsible for getting the local population hooked. The stuff was strictly for export. If people in some faraway land had to have the stuff, they would supply it. Business was business. . . .

It was on these donkey cart rides that Mancuso began boasting of his skills. The ice was broken and we got down to the hard details of business. He asked what my buyers wanted, how much, and I asked him what he had. We discussed price. How much he could produce. Our relationship blossomed. We shook hands. . . .

But where was that secret lab? This was my mission. I suggested maybe if I could work with him in his lab I'd be in a better position to tell my customers what grade stuff they were getting.

"Be patient, Pasquale."

A light rain was falling that night when he dropped me off at my hotel. "You'll hear from me," he said, and as he drove off in the drizzle, he seemed a strangely sad and lonely figure of a man.

That loneliness could be my leverage. Giuseppe Mancuso had no close family. One of his brothers was missing. The other was a fugitive. He wasn't married. What does a lonely man want? He wants a friend. And being the kind of man he was, he wanted a friend who understood how damn good he was at what he was doing. I almost whistled as I went into the hotel.

Now understand me, sympathy is a luxury you can't afford in this business, and I didn't waste any on a lonesome dope peddler named Giuseppe Mancuso. Better to save your sympathy for the family of the next dying junkie you meet. They aren't hard to find these days.

It wasn't until several days later that he touched me on the shoulder and said, "Tonight I will take you to my place of business."

"Giuseppe," I said, "you make me very happy."

"How is this?" he asked in his low, raspy voice.

"My grandfather, wherever he is, is happy because I have been taken under the guidance of a man as worthy of respect as he was."

I reached out for the usual handshake, but for the first time he solemnly gave me the Sicilian gesture of true friendship. He kissed me on both cheeks.

Mancuso blindfolded me with a black silk scarf that first night he took me to the lab, a moonless night and I rode in the back of a Mercedes-Benz as black as a hearse.

"Pasquale, this is necessary," he said almost apologetically as he knotted the scarf.

"Giuseppe," I said. "I've got faith in you."

I could hardly tell him I didn't but faith gets a little shaky when you're sitting in the back of a car in double darkness, black on black, speeding through the night. Imagination tends to work overtime. I thought of a hundred things that might have happened to tip my hand.

Suppose they had checked and found that the real Pasquale Lombardi was in cell-block D at Dannemora? Suppose they had discovered that the three Carabinieri in Room 204 were my back-up men? Suppose I'd goofed my lines when I thought I was being so damn clever. . . .

Before leaving the hotel I had alerted the Carabinieri. "If you want to put a tail on me, all right. But drop off quick if there's *any* chance of being spotted."

They took up positions downstairs, and I saw them trying to pass for bored tourists when I walked out into the night with Mancuso. We took a donkey cart again but only for about a half mile. Then we switched to the waiting Mercedes-Benz with two "muscle" guys sitting in the front seat. Even when Giuseppe had knotted the blindfold I could still see them, and in my mind's eye they looked even more unfriendly.

"Is the blindfold too tight?" Giuseppe asked.

"No," I said. "No, but I appreciate your asking." He really seemed concerned.

We drove about twelve minutes, near as I could judge, and stopped after what had to be no more than eight kilometers. From the lack of turns we'd made I thought we might be in the vicinity of Monte Pellegrino. I wondered if the Carabinieri were behind us.

Mancuso took my arm and helped me out of the car. Still blindfolded, I counted thirty-five paces. Then we walked up five steps and through a door. At this point Mancuso took off my blindfold.

The two friends were outside, and he and I stood in a typical Italian home, a combined living and dining room with high ceilings, marble floors and not much furniture. The windows were closed and shuttered and there were bars between the shutters and the glass. This wasn't unusual. Most Italian homes have bars on the windows. But I was disappointed. I had myself all primed to open my eyes and see a full-blown heroin lab.

"We'll eat, eh?" Mancuso asked.

"Sure," I agreed, although food was the last thing I had in mind.

He led the way into a huge kitchen where a heavy, hand-hewn table was all set. On the table were pasta and veal, that good Italian bread you break off with your hands instead of cutting, and Chianti in open-mouthed liter bottles. There was food aplenty but no other people. Just me and Mancuso.

Where was everybody? I kept thinking as I forced myself to push down the food.

"You enjoyed your dinner?" Giuseppe asked politely.

"Sure. It was just great."

The condemned man bit? You never know; not really.

He got out fruit and cheese. Then the coffee. It was all I could do to keep from asking about the lab. Don't do it, I told myself. Finally, he gave me the closest thing to a real smile I ever saw on him and motioned to me: "Come, my friend."

He led the way out of the kitchen and down a spiral staircase. At the foot of the stairs we came to a heavy door with a huge padlock. That huge, carved door was a work of art and designed to be around a while. Giuseppe took out a key. The door creaked open. We went down another step.

The lab.

My first thought, as we stood on the threshold, was that Commissioner Anslinger and John Cusack should see this!

My second thought was that I probably was the first agent in history to walk into a bona fide heroin lab without first kicking down the door.

"This is our place of business," Giuseppe said proudly.

The lab was a huge cellar with stone walls like a dungeon, a hard-packed dirt floor and no windows. What light there was came from dim bulbs hanging down from the ceiling by their own cords. Unlit candles sat in crude sconces on the walls.

Cordwood was stacked in one corner and two sides of the cellar were taken up with tubs and ventilating paraphernalia. Pipes connected to metal hoods turned at right angles and went through mortar and stone to the outside.

I looked around for the morphine base, or the raw opium or the heroin. All I saw were glass jugs of clear acid, thirty or forty of them, lined up in varying shapes and sizes. They had glass tops, or stoppers, because acid would eat cork away.

"Here is where we will work," Mancuso added rather unnecessarily.

"When do we start?"

He was surveying his workshop proudly. "I have a shipment of morphine base getting here in a few days and we will start immediately once it arrives."

I made a mistake. I asked him where the base was coming from.

"I have sources," he said quietly. "They are good sources." Subject closed.

I was making a mental diagram of the lab. In case for some reason I didn't get back again, the Carabinieri would want to know the dimensions, location of the door, the exits if any, other details.

Trying to ride over my gaffe, I asked Mancuso why he didn't do the whole operation there, starting from scratch with raw opium. "That would eliminate the middle man," I suggested. "We could make more money." (The first step in the manufacture of heroin is converting raw opium to morphine base. Step two is the conversion of morphine to heroin.)

"It is better this way," he said. As it developed, he had people in Lebanon and Syria, close to the opium fields of Turkey, who handled phase one. The logistics of drug-making dictated this, since the average conversion ratio is roughly one to ten—that is, it takes ten kilos of opium to produce one kilo of morphine base.

Mancuso put a firm hand on my elbow and ushered me toward the door. The visit was over. He led me back upstairs and out to the Mercedes-Benz, where the two other men were waiting. I climbed into the back with Mancuso and waited for the blindfold. There was none.

"No more blindfold." He shrugged. "I am satisfied, Pasquale."

"I appreciate this, Giuseppe." I really did.

On the ride back I didn't try to get a fix on our route. I couldn't see myself leaning forward and rubbernecking for landmarks. Besides, chances were good now that I'd be coming back anyhow.

Four nights later, I did.

And I was really startled when he led the way into the lab, whose location I had managed to pinpoint on this trip. "Good God, Giuseppe!" I said when he switched on the light bulbs in the lab. There were four large suitcases—big as trunks, actually—sitting open on the dirt floor. I'd never seen so much junk at one time before. Each suitcase was filled with transparent plastic bags that I knew contained morphine base. I opened one and rubbed the coarse light brown powder between my thumb and forefinger.

"How much is here?" I asked with an awe I didn't need to fake.

He actually laughed—a short, sharp laugh. "We got one hundred and thirty kilos."

I did some quick mental arithmetic and made it come out to about 286 pounds of heroin, enough to fix every junkie in New York City.

We worked the whole night. Mancuso, the maestro, hovering over me, the protégé, explaining, demonstrating, cautioning. It was hard, agonizing work. Mancuso was a perfectionist.

We started by putting the morphine base in large tubs for cooking—four bags of morphine base to a tub, spread out evenly with a wooden scoop. Then the acid.

"No, no!" Mancuso said. "Not like that, like *this!*" Then he showed me how to pour the acid (mostly from bottles with fake labels in German) so that it went around the edges and twice across like an X.

"You don't want globs . . . it's how you pour . . . don't lean over the tub . . . painful fumes. Watch the acid, it'll eat right through you."

It looked like mixing cocoa with water until the acid started to work, burning out the impurities and creating a chemical action that produced diacetyl morphine-hydrochloride—translation: heroin.

"Watch close, Pasquale," he ordered, beginning to stir. He moved the scoop in precise motions, away from him and back, then around and across. Mix. Cook. Cough. Mix. . . .

We wore gauze masks but the fumes got to me eventually. Three times that night I went outside and threw up. Working in a heroin lab wasn't something I wanted to make my life's work.

"Giuseppe, does it ever make you sick?" I asked him.

"Yes, sometimes it still makes me sick."

"I didn't want to say anything. But sometimes I don't feel so good."

"It's understandable," he told me.

Each batch had to be cooked three times and dried three times. It was the drying process that took the time. This was done over in one corner on a table with raised edges. He showed me how to use a piece of glass, something like a large jalousie, to fold the stuff over and over. And it got lighter in color with each drying, changing from light brown to beige to oyster white.

The result: pure heroin. Before it got to the addict in the street it would be cut over and over with quinine and sugar powder. How many times depended on how many dope peddlers handled it. But coming out of Mancuso's lab it was as pure as heroin ever gets, which is about eighty-seven percent. In this "pure" state it can also be a deadly poison. For example, if it gets into an open cut, it can kill a person. It causes a painful rash if it gets on the skin. Any dose over thirty percent is usually lethal, and such a high-percentage dose is often used by the underworld as a method of eliminating junkies who are considered unreliable and therefore dangerous. They give him a fix of pure heroin and after he shoots it by himself they find him dead the next morning of an overdose. No evidence. Case closed. . . .

When that first nightmare night ended, Mancuso suggested I sleep there in the house, which I learned he used exclusively for business. I told him I had to go back to the hotel because I was expecting some word from my people. He didn't argue and on each of the next two evenings he picked me up and took me back to the hotel about dawn.

By now the Carabinieri were getting impatient to move in but I persuaded them to hold off. I wanted to tie up the loose ends, such as making positive identification of the two men that rode in the front seat of the Mercedes-Benz as well as two other men who had visited the house one evening (Mancuso's cousins?). I wanted the whole lot.

When Mancuso picked me up that last night, he looked at me with only one eye. The other was closed and watery. It looked like hell.

"What happened, Giuseppe?"

"A splash of acid. I couldn't get to water fast enough."

"Can you see?"

"No, Pasquale, but I have another eye." He actually said that. No show of emotion. No self-pity. I started to tell him how sorry I was, but he shut me off.

"Think no more about it," he said.

When we got to the lab he was all business as we began working on the contents of the third suitcase. "We will finish in another week. I will need money for the next shipment."

"I understand, Giuseppe." Friendship was one thing. My getting up a couple of hundred thousand dollars was another. Our arrangement was cash on delivery.

"I'll go to Rome in the morning. The money is there. I'll be back in a few days," I told him.

"No need to hurry, my friend, but you understand these matters must be attended to."

Giuseppe drove me to the airport the next morning in the black Mercedes-Benz and when we said good-by I knew it was for the last time. Pasquale Lombardi had no intention of coming back. Still, I won't deny I felt a twinge as I watched him walk away, his pants baggy in the seat, his thin neck jutting up from his oversize coat. And a patch over the acid-scarred eye.

The next day I called him from Rome. "I have the money. I didn't want you to worry."

"I'm starting on the last suitcase tonight," he advised me. "I'll have it all finished in a few days."

The timing was perfect. The Carabinieri hit the lab that night with the help of the Palermo police. They got everybody.

The case made headlines and the Carabinieri got all the credit, which was a relief to me. The last thing an undercover agent wants is publicity. Pasquale Lombardi and his credentials went back in the files, just in case I might ever need them again.

They put Giuseppe Mancuso away for fifteen years, but not before the Palermo police worked him over pretty good. They quickly got it out of one of the two bodyguards that an American "gangster" had been working in the lab with Mancuso. The Carabinieri were under strict orders not to reveal my identity or my role in the case. The Palermo police were determined to arrest me or at least find out who I was. They put the full heat on Mancuso, and I can tell you that the Sicilians—police and Mafia both—have very persuasive ways.

Giuseppe Mancuso never cracked.

He never said who his friend was.

CHAPTER 4

The King in Exile

OPERATION LEPO, code for the Luciano operation, had priority over everything else. For almost three years, from 1959 until the day my target dropped dead at the Naples airport, I was periodically ordered to interrupt whatever case I was on and proceed to Naples.

I visited Luciano nine times in all. Each time it meant climbing back into my Air Force cover as Major Mike Cerra (later I got promoted), updating traveling orders and retooling myself mentally. After a while I found myself thinking about the pitcher that went to the well too often. I thought a lot about it. Charlie Lucky Luciano wasn't to be taken lightly. Playing up to him was like offering your head to a cobra. One mistake and out. He had killed a hundred men, maybe more than that, and he hadn't survived or gotten where he was by being careless.

Still, my job was to get so close to him that he thought of me as one of the family, the pilot who represented something he could respect on the other side of the tracks.

From a risk standpoint, my second visit to Naples was the most critical. By then, two months had gone by since my introduction by

Sam Cook. If Luciano was going to do any checking on me, he would have done it then. And as good as my Air Force cover was it wouldn't stand intensive scrutiny. No cover really can if it's put to a full test. You just can't cover everything. Any competent private investigator could have shot holes in mine. Who were my Air Force buddies, what girls did I date, where had I gone to school, what were my parents doing now and what did they think I was doing? Inquiries into any of these areas would have aroused suspicions. The point was, I had to be so plausible that nobody would be suspicious enough to check beyond the cover. Once they start to distrust you seriously, you're already in very serious trouble that no cover can totally protect you from.

When John T. Cusack called me in to say I was going back to see Luciano, he told me to go in with my eyes open. I told him that I already had this in mind.

"Other agencies in Washington have become interested in this investigation," he said. "They want to be kept informed of its progress. I don't have to tell you that Commissioner Anslinger has a personal interest. He read your first report and wants more."

Cusack said that headquarters was particularly interested in paragraph 16 of my original report, which noted that Luciano was about to make a tax payment to the Italian government of 2,500,000 lire, or about $4,000, on money received from the United States. A check had shown that Luciano had received no funds from the U.S. by way of normal channels. This meant that it was probably being delivered in cash by special courier and Luciano the respectable businessman decided he'd look good paying some taxes (just the reverse of Capone).

"See what you can develop in this area. We want to know how much Lucky is being paid and by whom. And, of course, the original instructions still stand. We want to know everything about him."

I boarded the train in Rome feeling the same kind of queasiness I used to feel when I went off the 50-foot platform in a diving contest. I had been a fair country diver at one time. Also a water-show comic. Any athlete will tell you that when you stop feeling those butterflies it's time to quit. You've lost your edge.

After checking into the Hotel Mediterraneo in Naples I headed for the San Francisco Bar and Grill and found it almost deserted. Luciano wasn't there. Neither was Joe the Wop nor Cockeyed Johnny Raimondo. But sitting at a table with a girl was Luigi Pappagallo, the stylish harbor pilot.

How he reacted when he saw me would tell me a lot. If anything had gone wrong, I hoped I would see it in Luigi's face. But his expression brightened when he spotted me—the look of one friend greeting another.

"Hey, Major," he said, jumping up and extending his hand. "I didn't know you were in town. Sit down and have a drink. The other guys will be glad to know you're here."

I relaxed and ordered a Cinzano. Luigi Pappagallo couldn't be that good an actor. He said he had an appointment that night but would cancel it and spend the time with me.

"Charlie will be sorry to hear he missed you," he went on. "He went down to Palermo on business and won't be back for a couple of days."

"That's too bad," I said. "I was really hoping to see him."

I was disappointed but I was also glad Luciano hadn't decided to go to Palermo two weeks earlier when I was there as Pasquale Lombardi going after Giuseppe Mancuso. If I'd had that unplanned rendezvous, two cases would have gone down the drain and I'd have gone with them.

Luigi asked me if I'd like to see the art gallery Cockeyed Johnny Raimondo ran for Luciano, and I quickly told him that would be fine. After all, everything owned by Salvatore Lucania, alias Charlie Lucky, alias Lucky Luciano, was of interest to me and the Bureau.

We took a cab to the Royal Art Studio, located on a hill not far from NATO headquarters. Raimondo gave me the big hello and proudly showed me around.

"I'm doin' real good here," he said. "Every cent I make Charlie lets me put back into the business. What the hell, he doesn't need the money."

I'm hardly an expert, but his place at least had a wide selection of paintings and there were several customers not only looking but buying. Maybe the real ownership had leaked out and people liked to come just to be somehow in the presence of the notorious Luciano.

Raimondo rattled on. "I got me a bunch of local painters lined up and I pay them five bucks each for these paintings—lots of scenes of Naples and other Italian cities. I put them in cheap frames and sell them for at least twenty bucks. Lots of servicemen come in here and when they can't pay cash I take cigarettes they get cheap from the PX and then I sell them at a good profit. Either way I come out way ahead. Hey, why don't you pick one out, Major?"

I told him I couldn't afford the twenty bucks, and he seemed offended.

"It's a gift. Charlie'd kill me if he thought I charged you. I couldn't do that to a friend of his."

I thanked him for the offer, telling him I had no place to put a painting.

Raimondo insisted on closing the studio for the rest of the day and going back with Pappagallo and me to the San Francisco Bar and Grill. When we got there we found Vincenzo Facchini, who also greeted me like an old friend and introduced me to a man he was sitting with named Pietro Ventimiglia. I made him from the files as a small-time hood who'd been deported from St. Louis some years before on suspicion of having smuggled heroin into the United States.

Ventimiglia was a talkative, arrogant type and after a quarter of an hour dominating the conversation without saying anything, he said he had another date and left.

Facchini took me aside. "He's a guy to stay away from, Major. He talks too damned much and he's always in trouble with the police for swindling American sailors. Charlie doesn't like to have him around."

I had dinner with Pappagallo, Facchini and Raimondo, and later Pappagallo took me to an outside terrace at a waterfront bar where we sat and talked.

"How do you like Naples?" he asked me.

"I think it's great."

"Well, why don't you ask the Air Force to transfer you here?"

I told him I'd like to, but that knowing the Air Force, if I asked to be assigned to Naples I'd probably be transferred to Japan.

Pappagallo laughed and then talked about his friendship with Luciano. "It ain't all cake and ice cream for Charlie," he said as we walked back to my hotel. "The local police are always looking for an excuse to arrest him or question him. They're not really interested in putting him in jail. They only want pay-offs and Charlie has to take care of them. Charlie's smart, though, and he never forgets anything."

Which made it very clear that if I ever did get crowded during my Naples operation I'd play hell looking to the local police for any help.

I'd missed seeing Luciano on this trip to Naples, but I had firmed up my friendship with his intimates, learned that Ventimiglia, a narcotics suspect, was one of their group however unpopular, and most important had established that my cover was intact and that Major Mike Cerra was beginning to have a home away from home.

The next time I went back I was in luck. Facchini was at the San Francisco Bar and Grill—he practically lived in the place—and Luciano was with him.

He seemed glad to see me and asked where I'd been. I told him that I'd been flying all over, to the Mid-East and back to the States, and that I was reporting to the Naples NATO hospital for a checkup on a neck injury. That's why I could get back so soon this time. He wanted to know about my neck, and I told him I'd crashed on a take-off and was lucky to get out alive.

Before leaving Rome I'd met with Cusack and we decided it would look better this early in the game if I had a specific reason for coming to Naples this time. Just dropping in for the third time in four months might arouse suspicions, so we invented the crack-up and neck injury and Cusack went through the motions of having somebody notify the hospital about Major Cerra and when he'd get there.

"I'd quit flying if I were you," Luciano said, and I told him I might if I could find a job where I could be as loose and make as much money as I could in the Air Force. He looked at me, but didn't say anything. He got the message, though.

I changed the subject and asked where Luigi Pappagallo was. I knew they spent a lot of time together and I didn't see the harbor pilot around.

"He sailed five days ago for New York on the *Constitution*," Luciano said.

With their being so intimate, I thought, Pappagallo would probably be contacting some of Luciano's people in New York.

"I'm probably going to New York the end of the month," I told Luciano. "Maybe I can see him there." I thought it would be better to get his address and maybe try to see him than alert anybody in New York right away and risk putting the finger on myself as an informant. If nothing happened after Luciano confided in me once, he'd be less suspicious that the tip came from me another time. And I'd take the chance there'd be another time for busy Luigi.

"Luigi won't get there until the second or third of October," Luciano said, "and he isn't sure where he's staying but he'll write me as soon as he has an address. I gave him a few names in New York so it won't take him long. I'll let you know where you can find him. He talks about you a lot and would get a kick seeing you in the States."

Pappagallo had gotten a six months visitor's visa, Luciano said, and planned to marry an Italo-American girl.

Luciano, Facchini and I ordered lunch, and while we were waiting a newsboy came in and Luciano bought an Italian newspaper and the Paris edition of the *Herald-Tribune*. He finally landed on a headline that he seemed to be looking for.

"You read this about Pici and Gioia?" He stared at Facchini, slapped the paper in disgust.

Facchini said he'd read it that morning.

"What's it about?" I asked. I already knew. Cusack had briefed me before I left about the arrest in Genoa of Giuseppe Pici and Giovanni Gioia—both suspected of being major suppliers of heroin to the New York operation. In fact, one of the reasons for this visit was to get on the spot Luciano's reaction to these arrests.

"Oh, nothing much," Luciano said. "It's just that some friends of ours got themselves arrested in Genoa." Luciano looked back at the paper and this time banged a fist on the table so hard that the dishes and silverware rattled.

When he pushed the paper aside I casually scanned the story. This account was in an early edition and neither Pici's nor Gioia's name actually was mentioned in the story—which meant that Luciano had first heard of their arrest by some other means, probably through the underworld grapevine. It also meant he was closely enough linked to them to be informed early about what had happened to them.

There was more news for Luciano in the *Herald-Tribune*—an article reporting the gunning down in New York of Anthony Carfano, better known as Little Augie Pisano.

"He got his retirement," Facchini said.

Luciano read the article slowly, then said almost to himself, "See what happens when you don't move for the big guy?"

The "big guy" would be the head of the sydnicate. Once it had been Luciano, and there were those who believed he still was. But New York was the center of the action, and after Luciano had been deported Vito Genovese moved up. When Genovese went to prison, Jerry Giancanno was supposed to have been the boss but we believe it was Tommy Ryan—real name Thomas Eboli, who was recently killed in New York.

I wanted to ask some questions about this, but I decided not to at the moment—especially not with Luciano in his black mood.

Luciano said he wanted to take a walk and get some air, and while we were strolling through the September sunshine, with Momo bringing up the rear, we came to a movie marquee advertising Bob Hope in a picture called "Here Comes Jesse James." And here I am, I thought, with a guy who makes Jesse James look like Shirley Temple.

Luciano pointed at a billboard picture of Hope. "Back in New York in '30 I invested five grand in a play Hope was in. I met Hope and saw the play early. It looked like a flop to me so I went to the producer and got my five G's back. No argument."

I could believe it.

Later I heard—I don't know if it's true or not—that Luciano said Hope came to Italy with Louella Parsons, called him and said he'd like to say hello. Luciano was supposed to have said he'd have gone to see Hope if he had not been with Louella Parsons—and called her a bitch.

We stopped for a while at the California Restaurant, and then he called the San Francisco and had a car come and pick us up to take us back there for supper. While we ate Luciano asked me where I spent most of my time when I was in the States, and I told him that I sort of commuted between New York and Miami.

"I envy you," he told me. "Just six months, that's all I want, three months in New York and three months in Miami. Then they could bury me. I'd be satisfied."

"How long have you been gone from New York?" I asked him.

"A lifetime, Mike, a lifetime. And I'd still be there if it wasn't for that son of a bitch Tom Dewey. He framed me, Mike, and that's the God's truth. I never took a dime from a woman in my life, let alone from a prostitute. For a while I didn't know what was happening. Some of the protection boys were going around to the whorehouses and shaking them down for twenty-five bucks a week for each prostitute. If the madam kicked they told her I sent them. When I heard about it I sent word that under no circumstances was my name to be used in any such kind of a business. But it was too late by then. Dewey was the D.A. and he got hold of it. He was looking to make a name for himself so he framed me. He sent his men out to tell all the madams that if they wanted to stay in business they'd have to testify that they were paying protection money to me."

Luciano stopped a moment and then went on. "They had me up there at Dannemora when the war broke out. Nobody ever officially gave me credit, Mike, but damn it, I helped the U.S. government."

I told him I'd heard something about that, but never a full story.

"Well, they were having a lot of sabotage on the New York and Jersey waterfront. They heard I had some influence with the longshoremen and the union bosses. So one day the warden calls me in his office and there's a navy commander with him. They want to know if I'll get the boys into a meeting and set up a kind of an organization that will watch out for any screwy stuff going on around the docks. I called a meeting of longshore guys right up there in the warden's office and we set up just what they wanted.

"Later on the commander comes back to see me again. He says don't breathe a word to nobody but we're getting ready to invade Sicily and they need my help again. They want me to get together a lot of the guys I know, Sicilians and Neapolitans especially, so we can give them people they can work into the underground in Sicily and tell them about troop movements, the enemy's military strength and anything else important going on there. Well, Mike, it was kind of funny. A lot of guys must have had a helluva bad feeling walking into that joint under their own power. But they all showed when I sent out the word I wanted them. It was some kind of muscle, let me tell you. We held a council of war right there in the warden's office, with the commander and some naval intelligence guys, and before it was over we had a whole bunch of meetings, all very hush-hush. My guys got so they waltzed right through the gates like they owned the place. I should of got a medal."

"Well," I said, "at least they let you out."

"Let me out hell, Mike! Dewey wouldn't have let me out in a thousand years if he had his way. But I'll tell you what happened. I had a whole damned battery of lawyers. I told them I didn't care what it cost but I wanted them to dig into Dewey's background. They came up with a pile of information on him that might have put his ass in the can. This much."

He held his thumb and forefinger three inches apart.

"My lawyer walked right into his office in the State House in Albany. He was governor of New York by then mostly because he sent me up. Big racket buster. I buried more than a hundred guys

and I go up on a lousy prostitution rap. Anyhow, my lawyer threw
that file down in front of him and told him if I didn't get out we
were going to make it all public. So he deported me. But at least I
got out. . . ."

Luciano suddenly stood up and said, "Let's go down to the Snake
Pit and hear some music." From somewhere behind me Momo the
bodyguard showed and followed us down the stairs. The same old
look was fastened to his face.

Luciano and I took a seat at a table and he motioned for two
girls at another table to join us. Both of them were attractive, one
dark and Italian, the other blonde and German. The brunette looked
no more than nineteen. "You like the blonde?" Luciano asked me,
indicating, I guessed, that he had already settled on the dark-haired
one for himself.

I said I did. I decided a dashing Air Force major had better not
cop out in an area so near and dear to the big man's heart.

After a few minutes Hilda and I got up to dance and then I noticed Momo sitting by himself at a table on the edge of the dance
floor.

I knew he didn't like me. You don't need that kind of a thing in
writing. I'm not even too sure I could blame him. Every time I
showed up Luciano shunted him into the background, obviously
even ordered him to keep away from his table when I was around.
He probably figured he deserved better than that for all he'd done
for Luciano, and no doubt he was right. He sure couldn't take it
out on his boss, so I seemed the safer target.

Now, as we danced past him, he suddenly stuck out his foot and
tripped me. I didn't quite go down but, as I swiveled my head in
Momo's direction, I saw that he could smile. I started for him but
Hilda pulled me back and held tight to me.

"No," she said. "Let's dance."

"O.K.," I said, and danced her out toward the middle of the

floor and then back again toward Momo's table. As we passed his table I reached out and tipped a drink onto his lap.

In one motion he was on his feet and coming at me. I pushed the girl aside and timed it just right. When he got close enough, reaching off balance to grab me, I gave him a karate chop in the throat and he went down on the dance floor.

He made some gagging noises for a few seconds and then grabbed for his gun. As he did I kicked it out of his hand and managed to get it before he did and stuck it in my belt so nobody would see it.

The band was still playing and Lucky was hollering, "What the hell's going on? What's happening?"

I went over to him. "Hey, Charlie, this guy's crazy. He pulled a gun on me."

He looked at Momo who was still out on the dance floor with one hand over his throat. "I don't know what the hell's wrong with him," Lucky said. Then he turned to Momo. "Get out of here. I don't want to see you no more tonight."

Momo left without a word but his look toward me said it all.

"Here's his pop gun," I said, holding out the .45 to Luciano.

He shook his head. "Give it to the bartender."

"O.K.," I said, but before I did I went to the men's room and made a note of the make and serial number. I debated about whether to remove the firing pin and decided against it. Too risky. The next time he tried shooting cans off a fence post he'd be sure to figure I was the one that had disarmed it. Worse yet, so would Luciano, who might not appreciate me taking that kind of liberty with his boy.

Back at the table with Lucky I found him looking at me with new eyes. "You're pretty good, Mike," he said. "Where'd you learn that kind of stuff?"

I shrugged it off. "They make all flying personnel take courses in it. You know, self-defense, jungle survival and all that kind of stuff. In case you're ever shot down over enemy territory."

It seemed to satisfy him.

"I like having you around, kid," he said. "You're O.K." Then he almost smiled as he added, "But you better take it a little easy with the rough stuff until you get that neck fixed up. Hell, you could get it broken."

I think he was trying to tell me something, and I was listening.

One of the matters I was briefed on before leaving for this trip to Naples was a recent two-part series in *Life* magazine on the Mafia, its notorious meeting in Appalachia in upper New York State, suspected and known Mafia members deported from the United States and the international narcotics problem. I was given copies of the magazines and told to use my discretion about showing them to Luciano. I also brought a gift for my new friend from the Embassy PX—a twenty-five-year-old bottle of Scotch.

I had held off a day in bringing him this explosive material until I had the feel of how things were developing for us. After the go-round with Momo, which seemed to impress him, and his fairly open reactions to the news about his Genoa friends Pici and Gioia, I decided to risk it and also give him my vintage booze. Besides, I'd already said I was here to check into the hospital about my neck injury and I couldn't very plausibly hold off on that much longer.

So the next morning, armed with my copies of *Life* and the Scotch, I found Luciano at a table in the California Restaurant, looking aloof and reserved and flanked by two young girls whom he introduced me to as an Air Force major and good friend of his (that *was* confirmation of progress, I thought). He asked me what I wanted to drink and for once I told him the truth—hot tea. When I said it one of the girls started laughing.

Luciano turned to the girl and asked her what she was laughing at. "He's a flyer, not a bar-flyer like you." The girl stopped laughing, and Luciano suggested she and her friend get lost. As we watched their rear ends going out the door, Luciano asked me, "Which one you want?"

"They both look like champions," I told him, "but I'm in no shape to play any more this trip—last night sort of did it for me. Besides I got to check into the hospital tomorrow morning about this damn pain in my neck."

He nodded and told me that Luigi Pappagallo had suddenly come back to Naples. I said that was one fast trip, and he said Luigi had had some trouble with his girl, didn't get married and decided to fly home right away.

I told him with a straight face that I was sorry to hear about that and looked forward to seeing Luigi again. Then I said I'd almost forgotten something the day before and took out the Scotch from a bag I'd carried it in from the hotel and handed it to him.

He seemed really pleased with the gift. "You didn't have to do this, Mike," he said. "I got plenty of this stuff up at the house. I get it off ships by the case. No tax." He didn't drink it himself, but free's free, and I'd already noted the deep-grained cheap streak in the man, despite his power and his flow of tribute from stateside sources. I also would learn that the steaks he served at home were free from the larder of ships whose pursers were also his couriers.

After giving him the bottle of Scotch, I unrolled the two issues of *Life* that I had under my arm and handed them to him. "Almost forgot something else," I said. "I picked these up when I was back in the States and thought you'd be interested. Charlie, you made the hit parade."

I turned to a page showing him sitting at a table right here in the California Restaurant. His face lit up when he saw a spread of several men deported for their illegal activities in the United States.

Then it darkened when he came to a second picture of himself standing on a street in Palermo.

"Those sneaky sons-of-bitches," he said. "You ain't safe nowhere in this goddamned world."

I told him that's what he got for being such a celebrity.

For the next ten minutes he sat reading the article, obviously laboring over some of the longer words. Finally he turned the magazine toward me. "My eyes ain't too good, Mike. Would you read this to me?"

I read it all to him and he kept his eyes fastened on me, sitting like a man in a trance. Whenever I came to a big word he didn't understand he'd ask me exactly what it meant. When I came to the parts about him he asked me to read them twice, and one part, about him being the king of the deportees, I had to read to him three times. When his name was mentioned, he would squeeze his hands into fists as if he were about to pound the table. Once, when the waiter came to take away my tea, Luciano chased him off with an authoritative wave of his hand without looking up.

The story on the sentences given out as a result of the Appalachian meeting sprung him from his trance. "You can go to jail for anything nowadays. You go visit a sick friend and end up with five years in prison. Barbara died later. That proved he was sick when all them guys went to see him."

He was referring to the grand conclave of Mafia leaders at the Barbara home in Appalachia. Federal agents and state police had raided the meeting, sending the concerned buddies of the "sick" host pouring out through windows and doors trying to escape. Most of them hadn't.

Seeing a chance to get in the question naturally, I asked what he would have done if he'd been at the meeting.

"I would have been the first to go to jail," he snapped out, and then paused a moment. "No, if I was in New York at the time, there wouldn't have been no need for the meeting. [By his now-and-then logic, Barbara wouldn't have been sick. Doctor Charlie would have dealt out preventive medicine?] If it hadn't been for Ass-slinger and his men, nobody would have known anything about the meeting."

He flipped through the magazine and jabbed a finger at a picture he found of Commissioner Anslinger.

"That's the son of a bitch," he said. "If it wasn't for him I'd be back on top in New York. He's worse than Hitler ever was. If I went back to New York, he'd be the first one to meet me on the dock." He also said that there were two things he really wanted to do before he died. The first was to spend six months in New York. The second was to piss on Anslinger's grave. (I filed this conversation without deletions in Bureau Report No. 18473, and a copy of it went to Commissioner Anslinger. He took real satisfaction out of Luciano's reaction. It meant he'd hit the Mafia where they hurt —pocketbook and pride.)

Luciano asked me if he could keep the magazines, and after I told him sure, I'd brought them for him, he said, "Come on, Mike, let's get out of here. I need some air. And don't forget my magazines."

He led the way out into the bright sunshine to his Alfa Romeo parked at the curb. It had a Naples 182727 tag, heater, a radio, and from habit I noticed the speedometer reading—six thousand kilometers. I got in the front seat next to Luciano.

After the trouble the previous night with Momo and what, despite my explanation, might have seemed a too expert disposal of him, the idea of a ride gave me a tight feeling between my shoulder blades. I knew Luciano carried a Beretta. But if he ever pulled it on me and I was within reach of him he was going to eat it. It was my nature and training to be always suspicious, but

I think I was right in believing that if I ever blew my cover with him this would be his move—to invite me for a ride, alone. This was a job he'd want to do himself.

So we went for the ride.

At best, Luciano was a bad driver. When he got annoyed he was murder behind the wheel. The little car jerked into motion, burning rubber. It piled up traffic at intersections, scattering pedestrians and motor scooters. We headed up the famed Amalfi Drive and took blind corners on the wrong side of the road. I held my breath. We ground to a stop in a sightseers' parking area high above the harbor, where he asked me to read again the sentences that had been given out to the Mafia leaders. This time I read them very slowly, stating the name, prison term and fine for each one convicted.

"A damned shame," he muttered when I was finished. "It's a crime, a damned crime." This final pronouncement from the man who straight-faced complained about being sent up on "a lousy prostitution rap" when he'd admittedly "buried more than a hundred guys."

Luciano drove in silence to the San Francisco Bar and Grill to his usual place right in front of the door. As we entered, he pulled a wad of $100 bills from his trousers pocket.

From a quick glance I guessed that there were twenty or thirty bills in that roll. He liked to carry a large wad of money and look at it from time to time. It wasn't that he was going to pay for anything. I'd never seen him pay for anything. Even the newspaper he took from a passing newsboy had been paid for by Momo or somebody else in his entourage.

"Charlie," I said. "If I had your money I'd throw mine away. Where do you get that kind of money around here?"

"Not in Italy, that's for sure."

I wanted a couple of those bills. There was a possibility the

Bureau could check the serial numbers against the numbers of marked bills used by agents in New York to make undercover buys of narcotics. The roll he carried could be part of his regular pay-off from the States.

"You know," I reminded him, "that I'm going into the hospital for a checkup on my neck tomorrow, Charlie. How about giving me one or two of your bills for a bunch of my small ones? It'll make it easier for me to keep track of my money." He agreed and I gave him five twenties and a handful of lire for two hundreds.

He looked close at me as we made the exchange. "That's a good idea, Mike. You're smart not to trust anybody."

The next day I checked into the NATO hospital long enough to make it look official and caught the afternoon express for Rome.

Cusack was waiting in his office for me when I arrived. He wanted the usual verbal briefing before I got around to my written report. I also gave him the two $100 bills I'd gotten from Luciano and the serial number of Momo's gun. One of the bills was a Federal Reserve Note, Series 1950 #B 07485233 A, and when it was checked out in New York it was found to be a listed bill that had been used in a large undercover heroin buy. I was impressed that Luciano trusted me enough to give me that bill, knowing as he probably did where it came from. Another confirmation of the solidness of my cover—or an invitation to trap myself?

One thing was sure. The king might be in exile. But it was now absolutely clear that the king wasn't dead.

Cusack let me know that there was somebody else going into exile. I would be moving permanently out of my apartment in Rome, which I'd hardly seen enough to call a home anyway, and transferred to Turkey—Istanbul to be exact—to head up operations there.

"Am I being taken off the Luciano case?"

"No. It just means that you'll be operating in and out of Turkey between your visits to Naples. We don't want to overdo that, and we do need to start moving hard against the sources of supply there."

"By the way," I said. "Exactly where the hell is Istanbul?"

"That way," he said, jerking his thumb in an easterly direction.

CHAPTER 5

Tough Turkey

THE TURKS are tough, with guts left over. They run at you when trouble starts instead of the other way. For example, Ali Kambur, a very tough Turk complete with mustache. He ran at me like a crazy man with only his knife against my gun the night we knocked over his opium-cooking factory out in the Turkish hills. It was near a village called Izmit.

I looked like a Turk myself, wearing a handle-bar mustache with the ends waxed to a point, my hair close-cropped under one of those old-fashioned, button-down caps. I straightened up from an opium vat cooking over a wood fire and tried to rub a kink out of my back. Stirring hot opium is muscle-tearing labor.

Ali Kambur looked at me in disgust. "A mustache like a Turk doesn't give you a heart like a Turk."

We were in a dirt cellar with some kind of black burlap covering the two small windows. What light there was came from two gas-burning lamps and a single electric bulb dangling naked from a wire. The foul air kept my stomach turning over. I checked my watch. It was almost time to signal my men to make their hit.

I went out the back door toward the outhouse, found my gun where I'd hidden it—a lightweight .38 special Colt Cobra—and tucked it inside my shirt. I looked toward the area where my men were supposed to be. It was a black night. I couldn't see a thing.

Fumbling for a cigarette, I jacked it out of the pack and lit a match. I shook that one out and struck another. That was the signal. To make sure, I struck a third. Then I went back inside.

Kambur was busy at work on the last batch of opium.

My men hit the place according to plan, breaking through the front door while I moved to block the rear exit.

Ali Kambur reacted like a crazy man. Letting out a roar, he came straight into my gun with his knife flicking out in front of him. I hated to kill him because the Turkish police wanted very much to have a talk with him. Ali knew a lot.

I tried to twist out of the way as he came at me, but the point of the knife caught me just above the right elbow. I didn't feel anything. I didn't even know I'd been stuck. I was too busy swinging my gun at his Adam's apple.

The gun caught him in the throat and he went down gasping, but still hanging onto the knife like a strap-hanger in a subway. He wouldn't let go. And because the blade was embedded in my arm he was pulling me with him.

I saw blood on him and realized that it was my own. I hit him again and the knife blade snapped off leaving the hilt in his hand. The other part of it was still in my arm but I didn't yet feel any pain. That came later.

Ali Kambur was lying on the floor making noises with his windpipe. The throat is a specially vulnerable part of the human body if you hit it just right.

We made quite a haul at Kambur's place. We loaded up more than two hundred kilos of opium, a few guns and other incriminating evidence and got ready for the long drive back to Istanbul.

My arm had now started to ache. I got a combat bandage from a medicine kit in one of our cars and used it on my arm. You break open the middle of the gauze which has powdered penicillin inside it. You apply it to the wound and it acts as a bandage as well as a tourniquet.

This worked for a while. But jouncing through a night as dark as Turkish coffee over those primitive Turkish roads soon had the arm throbbing with pain. My thoughts seemed mixed up . . . I kept thinking of little kids eating opium apples and wild shepherds out in the hills with their wild dogs and the whole crazy pattern of kill or be killed that Turkey had been for me. . . .

Dizziness came with the pain and I asked one of my men to get a morphine surette out of the field kit.

He got it and I had him pop the needle into my arm above the bandage. The pain subsided. It was hard to believe that a by-product of opium, which brought so much misery to the world when misused, could also give such blessed relief from acute pain such as mine.

Slowly I began getting out of my Turkish mountaineer garb and back into my city clothes. I had left Istanbul as Ismet Musret Kural but had told Ali Kambur, my target, that I was a Syrian hiding out from the police. Which is why he threw that line at me about a mustache not being enough to make me into a bona fide Turk.

Now I changed my name with my clothes. I would arrive back in Istanbul as Mike Warner, a commercial pilot who specialized in flying dynamite. Both aliases were covers I'd used before, and probably would use again because I had their I.D.s ready at hand.

I had the driver let me off at the Istanbul-Hilton. I had to see Dr. Dan Klein about getting this arm fixed. I figured he'd be having a nightcap at the roof-top bar about now.

I figured right. He was at the bar as I expected, twirling a brandy glass in his fingers.

Captain Klein was the medical officer for TUSLOG DET-29, which is short for Turkish-U.S. Logistical Group, Detachment 29. Dan and I were friends and partners, and we shared an apartment at Suleiman Nazif Sokak No. 34, located in the best section of Istanbul.

I pointed to my arm.

"My God!" he said. "What's it this time?"

"Knife wound."

"At least you're getting out of your rut," he said. "Usually somebody shoots you."

Across from the Hilton in the TUSLOG clinic he probed the wound and found the tip of the knife blade had gotten into the bone. It wasn't easy to get out. He finally removed it, shot me full of antibiotics and took me home. With the help of a sedative I drifted into a deep, nightmare sleep.

I was in some huge depot or terminal and a strange hollow voice was coming at me from all sides.

Sal Vizzini, will you please come forward, it said.

In my dream, a number of people were sitting erect on widely separated benches. All were looking straight ahead, unseeing. All were dressed differently and all had different names. But all had the features of Sal Vizzini. Me. I kept hearing that hollow voice. I kept trying to remember which of those people I was at the moment. . . .

Strange dream. But, then, Turkey was a strange country. Still, it was very productive if you're in my line of work. Other Bureau agents out of the Rome office had been there before, good agents too, but only for special assignments. I was the first man to be sent in there on a permanent basis. It was virgin territory and the pickings were good. Turkey was first class for making cases and being where the action was. In the three years I was there, I can't count the tons of opium we confiscated and the peddlers we sent to jail. Anyhow, it all looked good on the official reports going back to Washington.

The only bad thing about Turkey, other than a few incidentals like poor sanitary conditions, was the fact that nobody ever seemed to give up without a fight. You walked with your gun in your hand in Turkey. Too damn often you found yourself shooting it. And being shot at.

Commissioner Harry J. Anslinger made it possible for us to work with the Turkish National Police. Besides being Commissioner of the Federal Bureau of Narcotics, he was the number one crusader for control of world-wide narcotics. As a representative on the U.N. Board for Controlling International Drug Traffic, meeting with representatives from various countries, Anslinger spoke out long and hard.

He'd sit across the table from the Turks and say, "If it wasn't for you, the United States wouldn't have its problem. You grow 56.2 percent of the world's legitimate supply of opium. At the same time, because you're not enforcing properly, the same amount if not more gets out on the illicit market. If you stopped the stuff there, it wouldn't wind up in the United States in its purest form—heroin. You're causing us one of our major narcotics problems."

Everybody in the Bureau knew about Anslinger's tirades against the Turks. Likewise the French.

At first the Turks were angry. Then, as he kept shoving facts at them, they became embarrassed. Finally they agreed to accept help from American agents. In fact they welcomed it—anything, I suppose, to get the Commissioner off their backs.

I heard about the assignment to Turkey shortly after I was sent to Rome and after getting back from my first meeting in Naples with Luciano. Cusack summoned me to his inner sanctum across the Via Veneto from the Embassy and broke the news to me in his usual cheery fashion.

"How'd you like to take a trip?"

"Which way and for how long?" It was our stock q. and a. routine.

He shuffled some papers on his desk and cleared his throat. He looked like a bald-headed travel agent about to offer the De Luxe Tour at off-season rates.

"Istanbul."

He told me I'd be assigned there for at least six months, officially as an Interpol representative, to help the Turkish National Police set up an anti-narcotics squad with teeth.

I didn't say anything. I sat there looking at him and wondering what special genius prompted executive decisions. I was just getting myself settled in Rome. I was just getting started in the undercover project against Luciano. I didn't know the Bosporus from a belly-dancer. I spoke fluent Italian but no Turkish. So naturally they were sending me to Turkey.

"You know how Anslinger feels about opium coming out of Turkey," he went on. "We can't wait for the Turks to do it. Move things along, Sal. Set up your own informants, develop your own cases. The stuff coming off those dope farms keeps getting into the States in greater volume every year."

"What about the Luciano operation?" I asked.

"You can do it from Turkey as well as here, maybe better. There's a U-2 base near Adana, the Inchlick Air Force Base. You can use it as a mail drop for any correspondence you might have with Luciano. We'll set up the Major Mike Cerra cover with the base commander there. You'll be a transient officer with temporary quarters, and can touch base from time to time when you're in the area."

He said he didn't want me to use my Air Force identity on other operations in Turkey. Too risky. I would check in with the Turkish authorities as Sal Vizzini. My contacts would be two Turkish police officers named Ali Eren and Galip Labernas. I would work with them, using what covers I thought appropriate. I would have an office in the American consulate in Istanbul. I would receive messages there. I would get money and anything else I needed by diplomatic pouch.

"When do I leave?"

"In a week or two. Meanwhile, go to work on the Turkish files."

There were a dozen of them in the office, steel cabinets containing confidential reports from agents along with Bureau memoranda, Interpol data, a list of known criminals and smugglers and general background information. Every day until I left I pored over it all like a college kid cramming for an exam.

I briefed myself so thoroughly that when I got to Istanbul I had the feeling I'd been there before. I knew the layout of the city, the official and black-market rates of exchange from U.S. dollars into Turkish *lera* and the fact that Allah was supposed to return some day through the rectum of a Turk. That was the reason for the baggy pants some of them still wore—they were supposed to keep the Holy One from having a hard fall.

It was a city of unending intrigue, half-Asian and half-European, an ancient metropolis where corruption had been a way of life for thousands of years. And in the back of my head, implanted there from studying the files, were two Turkish names: Hussein Iminoglu and Ali Asman Tutter.

They were my two prime targets in Turkey.

Hussein Iminoglu, I discovered, was the Lucky Luciano of Istanbul. He had his slick hand in everything—contraband goods, guns, gold, counterfeit money. He was also Turkey's biggest mover of illegal opium. No way to ignore Hussein Iminoglu. And Ali Asman Tutter was the number two man, only a half a rung or so down the ladder. It would be something to nail both of them.

But first I had to set up shop and get organized, so I checked into the Istanbul-Hilton and promptly decided to make the roof-top bar my operations base. Nobody could ask for a better headquarters. It overlooked the harbor. It was a swinging place. And it boasted an accomplished Greek bartender by the name of Chris Christopoulos.

I tipped him well right from the start. Bartenders never forget a customer who tosses money around freely. My cover name was Theodore (later mostly known as Mike) Warner and I was a commercial pilot flying dynamite for an oil company. That was all he needed to know. By the end of the second day I had only to appear and he'd begin making my favorite drink.

I had a special seat at the bar and another at a table where I could observe everybody who came in or out of this sky-high oasis. I negotiated with a stream of informants and opium peddlers right there while watching ships ply in and out of the Bosporus.

My other office was in the first-floor rear of the American consulate, back where the janitors kept their brooms. Next door to me was the Istanbul CIA chief. I'll call him Napoleon. He was to come in handy. Meanwhile, I wasn't there very much. I used it mainly for sending and receiving cables and getting my own brand of CARE packages by diplomatic pouch.

The first week I got several of these packages. One contained the I.D.s for all the covers I'd established before and planned to use in Turkey. You just don't risk traveling with more than one phoney I.D. unless absolutely necessary.

Another of my packages contained two guns. One was a .38 Colt Cobra, the other a 9mm. Walther—the Walther was the only automatic that fires double-action, which means you don't have to cock it before firing the first round. There was also ammunition for both guns. The third package contained $5,000 in U.S. currency, mainly hundreds and twenties.

This was the amount Cusack and I had agreed on before I left

Rome. Other shipments of cash, up to as much as $15,000, would be forthcoming as needed. They would be used mainly for the purposes of setting up a network of informants. Informants didn't come cheap, if they were any good at all, and they took risks. Of the thirty or so I recruited in Turkey, eight ended up on slabs. But the good ones didn't. And I've paid up to $12,000 to a man for setting up a prime target.

If I was going to get to Hussein Iminoglu, or any other peddler, I had to have reliable informants. It was step one in any kind of a successful undercover operation, and I worked almost full time on it for the first few weeks.

I hit some crummy waterfront bars. They're pretty much the same in every city. I looked for types that spoke a little English or Italian, and managed to get by with hand gestures as well as scribbling notes from a Turkish-English dictionary. Larceny, after all, is an international language. I followed my nose and instincts. It's really amazing what you can do, in almost any city in the world, with some money and a lot of patience.

When I felt I had a live prospect, I'd borrow an interpreter from the CIA at the Consulate to help international understanding. Often small fry who couldn't help passed me along to bigger people who could.

Recruiting informants is a fairly universal procedure. You dangle the carrot and eventually the conversation gets around to cash. Nobody works on promises, and you don't want to play Santa Claus either. So you compromise. If the prospect seems to check out, you front him $500 and say, "O.K., let's see what you can do." If he doesn't check out so good, you lay some money on him but take his watch or his car keys as collateral. You play it close, hope for the best.

The trouble with getting informants in Turkey, at least at the start, was the police. When you paid an informant you could almost count on the Turkish police shaking him down for most of it before he got home. It took all the incentive out of the informant's work. So I devised another method of payment. I would give the informant a token pay-off when I was sure there were police eyes watching and let them strip him of most of it. Then, later, I'd give him a large amount the police didn't know about.

My informant network was my own. The police didn't even know who most of them were. I didn't feel it was necessary to share this knowledge with the two Turkish police officers, Ali Eren and Galip Labernas, assigned to work with me. They were my good friends. They saved my life more than once. But I didn't tell them about my informants.

I had some of the most talented thieves in Istanbul on my payroll and it gave me a better intelligence system than the Istanbul police ever had. I finally got to Hussein Iminoglu through one of my informants. But I got to number two, Ali Asman Tutter, on my own—with the special help of Dr. Dan Klein.

I hadn't been in Turkey a week before I began putting out feelers on Ali Asman Tutter. I found out where he lived and cased his place of business. I learned that he knew no English but spoke perfect French. In the beginning I spoke very little Turkish and almost no French, which situation led to my alliance with Klein.

I met Dan Klein the second week I was at the Hilton. As a freewheeling, free-spending pilot, I made it my business to know everybody. He was a young doctor in his thirties and just about as inhibited as I was outgoing. I liked him right from the start.

He had studied medicine in Lucerne and spoke flawless French. As he was an Army captain and the medical officer assigned to TUSLOG-DET 29, I decided he could be useful and asked intelligence to run a background check on him. It came back clean—Dr. Dan Klein was a most solid, reliable citizen.

I made my pitch one day while we were having a hamburger out by the hotel pool.

"Dan," I said. "I'm not the guy you think I am."

"Good," he said. "I didn't think anybody would be fool enough to fly dynamite around in this part of the world."

"I'm serious, Dan. I'm an undercover agent for the U.S. government."

"C'mon, Mike. What have you been smoking?"

I threw my I.D. on him. The real one with my commission from the U.S. Treasury Department.

"Salvatore Vizzini!"

"Yeah, I'm a guinea. Dan," I told him. "I've got to put something on you, and I hope you take it in the right way because I need your help."

"How can I help?"

"Well, first of all, your French. I have a target here and I need a reliable translator. It's not something I could trust just anybody with. If things go wrong, somebody could get hurt. And if you agree to go along, there will be some risks for you. These guys aren't amateurs."

This didn't seem to bother him. I'd figured him right.

"You can count on me in any way," he said. Then he added, "But you don't know anything about me."

I looked at him for a minute. "I know everything about you starting from the day you were born. I know that you were called Din as a baby, and that you have a single sister; further that you were the best fly-tier in your high school hobby club but you got so upset about killing fish that you stopped fishing altogether. You didn't want to kill anything. That's why you went into medicine."

I told him to think about it. "You don't have to give me your answer right away. But if you refuse, I'll have to go with you to your C.O. and he will take steps to make sure you keep everything I've discussed absolutely confidential."

"I don't have to think," he said. "Is there anything else?"

I explained that I made frequent trips to the interior, and also out of the country, and that I needed someone to cover for messages while I was gone. In effect, what I was offering was the responsibility of being a part-time partner and colleague, for kicks. It might at times be dangerous but it would never be dull.

I also told him I wanted to share an apartment with him. It would help both of us cut expenses. I didn't say it would be handy to have a doctor as a roommate, especially if Turkey was as unhealthy as it figured to be.

He agreed. He liked it. He bought the whole package.

Then I told him about Ali Asman Tutter, the immediate target, a crafty little man of Turkish and Syrian descent. On the surface he was a respectable businessman in Istanbul. He was also the middleman between the opium growers and the opium peddlers. He took little risk but got a big slice of the pay-off.

"A target worth cultivating," I said. "How's your French?"

"Mon français est très, très bon," he answered, by sample.

I decided to try to meet Tutter without using any of the local informants I was developing. For one thing, I wasn't yet sure exactly which ones among them I could trust. None of them had much of a track record. Second, walking in cold just might work. It would be what a wild pilot with an eye out for an easy buck might well do.

As a bit of preliminary groundwork I had the Rome office send Tutter a message from an old business associate of his in Rome. The Italian police had managed to pressure this bird into becoming an informant. The message he sent Tutter was vague. It said that an associate would drop in on him and asked him to extend every possible courtesy.

When the time came, Dan and I walked up to Tutter's home about dusk. It was a dark, two-story house on a narrow street near the Galata Bridge. I took a sideways look at Klein. He was as cool as if he had been doing this sort of thing all his life. A natural, I thought. We knocked and a maid answered. She asked us to wait and disappeared into a nearby room.

"Qui?" I heard a voice from a room off the hall where we were standing.

I nudged Klein, who called out something in French about a letter. The maid came back and motioned us in.

Tutter had glassy, black-marble eyes and, I swear, glistening patent leather hair. His face was thin, reminding me of a ferret, and he sat in a huge chair covered with Moroccan leather. Two clear but very dim bulbs shed almost no light in the room. Most furtive animals avoid light, I thought, as I watched him.

Klein and Tutter talked in French and it didn't take a language scholar to realize we were getting a chilly reception.

Yes, Tutter told Klein, he had received a message of some sort, from a person he may or may not have known. Anyhow, he wasn't active any more. His health hadn't been very good.

"Tell him O.K.," I said impatiently to Klein. "If that's the attitude he wants to take, maybe I'm wasting my time. I thought we could talk about business that would be beneficial to both of us."

Tutter's tone softened a bit but he insisted that he was sincere about his retirement. Still, he offered us Turkish coffee and we settled for tea. I've smelled shellac that had fewer muscles than that Turkish coffee; later I became accustomed to the thick brew.

The meeting didn't last long. At this point, neither of us had much to say. Tutter obviously liked Klein, and even ended up smiling at me after I fed him a few lines about his being a fine host and what a good businessman I'd heard he was.

"I will communicate with you," he said as we were leaving. This time he stood up to shake hands.

On the way back to the Hilton I told Dan Klein I had a feeling our visit had been very worthwhile.

"What do you think we accomplished?"

"Dan, now I have a reference. And it's one of the best references in all of Istanbul."

From time to time we'd meet him for tea. When discreet inquiries about opium and morphine didn't get a response, I had Dan, acting as my interpreter, switch the talk to other commodities. One of my side lines was cigarettes, I told him.

"I'll see that you get a steady supply," I told him through Klein.

Tutter's eyes lighted up. Like Charlie Luciano, there was a cheapskate in him. Like most successful men, he liked to get something for nothing. I sent him ten cartons of Pall Malls. I had authority to buy up to a hundred cartons a week at the PX. They cost me fifteen cents a pack and brought up to $20 a carton on the black market. American cigarettes were like gold in Turkey. For $15, I made a lot of points.

I used Tutter over and over as a reference. It was a magic name, an open sesame, that helped lead me to smaller fry in the Istanbul underworld. Just by saying I knew Ali Asman Tutter I made a half dozen cases in one month.

The first was an opium peddler named Yucil. Then tougher types like Refik Ahmet Sarakos, Cemal Boybeyi and the rugged Izzettin Biyikbey, who forced us to shoot it out with him. The Bureau wanted seizures and arrests, and I was keeping them happy. The action I was producing earned me a $500 award and a promotion to Grade 12.

I would get around to Hussein Iminoglu in due time.

I moved into a bachelor apartment with Dan Klein. I was known around town as Mike, the swinging pilot nutty enough to fly dynamite for an oil company. Unless, of course, there was some reason for me to be Pasquale Lombardi, Joseph Angelo Vento, or Ismet Musret Kural. In the interior, I usually went under the Turkish alias.

But Galip Labernas and Ali Eren, my two Turkish police liaison officers, called me Mike no matter where I was. At National Police Headquarters, soon after I arrived, Labernas had asked apologetically, "Signor Vizzini, do you mind if Ali Eren calls you Mike?"

Labernas was the younger of the two and spoke some Italian. I spoke no Turkish at all at the time. Ali Eren spoke nothing but Turkish. This made him the silent member of the pair. Until I could handle his language, the only thing I ever heard him say in English was "Tank you very much." He said it all the time, whether we were shooting at opium peddlers or boiling tea over a campfire out in the hills. He was really proud of those words, although I don't think he knew what they meant.

"Why does Ali want to call me Mike?" I'd asked Labernas.

"Because you remind him of Mike Hammer, the American detective."

He showed me a copy of a Mickey Spillane paperback, printed in Turkish, and pointed out that Mike Hammer carried his gun in the small of his back, as I sometimes did.

"Sure," I said. "He can call me Mike if I can call him Ali Baba."

So Mike became my name with them and I even took out a cable address under the name of Mykham. I had never read a Mike Hammer story in my life. I carried my gun in the small of my back, the holster fitted on the inside of my pants with a small metal clip extending down on the outside, because that was the most inconspicuous place.

Sometimes people on the other side would have a woman brush

up against you at a bar, as if she had lost her balance. Grabbing at you she'd give you a quick frisk and see if you were carrying arms. They still work this gimmick. If you've got a gun, and you're wearing it on a belt, nine times out of ten you're a cop.

In the first month I became very impressed with Ali Eren's capabilities. He was a major in the Turkish National Police and deserved his rank. Ali had a little black mustache and dressed like an undertaker's helper. He had two wives, an old one and a young one. Not so surprisingly, he'd take the young one out and leave the old one at home. Ali always unrolled his rug three times a day and prayed to Allah. He was quiet, sincere and damned resourceful.

I wanted to talk things out with him and avoid any misunderstandings so I went to Napoleon, my CIA friend at the consulate. By now I had learned that there was no end of things Napoleon could produce on a moment's notice. If you wanted a Thompson submachine gun to impress a customer, or a forged letter from the King of Araby, or a vintage passport appropriately aged, there was never any problem. He ground out visas and routine I.D.s while you waited. Now I told him I needed an interpreter who was without a doubt one hundred percent reliable. And I wanted to talk in a place where I would not be overheard or recorded. Everybody was bugging everybody else in Istanbul.

We sat down in the annex of the consulate—Ali Eren, the interpreter and me.

"I want to stay here and get a job done," I told him. "But I won't be allowed to stay here unless I produce. I need your help."

He contemplated me in silence for a few moments, then put out his hand. "Starting right now, you can consider me your blood brother. I will never lie to you. I will swear that in the name of the Prophet."

As far as I know he never did, which had to be a record when dealing with the Turkish police.

He told me I had to be very careful. Life was cheap in Istanbul.
I asked him who was the top opium smuggler in Turkey.

"Iminoglu."

"How do we get to him?"

He said it would be very difficult. Hussein Iminoglu was a careful man. But Ali knew a man who worked with him, one of the
top people in his organization.

"The man's name is Nar," Ali Eren explained through the interpreter. "He owes me a debt. He owes me his life. I can arrange for
you to meet Iminoglu through him."

I told him to go ahead and set it up. The interview ended with
Ali Eren and me clasping hands like blood brothers.

"Tell Ali Baba I thank him from the bottom of my heart," I
said to the interpreter.

Ali laughed and I caught the word *"sakarin."* The interpreter
told me this was a term of affection commonly used by Turkish
men.

Several weeks went by before Ali was able to produce any results. Then I received a note written in poor but understandable
English. It told me to be at a certain restaurant at nine o'clock
that night, that Hussein Iminoglu would be there, and that he
would be expecting an American pilot named Mike. And it ended
saying that Ali Eren would be covering me from outside. I felt like
a kid at Christmas—I was going to get a whack at the big guy.

I showed up right on time. The restaurant was on a side street
down by the waterfront, near the point where the ferry leaves on
its run to the Asiatic side. It wasn't much of a place. About all
you could say for it was that it had tablecloths, most of them
dirty.

The fat proprietor greeted me with a bow, and I told him I was
there to see Mister Iminoglu. I had been boning up on my Turkish
and felt I could handle the situation with the help of Sicilian hand

gestures. Put a Sicilian's hands in his pockets and he's practically speechless.

Hussein Iminoglu was sitting alone at a corner table, a napkin tucked in at the neck, attacking a dish of lamb with noisy gusto. He waved me to a chair and kept right on demolishing the lamb. I sat there and sized him up. He was stout, but despite his table manners, well-groomed. Steel-rimmed spectacles perched over baggy eyes and with every king-sized bite he dabbed at a large handlebar mustache and a pointed Vandyke beard sprinkled with gray.

When he finally came up for air, I offered him a cigarette and he accepted fast. I've never seen a Turk yet who refused an American cigarette.

"What can I do for you?" he asked in good English.

"I thought we might do some business."

"What kind of business are you in, my friend?"

"Any kind of business there's a buck in. Let's start with morphine base."

"Why do you not want heroin?"

"Because, to be frank with you, you're a lousy chemist. We Sicilians are the best chemists in the world."

"I thought you were an American."

"I am, but by way of Palermo."

He asked me if I planned to convert the morphine base.

"If I have to."

I told him I'd worked in labs and could handle the job myself. He wanted to know how much could be rendered out of so many kilos, and I said it depended on the morphine content and the chemist.

I was giving all the right answers and being aggressive about it.

He sat there brooding, no expression behind that mask of hair. Well, I'd heard he was a cautious man. He wouldn't be around if and when a sample was delivered. You stop being a delivery boy when you're as big as Hussein Iminoglu.

I tried another tack. If you can't get in the front door, try the back. Or come up through the cellar or in a window. He dabbled in contraband of all kinds—coffee, cigarettes, English nylon, gold, machine tools, guns and even baby's pacifiers. Anything you could get tax free and sell at a profit. I told him I could furnish American cigarettes at a reasonable price.

He seemed interested for the first time. "In what quantity?"

"Two thousand dollars' worth at a whack. That's two hundred cartons at $10 a carton, half the going retail rate. And I have a steady supply."

"I think we can do business, my friend."

I told him it was cash-and-carry, but that I wanted to put my cash to work right away. If he wouldn't deal in morphine base, what kind of goods did he have to offer?

"I have a ship arriving in a few days with a miscellaneous cargo that might interest you. I'm a businessman, Mr. Warner."

"So am I. I fly airplanes for a profit."

He said he'd be in touch with me shortly.

I didn't wait for the message. I told Ali Eren to contact his friend, Nar, and squeeze a little harder. I wanted to know what ship Iminoglu was expecting in the next few days, the exact time of arrival and whether Iminoglu would be at the dock when it came in.

The answer came back that he was expecting the Greek ship *Adana* on Thursday, that it would come in on the morning tide and that he would be on hand, as usual, to supervise the unloading in person. I began planning a surprise reception for the *Adana*.

It wouldn't be the regular police that met the boat but a hand-picked crew of local Turks under the command of Ali Eren and Galip Labernas. I set down a blueprint for deploying the men around the main dock, just across the bridge from police head-quarters. We set it up so we really did cover that waterfront.

I couldn't afford to risk blowing my cover on an operation as public as this one was going to be, so I contacted TUSLOG-DET. 29 and arranged to have a helicopter put at my disposal. From my airborne command post I could run the operaton without any chance of being identified, meanwhile giving radio directions to the men on the scene.

We planned to take Iminoglu at the dock, or at the warehouse, but it worked out differently than we had anticipated. Iminoglu appeared at the dock on schedule but when the ship ran into a delay in arriving at its berth he jumped aboard the harbor pilot's boat and rode out with him.

I was watching it all through binoculars from my vantage point in the chopper and grabbed up the radio headset. It wasn't instant communication, by any means. I had to talk to the military authorities at the airport. They, in turn, telephoned my instructions to police headquarters which relayed my orders to the men below by police radio. It was a risky procedure because between translations and relays there was always a chance of a foul-up. Luckily, they got my message through.

"Go out and hit him on the ship," I told them. "Don't wait any longer."

Ali Eren and his hand-picked detail rode out in a police boat and boarded the *Adana*. I watched as they pulled up beside the harbor pilot's boat, jumped across it to the ladder and rushed aboard. A seaman at the head of the ladder took one look at this group and led them directly to where Hussein Iminoglu and the captain were going over bills of lading which proved that together they were smuggling in twenty-five tons of contraband coffee and ten tons of English nylon, along with various other goods. Iminoglu and the captain were taken ashore in handcuffs.

Iminoglu was convicted of smuggling and sentenced to ten years in prison. If you can't get them one way, I told myself, you try another. The result was what counted and it was good enough for me.

As for Ali Asman Tutter, he had served his purpose by now. Besides, he was number two. And with number one out of the way, he had more heat than he could stand, for all his suave mannerisms and cautious fencing. I helped put him in jail on a conspiracy rap, and he never knew it was the hot-shot dynamite pilot who put this phoney businessman out of business. Others, like crazy Ali Kambur, would go harder and draw more blood.

6

Ill Wind in Marseilles

I HAVE a theory about guardian angels. It's that we all have to put in a stint as one, the length of service depending on how good or bad we were while in the mortal vale. My angel must have had a lot to account for because he certainly has been overworked.

This theory makes me a little nervous. Because after I die, I will wake up and there will be St. Peter staring down at me.

"Is this heaven or hell?" I will say, not knowing off my track record which direction I have gone.

"Probation," he will say. "Here's the assignment."

He will fly me to one of our Bureaus somewhere. We will flap in, invisibly. Over in one corner will be a young guy with a headful of black hair, a mind filled with wild ideas, an eye for broads, a nose for trouble, not enough sense to be scared and a Sicilian cast to his features. My counterpart.

"See that character?" St. Peter will ask me, and I will nod.

"You're to be his guardian angel," St. Peter will say. "Your assignment is to see that he lives to be 88 and dies in bed."

And that will be one helluva job. Particularly if the young guy happens to be sent to Marseilles, one of the most deadly cities in France, on an undercover assignment. Guardian angels have it rough in Marseilles. Mine certainly had to work overtime when the Bureau sent me in there.

I got to Marseilles with a vague assignment, a head packed with a miscellany of information, and a gut instinct that suggested a bullet, a knife or a garrote could be waiting.

The railroad station, Gare St. Charles, was large and gloomy, matching my mood. So did the hot, humid, everlasting wind that blew outside, the mistral that wafted in from Africa at various times of year, sweeping trash and litter before it. It fanned the city's narrow, twisted streets, picking up odors like an airborne garbage truck. If you weren't feeling bad before, the mistral took care of you.

An ill wind, I thought, and an evil city.

On the sidewalk I gave a legless beggar a few francs for luck. Instead of thanks he cursed me and spit at my feet. The cab driver didn't like me much better after I turned down his offer to supply female companionship at bargain rates.

"The Grande et de Noailles," I said, giving him the name of the best hotel in town. "And please don't take me the great circle route."

He scowled and drove off down the Boulevard d'Athènes. I leaned back against the seat with an empty, gut-fluttery feeling.

For me, cities have personalities much like people. New York is a hip, no-limit player. New Orleans is an old-family dowager who keeps slyly nipping at the gin. Marseilles, from what I could see, was a tough old harlot with an eye out for the main chance.

I was there to infiltrate Corsican mob society or at least to find out who made it tick. I had been in Turkey, running down opium smugglers, when the message came. It wasn't in code. It said simply: "RETURN ROME IMMEDIATELY FOR URGENT ASSIGNMENT." The message was unsigned. But only one man could have sent it.

I packed my scivvies and caught the next plane. At Donet's, near the Bureau office, I paused long enough to have a drink and check the five o'clock promenade of high-class whores along the Via Veneto. Nothing had changed. I went down the street to the blank-faced building across from the Embassy and took the world's slowest elevator to the second floor.

"Sit down," Cusack said shortly after a perfunctory greeting. He was in no mood for pleasantries.

"We've got to do something about Marseilles," he told me.

"Let's burn it," I suggested.

He didn't think it was funny. Marseilles and the French police had been a burr under his hide for some time. And I knew enough about the situation so that he expected me to be reasonably sympathetic, at least responsive.

Marseilles was home base for heroin makers. At the time, about eighty percent of all heroin smuggled into the United States originated in Marseilles. The rest came from such points as Mexico and the Far East.

The greatest difficulty was that the operations in Marseilles were conducted with the knowledge and cooperation of the local police. The heroin makers were Corsican, the police and customs officials were Corsican, the pimps and prostitution overlords were Corsican. Vice in Marseilles was almost exclusively a Corsican affair.

The Bureau had sent men into Marseilles before, but always officially. It notified the French police that an agent was coming and the agent would be met by a man from the Sûrêté. He would be wined and dined. He would be given false leads to follow. At the end of a happy and fruitless week, the French would shrug their inimitable national shrug.

"Very sorry," they would say. "As you can see, we can do nothing."

"This time," Cusack informed me, "we're not going to notify the French authorities. We've decided to send in somebody illegally and unregistered."

"Meaning me."

He nodded and kept talking. "If you're caught, you're on your own. You'll take the heat and we'll deny knowing anything about you."

I told him I got the picture.

It was flattering in a way to be the first unregistered agent named to go into Marseilles. But I wanted to be the first unregistered agent to come out again. An unregistered agent in a foreign country can get it from both sides: from the guys running drugs and from the guys running the government.

"We want to know what's going on up there," he explained. "But mainly we want to develop an informant in Marseilles. We need a reliable informant to give us names, addresses, output, deliveries—anything we can use as leverage on someone higher up in Paris. If we can embarrass the bastards officially, maybe we'll finally get some action."

"Informants cost money," I pointed out.

"I know. You'll be carrying money. And there'll be more on a regular basis if the informant works out. Now what about a cover?"

I told him I had several which seemed to fit the situation; he could take his pick. I had forged Italian seaman's papers under the name of Pasquale Lombardi. I also had a United States Merchant Mariner's document issued by the Coast Guard. It was made out to Joseph Angelo Vento and had a "Z" number, which meant that the papers were in order and the bearer was cleared to sail. The address on the card was 320 East 148 Street, Bronx, New York.

We decided on the Vento cover. I would be a purser waiting to rejoin my ship, the S.S. *Mormacsea,* scheduled to dock in Marseilles about two weeks hence. This kind of cover seemed most suitable for the assignment. For one thing, merchant seamen transported most of the heroin which was illegally getting into the United States, at the going rate of $500 a kilo, and pursers had more standing on shipboard than stewards or other functionaries.

We agreed that I would be a big spender with a mysterious source of money. I would check into the best hotel in town.

By daybreak, I had committed to memory the names and faces of all known smugglers, vice lords and drug traffickers in the Marseilles area. At least all of those contained in the Bureau and Interpol files.

It read like a Who's Who of the Corsican Mafia. At the top of the list were names like Antoine Guerini, the Venturi brothers (Jean and Dominic), Paul Mondaloni and Antoine Cordeleoni. I knew about Cordeleoni from the Giuseppe Mancuso affair in Sicily. He was Giuseppe's connection in Marseilles.

In reading the files, I saw too that the Corsicans didn't have it all to themselves any more. The Algerian Moslems from North Africa had been muscling in on their cartel, especially the prostitution division. In the previous twelve months, a total of twenty-eight persons had been knifed, shot or strangled in Marseilles. It was Europe's biggest recorded gang war.

I felt sorry for the prostitutes. They were the ones caught in the middle of all this. They couldn't work their trade any more, it seemed, without being forced to pick one side or the other. Either they had to work for the Corsicans or do business with the Algerians. Unless they played it right, they got slashed on each cheek with the Croix des Vaches, or Cross of the Cow. Such decorations swiftly put them out of business as desirable commodities of the evening.

It was too late to sleep. I showered, ate breakfast and began thinking like Joseph Angelo Vento, ship's purser. I wouldn't be Sal Vizzini again until I got back.

I debated about whether to take along a gun, but not for long. I attached a Walther 9mm. automatic in an elastic bandage on the inside of my left thigh. By unzipping my fly I could get to it almost as fast as I could in a shoulder holster. One clip of ammunition was enough. By nine o'clock, I was on a train heading north toward the French Riviera.

I arrived in Marseilles on The Mistral, same name but faster and cooler than its namesake wind out of Africa. This train leaves on time and arrives on time. If it is more than forty seconds late, the guy running the Wagon-Lits company has a mild heart attack, the engineer gets fired and everybody along the line is called in for an accounting.

You could rely on The Mistral. It was one of the two things I could count on during the Marseilles venture. The other was an extraordinary French prostitute named Susu.

The cab driver, out of spite, took me the great circle route to the Grande et de Noailles Hotel. I told him he had used up his tip doing it and gave him what was on the meter. If looks could have killed, my assignment would have ended right there.

The hotel concierge appeared simultaneously with my money clip. It was large and gaudy and stuffed with French and American banknotes. I peeled off five dollars and he bowed me all the way to the front desk.

"My room," I informed the desk clerk, still fondling my money clip. "It must be the best."

"Of course, monsieur," he agreed, pocketing a twenty. I had no reservation at the Grande et de Noailles. I did now.

"Will my valuables be safe at the hotel until I can get to a safety deposit vault?"

"My personal guarantee, sir."

I didn't tell him what I thought of his personal guarantee as I handed him my attaché case.

It contained two dirty shirts and an alarm clock. The $5,000 I carried to buy an informant was in a special belt under my shirt. The attaché case was window dressing.

This was a good French hotel, proud of its plumbing and excellent service. I'd been put in a fairly low-level penthouse suite. The hotel only had six floors and I was on the top. I gave the bellhop a five-dollar American bill. For that he was ready to toss in somebody's younger sister, but I told him to bring some ice and forget it.

He left to spread the big-spender news and I took a shower. By now, three people in the hotel knew I had money and tossed it around rather freely. It was better than putting an ad in the paper. I flopped on the bed and awoke an hour later wondering where in hell to start this flaky assignment.

Hustlers, cabbies, bell boys, newspapermen and cops, in that order, usually know their way around most towns. Paid informants, a breed apart, know more than all of them put together, but first you have to find one. I checked the list mentally and decided to start with the first. But it couldn't be just any hustler. It had to be one of the ritziest whores in Marseilles.

I found her at the Cintra, a few blocks away, but not before some preliminary negotiating. The Cintra was a high-class bar and restaurant. The bartender was a tall Algerian who spoke perfect English. I ordered a brandy Alexander and pushed a ten-dollar bill his way, telling him to keep the change.

He smiled and waited.

"What's your name?" I asked.

"Ahmed, sir."

"Well, Ahmed, we might be able to do some business."

I explained that I was looking for a special kind of lady, to use the word loosely. I didn't want an acrobat whose principal talent was jumping in and out of bed.

"Not like that one," I said, nodding toward a poodle-cut blonde sitting alone a few stools away.

I explained that I wanted one with some class, one that knew her way around. I'd be hitting some posh places and some dives, too. So don't waste my time or his. Could he produce?

Ahmed was very understanding. He knew just the girl.

"Magnifique!" he explained, rolling his eyes. "I sigh for her myself but she is too, what you say, expensive. It is only a question of whether she is available."

"Give it a try," I said. Ahmed made a telephone call and she was.

Susu made quite an entrance. Whores have last names just like other people, and hers turned out to be Deschamps. Who cared about last names? On her little high heels, she click-clicked toward me as though I was the only one in the place.

She was something else, and not hustler-hard pretty. She wore a red tam from under which jet black hair fell to her shoulders. There was no jewelry and the dress was plain, yet expensive. She had little-girl legs. She looked like a student. Only her eyes, big and brown and flecked with green, said she was otherwise. They were wise, extremely worldly.

All eyes followed her into the Cintra. She had that quality about her.

Susu slipped onto the bar-stool next to me and ordered a tomate, a local drink made with pernod and grenadine syrup. Then she opened her purse and put a ten-franc note on the bar.

"I always pay for my first drink," she said, giving me a searching look with those know-it-all eyes. "Then if I should decide to leave, there is no unpleasantness. I don't like everyone, m'sieu."

Now, I thought, I have heard everything. Ahmed had told me that she was a special kind of woman, that she went out with rich old men as a sideline because they could buy her expensive trinkets, and that her father was a respected merchant in Marseilles. I was beginning to believe him.

"Do I pass the test?"

"I don't know yet. Talk to me."

I told her my name was Joe Vento, that I had been born at a very early age in Waukegan, Illinois, that I was waiting for my yacht to pick me up in a few days, and that if she would come down off her God damn high-horse we'd see something of this God damn town.

"All right, Mister Joe Vento, you can buy me a drink now." She smiled.

Susu filled the bill all right. She knew the best side of Marseilles and the worst. We went to a dockside restaurant on the Quai des Belges where she ordered bouillabaisse. She said they invented it there. I ate clams. I ate escargots. I ate the best shrimp I ever had, little gray ones with a special sauce. I stuffed myself.

She led me through the narrow, crooked streets of the Vieux Port section, the part that the Germans hadn't burned in retaliation for French resistance activity during the war. Susu was at home.

In one evil-smelling place after another, her perfume was the only tolerable scent I encountered. She knew the proprietors at every joint. She called the pimps and thugs by name. She sipped Marseilles tea, the usual B-girl drink, while I drank Courvoisier.

"Which side are you on?" I asked.

"What do you mean, Joseph Vento?"

"Are you with the Corsicans or the Algerians?"

It was a shot in the dark, but her face lost all expression.

"It's getting late, Mr. Vento. What else do you want with me?"

It was an obvious invitation. Sooner or later, most prostitutes get around to the subject of going to bed. I admitted to her that the thought had crossed my mind but explained I seldom mixed business with pleasure.

I told her that I was in Marseilles on business and that it might be profitable to both of us.

That got her attention immediately.

"What kind of business?" she asked.

Girls, gold, counterfeit money and drugs all were thriving industries in Marseilles.

I didn't answer right away.

"If I have to tell you it's not worth it," I finally said. "You think about it and we'll talk again."

She nodded and got up to leave. I gave her a $100 bill for "cab fare," put her in one taxi and got another myself. But not before arranging to meet the next day in the Café Ponti, one of the places we had visited earlier.

I woke up the next morning with an uneasy feeling. This wasn't my town. I knew that already. Maybe it was the mistral. That moist wind from Africa clung to you and you couldn't even wash it off in the shower.

Downstairs I had coffee and then ambled around. I smelled a tail and couldn't spot it. I went into a park and bought some stale peanuts and sat on a splintery bench feeding the sorriest-looking pigeons in the world. I will always associate the word "Marseilles" with loneliness. The evil and the danger seemed secondary.

Finally I spotted the tail as I strolled down the Cannebière, Marseilles' main drag. He stopped when I stopped, walked when I walked. He was doing his follow-the-man thing right out of the detective correspondence-school book. Hood, pimp, informer, cop? The last seemed most likely. He looked like a pallbearer and wore a black felt hat.

After a couple of blocks he was joined by another pallbearer in a similar black hat and the two converged on me.

"Identification!" one of them demanded.

They showed me their badges and informed me politely that I was acting in a suspicious manner.

"But my identification is in perfect order," I said, handing them my Joe Vento credentials with a twenty-dollar bill peeping out from under the I.D.

"You cannot be too careful in Marseilles," one of them said, giving me back my papers. I knew without looking that the twenty was gone.

"You seem to have a great deal of money for a seaman, m'sieu," one of them observed.

"Yeah, I'm thrifty."

I hadn't counted on attracting attention from the police so soon. They didn't figure in my plans.

They walked off, apparently satisfied, and I took a cab to the Ponti. It looked even dingier by day than it had the night before, a truly crummy little dive. A few sleazy characters sat around at tables, staring into their wine glasses. For ten American dollars you could get anything done there.

Susu hadn't arrived. I ordered coffee with milk.

She got there about five minutes later, looking fresh and lovely —no make-up, a demure dress, very chic. I offered her a cigarette. She tore the filter off one end, stuck the other end in her mouth and accepted a light. Susu didn't like American filters.

"What's up?" I asked.

"Money, Mr. Vento. Just money. When an American seaman

shows a big roll and puts an empty brief case in the hotel safe he is either stupid or advertising. You are not stupid, Mr. Joseph Vento. Susu is just answering your ad."

"You certainly are a bright girl, Susu," I said. "How do you know all this?"

"My cousin is the clerk at the Grande et de Noailles."

"And what else do you know?"

She flashed those amber-green eyes at me.

"I know you are too wise to take a prostitute to your hotel, Mr. Vento. I know that the police have been interested in what you do. I know you have more than shows in your money clip. And I also know that you keep a gun in your hotel room. That isn't very smart, Mr. Vento."

"You seem to have a lot of cousins."

"Everybody in Marseilles is my cousin. Now what is this business you wish to discuss?"

I sat there taking stock of the wisest prostitute in Marseilles, and still not believing. The black hair was in pigtails now, red ribbons at the ends, and she tapped the table with large black oval sunglasses. Amusement was on her lips at my inspection and obvious approval.

Susu was a player and Susu knew the score. I had to figure she might have a better intelligence network than the Marseilles police. At any rate, she seemed to have a hell of a lot of cousins. I needed someone like that. It was my main reason for being in Marseilles.

I began probing.

Normally, in recruiting an informant, you get right to the heart of the matter. You ask about the availability of heroin. They give you that wide-eyed look. They say they don't know what you're talking about. They say they didn't know you were a user. You tell them you're not, that you're a buyer. Then you play a little game with a $100 bill, or maybe two, depending on the circumstances, and see what happens.

They always want more and you hold out for less. If they ask for five, you offer one and settle for three. In the jungle, they'd be contemptuous if you played it any other way. But this was different. I decided to work on Susu from another angle. Besides, I had to know more about what she knew.

"What would you do if you had five hundred dollars in that purse right now?" I asked her.

Those big eyes softened.

"I would make you my partner, Mr. Joe Vento, because you are the only one who would give me five hundred dollars to use as I wish. But it wouldn't be enough."

"Enough for what?"

"For the business I have in mind."

"And what business is that?"

Then Susu sat there, smooth as a Vassar receptionist, and told me about the business she desired.

Her life's ambition, she said, was to have her own stable of high-price call girls. Not just an ordinary stable but the finest establishment of its kind in France. Susu was thinking large. She would go to Nice, away from this hell-hole called Marseilles, rent a villa, sprinkle some money around and operate in the grand manner.

"And you would be my partner, Mr. Joe Vento."

It wasn't the ordinary proposition you run into even in this business. I'd been offered deals in drugs and queer money, in heisting banks, shoving hot bonds and smuggling gold. But this was the first time I'd been offered a chance to get in on the ground floor as a whorehouse proprietor.

I asked her for more credentials, and Susu wasn't bashful.

She was an independent, she said. She worked for nobody, which was quite a trick in a city as full of pimps and prostitution overlords as Marseilles. It had been crowded even before the Algerians moved in, but now it was overwhelming. To top it off, there was the racial thing.

The Algerians hated the French; the French hated the Algerians; the Corsicans tolerated the French but hated everybody else. The Corsicans had the upper hand, whether it was the police, customs, heroin labs, smuggling operations or prostitution.

Part of the price Susu had to pay for staying independent, she revealed to me, was sleeping with one of the Corsican mob bosses. He wanted to make her his full-time mistress, but she wasn't partial to Corsicans. They had given the Croix des Vaches to the nearest thing she had to a mother, a prostitute who had found her in an alley when she was a baby, and Susu had vengeance on her mind.

Susu wanted out of Marseilles. She wanted to go where there was no gang control, no intimidation, no Cross of the Cow and plenty of rich men who appreciated knowledgeable females.

"There is very little danger this way," she insisted. "It isn't like dealing in heroin."

"What do you know about heroin?" I asked.

"I know the people who make it."

That was enough for me. She seemed to have all the qualities you look for in a good informant: knowledge, a desire to get even and a need for money. With a female, it also helps if they like you.

I gave her another $100 bill for cab-fare and told her to meet me at four o'clock at the landing where the boats go out to the Château d'If.

"Bring a picnic lunch," I said. "We'll talk more about your business."

I acquired a tail leaving the bar. I was getting used to it by now. The question was, is he a cop or a hood? I stopped to inspect the wares of a street vendor displaying sea urchins in one of the square baskets which are part of the Marseilles scene. Hood, I decided, watching a short hippo-fat character trying to act non-chalant a few yards back.

There are ways to shake tails. My favorite method is dumping one. You duck into an alley and cold-cock them when they follow. Another way, if you're in a strange city and want to avoid a fuss, is to walk into a restaurant and head right for the kitchen. You look around befuddled, like you're lost, and keep right on going out the back door.

At the moment, I wasn't too anxious to shake the Hippo. Let him earn a living. I caught a cab and headed back to the hotel. At 3:30, I took the back stairs down, went out the rear door and headed for the docks.

The Château d'If, sitting out on an island in the harbor, is one of the city's top tourist attractions. It has the smell of history, complete with ancient dungeons. Legend has it that the Count of Monte Cristo and The Man in the Iron Mask once were imprisoned there. For ten francs you get a tour in three languages showing where the Count burrowed through a five-foot-thick wall. It was a good front for someone who might be sightseeing, and a good place to talk business.

Susu appeared wearing a scarlet cashmere sweater but carrying no lunch basket. The French don't go for picnics, it seems, but they can bargain like hell. She got the boat captain down to half of what he was asking. I was beginning to like this girl.

The boat to the Château took a leisurely twenty minutes. The place looked small and decrepit, a forlorn fortress with a forlorn history. But from the terrace at the top, where the soldiers once stood guard, the view of Marseilles and the harbor was magnificent.

Susu got right to business.

"What do you want, Joseph Vento?"

"Information."

"About the Corsicans?"

I nodded.

"Are you a policeman, Joseph?"

I told her that wasn't important. All she needed to know was that she wouldn't be compromised and that she could be in business with her call girls by next week if she produced. I showed her five $100 bills and said this was a down payment for a sample of her information. Now let's have the sample.

"All right, Joseph," she said, leaning against the stone rampart of the terrace. "You see it all right out there."

In a low voice, sometimes bitter and sometimes vibrant, Susu told the story of drug traffic in and out of Marseilles harbor. Ships from Beirut, from Izmir and Istanbul, brought opium and morphine base right into the docks. Customs officials and the police looked the other way while it was unloaded and hauled to the labs for processing.

She said she could pinpoint eight labs operating in the area, each capable of producing from fifty to a hundred kilos of heroin a week.

Sometimes, she said, when a tramp steamer plying the Mediterranean run had no legitimate cargo for Marseilles it was met off the coast by small fishing boats. A few bags of contraband transferred by night, or even in broad daylight, took only a few minutes. On top of that it saved dockage and pilot fees.

The fishing boats took the stuff right into the beaches where the labs were located. She pointed to the shoreline off to the west and said she could almost see the locations of two laboratories. But what was a lab last week might not be a lab this week. Villas used for labs were changed frequently, almost from batch to batch, even though it wasn't really necessary. The Corsicans were cautious people.

Her throaty voice went on. The Guerini brothers had been the kingpins of the heroin makers until the internecine war with the Algerians. Then one brother had been slain by the Algerians and the other had been killed for killing his assassin. This made more room at the top for the Venturis and Jean Claude Rivard, the Corsican whose favors she accepted so reluctantly.

"How well do you know Rivard?" I asked.

"Better than I want to."

"Does he keep a record of his lab operations—names, deliveries, output, suppliers, etc.?"

"Yes. It's a black book and he usually keeps it in the café he owns in the Vieux Port."

"How many of your cousins work at the café?"

"Enough."

"Good," I said. "I think we're beginning to get somewhere."

I sweetened the kitty with another two hundred. Then I told her if she could deliver that little black book within the next two days, or a reasonable facsimile of its contents, she would be on her way to Nice with another $4,000 in her stocking, cash-on-delivery.

Susu gave me those big eyes again and said she would try. I told her I would wait in the hotel until I heard from her. She could send a message with one of her "cousins."

The only thing worse than being outdoors in Marseilles with nothing to do is being indoors in Marseilles with nothing to do. I read paperbacks that didn't interest me and week-old copies of the Paris *Herald-Tribune*. I checked departure times of The Mistral and commercial flights, and made both rail and air reservations in the names of Joseph Vento and Pasquale Lombardi. Although I had come in under one name, I might have to go out under another.

I took brief walks outside and discovered that now I had grown three tails. They were sitting on benches or leaning against lamp-posts. I wondered why they didn't pool their resources and save manpower.

At 11 A.M. on the third day, one of Susu's cousins appeared. She was my chambermaid at the hotel. I was to be at a place called Chez Tonio at three o'clock that afternoon.

I checked a map of Marseilles and discovered that Chez Tonio was four blocks from the hotel, six blocks from the railroad station and a hell of a long way from the airport.

Knowing that I might be forced to leave town suddenly, I had paid for my room two days in advance. I also had taken the precaution of buying a railroad ticket. After retrieving my gun from its new hiding place, taped under the bottom of a clothes dresser, I gave the room a final check. They could have my bag and its dirty laundry.

I slipped out of the hotel by way of the kitchen.

Chez Tonio was a place featuring bar and dancing, but only the bar was working when I got there. I picked a dark booth over on one side and sat down. I had lost my tails for the moment.

Susu arrived looking a bit edgy.

I greeted her.

"Hello, Joseph."

"You have something for me?"

Looking around to see if we were observed, she opened her purse and extracted a small black book.

"I think everything you want is here," she said, placing the book on the seat between us. "Names, addresses, phone numbers, delivery dates."

I slipped it into my pocket.

Asking her to order me another Cinzano, I excused myself and went to the men's room. I needed to check out the merchandise.

In the light of a dim bulb above the wash basin, I checked random entries made in French in precise, compact handwriting. Quite apparently it was the real thing.

Back at the table, I slid Susu an envelope containing forty $100 bills and told her not to spend it all in the gum machine.

"Now listen," I instructed. "I want you to finish your drink and walk out of here. Go where nobody can find you. You might even take that trip you've been talking about and if I were you I wouldn't stop to pack."

I had begun to like this girl and I didn't want her hurt.

Maybe it was mutual. She leaned over, gave me a kiss on the cheek and whispered in my ear, "You're a nice man, Joseph Vento, or whatever your name is."

Then she got up and left.

I made sure nobody was following her. Then I tried to relax over my drink. But suddenly all of the apprehensions I had felt since arriving in Marseilles surged up inside me. Once again I had that empty, gut-fluttery feeling.

With possession of that little black book my position had changed abruptly.

I no longer could afford to play tally-ho the fox with my pursuers in the hope of stumbling on a source of information. I had it now and a frisk would be disastrous. Being caught with that little black book would get me killed by one side or put in a French prison by the other.

Things began to close in about fifteen minutes after Susu departed. I wouldn't have waited that long except that I wanted to give her time to lose herself before leaving myself.

I saw Hippo waddle through the door and take a seat. Hippo didn't worry me; he was just a fat man with a sharp pair of eyes. But the man with him did. In the business of working undercover, you wonder when your luck will run out and someone you have busted somewhere along the way will show and say, "Hey, that sonofabitch is a federal agent."

My luck had just run out.

The man with Hippo was Francisco Frechetti, a Corsican seaman I had arrested walking three kilos of heroin off a ship a few years earlier back in the States.

Frechetti was followed by another tail I had come to think of as Snake, a slippery, unsavory type. They were closing in and the time had arrived to make a decision whether to run or fight.

In one pocket of my coat was the black book. In the other was a black gun. But the gun could be used only in an extreme emergency. They put aliens away for life in most foreign countries just for carrying one. I decided to run, and I hoped this place had a back door.

It did.

I got out ahead of them. Though not by much.

I could hear them grunting and sputtering profane French immediately behind me. I did some broken field running through some of the world's smelliest garbage cans. I climbed fences and moved through the dirtiest alleys I have ever seen.

In one yard I grabbed a red turtle-neck sweater off a clothes line and stopped in an alley to ditch my jacket. They wouldn't be looking for a guy in a red turtle-neck sweater. But with the sweater on, that hot, everlasting wind made it feel as though I was running inside an oven. Stopping to listen, I heard no sound and then I spotted a run-down movie house and ducked inside.

I sank into a seat to catch my breath and collect my thoughts. I realized that getting out of Marseilles wasn't going to be as easy as getting in. Going back to the hotel was out. They'd have it covered. The airport was too far and too risky. I decided my best chance of getting out of town with that little black book was the railroad station. The Mistral left in less than an hour and I planned to be on it.

I had a train ticket in my pocket and a quick check of the theater revealed that it had a back door. Twenty minutes before train time, I let myself out the back door and began working toward the Cannebière. I spotted Hippo going down one side of the street and Frechetti working the other side. I didn't know how many reinforcements they had by now.

A low-flying Citroën almost picked me off as I took cover behind a parked truck. I found momentary refuge in a second-hand clothing store and, for a few francs, bought a seaman's beanie to go with my red sweater. I waited until I saw a cab heading the other way and flagged it.

"Gare St. Charles," I said, handing off a twenty.

I told the driver to circle the station once he got there. I'd let him know when to let me out.

Whether I became the first unregistered agent to get out of Marseilles depended on The Mistral. Its tradition is absolute, I reassured myself, and it leaves on the second.

I gave myself one minute to get from the cab to the train gate. Once past that point I would be safe, unless the police as well as the Corsicans were following. Nobody gets through that gate without a ticket.

I entered the station and tried to walk at a normal pace. My footsteps seemed to be making far too much noise. Only twenty paces more. When would it happen? I presented my ticket to the control agent, had it punched, and walked on the platform where the Mistral waited.

The commotion behind me started as I was boarding the train. I looked over my shoulder long enough to see a couple of them try to storm the gate only to get thrown back. Those guards were tough.

"I think," I told the porter as the train pulled out exactly on time, "I would like a bottle of champagne."

"Any special vintage, sir?"

"The best year you've got," I said.

Sitting there with that little black book in my pocket, watching the bubbles bead up in the glass, I thought about Susu and her future.

If I ever got to Nice and desired a call girl, I told myself, I wouldn't settle for anybody but the boss.

CHAPTER 7

Eve's Apple

WHEN DAN KLEIN became my roommate in Istanbul we ran a pretty fancy pad. We occupied a duplex with oriental rugs, ottomans everywhere, two Sultan-sized bedrooms and plumbing that actually worked. The second floor was almost all glass, practically a solarium. We used it as a combination den and hi-fi room. I was sitting there, telephone in hand, trying to order a fancy dinner from the chef at the Hilton.

"The cold pressed duck sounds good," I told him. "Now what about the trimmings?"

I was talking as though I was spending somebody else's money, which of course I was. I ordered some lobster and shrimp, a little caviar, something with capers and truffles, some of that sticky-sweet dessert they call baklava, and four bottles of the best sake he had in the house.

Dan stood by, shaking his head. "Boy," he said, "this guy must really be important."

"You don't catch big fish with little hooks," I replied.

Asim Bentepe was the big fish I was after.

There were lots of little fish in Istanbul who'd say they could get you opium. Then they'd have to go out and look for it in the interior where the stuff is grown. Asim Bentepe was a top target because he had his organization and source of supply already set up.

He was a businessman who manufactured sickles, axes, knives and other implements, but his most profitable venture was dealing in illegal opium. He dealt in big lots as the jobber and middleman. When he traveled into the interior to sell his regular wares he easily made contact with opium growers and Turkish government agents, who were also sideline bandits—in fact, the government opium agent is the real bandit. On Thursday he sits down on the side of the street in a little town and negotiates with the farmer for his crop. The farmer sells to the highest bidder and the agent buys from the one with the highest grade opium.

After the transaction, the agent stamps a paper which allows the farmer to grow next year's crop. The agent will mark down that he got eight kilos—but actually he got ten. Those extra two belong to him, while the eight listed belong to the government. During the opium season, which is May through August, he does this all day long, two days a week, and at the end of the season he might have 500 kilos that belong to him.

In addition, depending on the weather, he'll steal more from the government at the warehouse. If it's dry, he'll claim that due to dehydration the opium ball that should weigh one pound only weighs half a pound. That gives him quite a haul, which he buries or stashes with a friend.

Then he says to a close associate, or even a relative, "I got half a ton. You want to make some money? Find me a buyer." And the connection has to come to Istanbul to find a buyer, because who has that much money out in the sticks? That's how the racket works.

I had been cultivating Asim Bentepe off and on for more than a month, posing as the captain of an Italian freighter plying between Istanbul and Naples. My undercover name was Giuseppe Antonio Vento. I called Bentepe whenever "my ship," the S.S. *Adriana,* was in port and kept out of his way when it was not. It was easy to check the ship's sailing schedule.

I had met Asim Bentepe through an informant and entertained him at the roof bar of the Hilton. He was short and stout but quite a sharp dresser from a Turkish standpoint. He wore yellow ties and pointed shoes with brass buckles, a gold tie-clasp and large gold cuff links.

He affected a cigarette holder as most Turks do, and constantly flashed a sterling silver cigarette case. It held only fifteen cigarettes, and he carried an extra pack in his pocket. After our first meeting, I kept him well supplied with free Parliaments. He also loved American whiskey and could put it away without any trouble.

It wasn't necessary for me to wear a captain's uniform. If he ever asked to visit the ship, I'd meet him on the bridge with a captain's hat and four wide stripes on the sleeve of a borrowed coat. That would be easily arranged through the Turkish police and the Italian consulate. Or if he checked and found that the *Adriana's* real captain was named Carlo Talamani, I had an answer ready for that, too.

I'd say to him, "You didn't think I'd tell you my real name? Supposing we got caught? Then you'd be able to pinpoint me. I can't take chances like that."

Sometimes that sort of lie doesn't work. But ninety-nine percent of the time it does. There's nothing sure in this business. In this case, the guy never checked.

In our first meeting, Bentepe wanted to know what price I'd pay per kilo of opium, and I told him it depended on the morphine content of his supply. The higher the morphine content the higher the price it brings. I said I was already negotiating with another dealer who was offering me fourteen per cent morphine.

"I want the best," I told him. "If you can't beat that, I'll do business with him."

He assured me that his product was fifteen or sixteen per cent.

"I'll guarantee it," he said. "If it tests lower, I'll throw in an extra ten kilos."

It's a little game you play—like jewelers arguing over the grade of gold—when you're working undercover against criminals. You think the way they do. You forget about the badge and the flag. You think like a criminal, you act like a criminal, and you catch a criminal.

After the first few meetings, I asked him for a sample. I did this for two reasons. First, it would show that he had access to opium and that I wasn't wasting my time. Secondly, the moment he handed me a five-ounce package of the stuff it would make him a defendant.

Bentepe said he would bring me a sample the next time my ship was in port. I invited him to be my guest for dinner and this was my reason for ordering the big spread. Dan Klein was to be on hand in the guise of the ship's medical officer. He would also be a witness.

Asim Bentepe dug into the food as though he hadn't eaten for a week. He also hit the whiskey pretty hard. He asked for bourbon with water on the side, but I didn't see him pick up the water. Taking it neat mellowed him quickly, and after he got nice and congenial, I asked to see his sample.

With a flourish, he produced a cloth bag from the large pocket of a raincoat he had carried on his arm and thrown over an empty chair.

I opened the drawstring and took out a ball of raw opium. It weighed about two pounds and was wrapped with cabbage leaves, the customary method of storing or transporting opium.

You can't take off the cabbage leaves because they stick to the gummy brown substance on the surface. So I took a switchblade knife and dug into the opium ball, bending the blade so some of the center would stick to the knife. This is the professional method of testing the contents. It enables you to see the opium and make sure the center core isn't something else, like a rock or just a ball of mud.

"This appears to be good," I said, nodding approval. "You've told me how good it's supposed to be. But you're not a chemist. And I'm not a chemist. So, with your permission, I'll give it to my chemist, and then I can be certain what I am purchasing, my friend."

I turned to Dan Klein. "How soon can I get a test on this?"

"We can have it by tomorrow morning," Dan replied.

Of course, this by-play was all for Asim Bentepe's benefit. I had no intention of getting it tested, except to send a sample back to Washington for origin analysis. They have ways of pinpointing where the opium was grown within a few miles. I asked the price and Bentepe quoted twenty-two dollars a kilo.

I went through the motions of adding and subtracting figures on a piece of paper, wondering aloud who'd be getting it off the ship, and how much my men would have to be paid.

Then I turned my attention to Bentepe. "How much can you deliver right away?"

He said he had two hundred kilos, plus another ten kilos thrown in for me, his good friend. "But," he said, "you will have to take delivery in Kutahya."

"In Kutahya!" I said with dismay, not altogether feigned. "But that's way the hell and gone out in the interior. Why not here in Istanbul?"

Bentepe was adamant. "There are so many hazards, my friend. There are bandits. There are the police. There is the military. They all steal opium, my friend. No, I absolutely cannot make delivery here in Istanbul. You must take delivery in Kutahya."

Finally I said, "O.K., if that's the way it must be. But you'll have to cut the price to seventeen dollars a kilo to make up for the inconvenience."

We haggled about that for a while and finally compromised on nineteen dollars a kilo. I told him the ship didn't sail for five days and that I'd be able to leave for Kutahya the very next day. Asim Bentepe told me he would be there himself and gave me an address at which I was to meet him.

I knew Kutahya well. I had been there many times under the name of Mike Warner, posing as a pilot for an oil company. It was right in the heart of Turkey's opium-growing belt, a section which produced more than half of the world's legitimate supply of opium.

It rounded out to about three hundred tons a year for hospitals and the ethical trade, and another three hundred tons for the addicts. Most of this tonnage goes to Syria or Lebanon for conversion into morphine base. From there it goes to the heroin labs in France or Italy. The final product eventually reaches the addict in the form of a deadly white powder, mostly in the U.S.A. The Soviet Union and the Iron Curtain countries obtained their supplies mainly from Bulgaria, which produced an even better grade of opium.

The poppy plant grows to approximately three feet in height and has either a white or purple flower. When the green opium apples are out, the harvest starts. In the mornings a cut is made around three-quarters of the apple's circumference and a white sap is allowed to bleed out.

Through the day, the apple follows the sun and the sap turns brown and gummy. It looks much like molasses. The farmers scrape off this gum with a knife, being extremely careful not to touch the gum any more than absolutely necessary because if too much enters the pores of the skin they can become addicted. Yet I've seen Turkish kids eat the opium apple. And the grown-ups use the seeds on their bread and mix them in salads. The Turks say these seeds make you strong and good in bed. I wouldn't know myself. I never tried them.

From past experience, I knew that almost any arrest made in this cradle of international drug traffic would not be peaceful. In the province of Usak, right next to Kutahya, an opium trafficker had stuck a gun in my belly a few months before and pulled the trigger. Nobody but the Lord knows what made it misfire then— it went off with a bang when I tried it later myself. That was a Browning 9mm. automatic, serial number 4756. The man's name was Durmus Tobuk and I got him with 170 kilos, 400 grams of opium.

But he almost got me first.

So you go into the interior prepared for trouble. Thus after making my arrangements with Bentepe, I told Ali Eren and Galip Labernas, my two Turkish police officers, that we were going to the Kutahya area on what looked like a shoot-out, and told them to pick four additional good men to accompany us.

We traveled in two vehicles, a Land Rover and a 1957 Chevy, and because we usually by-passed towns and camped out at night when we traveled as a group, we took all of our own supplies and necessities.

I worked up the supply list myself and supervised the loading. We had extra jerry cans of gasoline, spare tires, large plastic containers of fresh water, sleeping bags, a small tent, soap, toilet paper, Clorox, disinfectant and a complete first-aid kit as well as food.

I was careful now about food. Except for Labernas and myself, all the others were Moslems and their religion forbids them to eat pork. On our first trip together I had loaded up with canned pork and beans at the PX and they ate it without knowing what it was. Then when the laughing Labernas brought it to their attention it threw the whole expedition into an uproar.

You learn to respect their religion. Three times a day Ali Eren and the others got out their basins, washed their hands and faces and turned to the East to pray. Having learned my lesson, this time all of the canned beans containing pork were labelled *domus,* the Turkish word for pork, and that made for harmony.

Along with everything else, we carried our own fire power. This included hand guns, carbines, automatic rifles and a "rising .45." That's a submachine gun. I also toted a double-barreled shotgun. We went prepared to fight a small war.

The trek to Kutahya was about a hundred and fifty miles—and they were rugged. Once you get out of Instanbul there are almost no roads worth the name, and in the dry season, which this was, the dust is unbelievable. Ali Eren and I were in front in the Chevy and had good visibility. Labernas and the others in the Land Rover had to eat our dust all the way.

It is a wild and ominous country, hilly without being mountainous, the brown terrain broken here and there by trees and patches of ground under cultivation. It is primarily the domain of roving shepherds, who move their flocks from area to area with the assistance of large, savage-looking wolf dogs. I've seen shepherds with as many as twenty of these fierce wolf dogs. They feed them a mixture of bread and milk, but never any sheep meat which could provoke a destructive appetite.

Because of the jagged, rocky terrain, we had six flat tires the first day. Every time we stopped to repair the tires we changed license plates on both cars. Tags don't expire in Turkey, so I carried a plentiful supply, changing them just in case anybody (such as the military) became curious and phoned the license numbers ahead. We couldn't afford to let anyone know where we were going or what we were doing.

That night we pulled off on a side trail and camped in a pleasant, secluded meadow where we were somewhat hidden and yet still could observe the main road. We could build a fire, since campfires were not unusual in that area. In fact, you could look out at almost any hillside and see fires twinkling in the distance. The shepherds almost always slept out in the open, and sometimes the farmers did too.

While we made camp, a shepherd stopped to visit us, chatting with our men to obtain news of the outside world. He was, he said, moving his sheep in the cool of the evening so that they would have fresh grazing on the morrow. He carried a long staff and wore baggy pants and an all-enveloping cape that was almost a blanket. He could sit down and practically be in his own tent, which was actually the purpose of that flowing cape.

Those shepherds could drop down and sleep peacefully almost anywhere, awakening only if there was restlessness among the flock or uneasiness among their dogs. The shepherd directed the dogs with shrill whistles through his teeth, along with sharp, shouted commands; and he ruled them rigidly and with no show of affection. It was work by stern domination. If that seems strange, consider that Turks seldom demonstrate any outward feeling or emotion. They don't even kiss their wives, at least not publicly.

At our invitation, the shepherd ate with us and drank some tea. Several of his dogs whined from just outside the ring of light cast by the fire, their eyes gleaming eerily from the darkness. As long as you made no sudden movement and their master remained tranquil they kept their distance. They were huge dogs with long, sharp teeth and, I thought privately, I'd rather take on half a dozen smugglers than one of those wolf dogs.

In the morning I drove into Kutahya and, as arranged, met Asim Bentepe at an inn about ten o'clock. He was filled with apologies as he told me he couldn't make delivery until midnight, and that it would have to be at a spot about twenty miles due south of Kutahya. Painstakingly he drew me a diagram showing the location of the rendezvous. But then he decided it would be better to avoid any possibility of a slip-up, so he took me there himself and showed me exactly where to wait.

"This is the spot," he said, stopping after a bumpy ride. "You will wait here with your lights off. See that hill? We will come that way and flash our lights off and on twice. You will answer in the same manner so that we will know everything is all right."

"Fine," I said. "But why are you going to all of this trouble?"

Bentepe frowned. "There are many reasons for worry, my friend. First of all, we must be careful that no one steals our merchandise. Banditry is a thriving profession in this area."

"Get the stuff this far and you won't have to worry about bandits," I told him. "I've got enough artillery to handle any hijackers."

"That is not all," he said. "We must be extremely careful to keep out of the way of the military. They have been very active lately looking for guns. As you may know, the government situation is very unsettled. So the military is always searching for guns. If, in the process, they find you with opium they will confiscate it. Then you must pay a bribe to get it back. Such an unfortunate incident can cut heavily into one's profit. Which is another reason why I must be very careful."

We drove back into Kutahya and I let him off in front of the inn.

"I do not like these flea-bitten places," I told him. "So I am going to drive out of town a ways where I'll be able to pull over to the side of the road and catch some sleep without being bothered."

Bentepe nodded and walked away as I drove off.

He didn't know that I had two of our men tailing him so he went directly to the home of the man who owned the 210 kilos of opium for which we had negotiated. The man's name was Mehmet Akyar, and he had a two-story house just off the main street, with outside walls made of mud or clay. Kutahya wasn't a very big town. At least we now knew whom we were dealing with besides Asim Bentepe.

I went back to our camp and made preparations for the midnight meeting. We left after cooking supper and were at the rendezvous well in advance of the scheduled time.

The rendezvous had good cover. There were trees on both sides of the road. We stashed the Land Rover in a wooded area about a mile away and I went over the plan with my people.

I would have Labernas with me in the Chevy and the others would be deployed in the brush at the roadside. I warned the men against becoming overanxious and thereby spoiling our trap. The plan was for me to go out to meet the convoy when it arrived and to greet Bentepe by calling out "Asim, Asim!" as though I was overjoyed at seeing him. Then I would inspect the cargo to make certain that it was opium. The next time I said, "Asim!" it would be the signal for them to move in with their guns.

It looked like as good a plan as any.

The men took up their assigned stations and I sat in the Chevy with Galip Labernas. Our lights were off and a pale quarter-moon did very little to cut the blackness. A few fires twinkled off in the darkness.

Midnight came and nobody appeared.

Another hour went by and Labernas asked anxiously, "Do you think they are coming?"

"They'll be here," I said, with more conviction than I felt.

The night was chilly. I got out of the car to loosen up my legs. I checked my gun again. I was beginning to wonder myself whether something had gone wrong and they wouldn't show.

Finally, at about 1:30 A.M., I saw lights coming down the road. When they reached the rise of the hill the lights flashed off and on twice. I gave the recognition signal with my lights to tell them that all was well.

A truck of a German make, with a wooden frame in the back and a tarpaulin over it, appeared out of the darkness and drew up alongside. Asim Bentepe was riding in front next to the driver. He got out and I greeted him with a joyous cry: "Asim, Asim!"

He introduced the driver, who was Mehmet Akyar, the man who actually owned the opium.

I asked Bentepe if he had the merchandise and he said that he did.

Then he asked me, "Have you got the money?"

"Yes, but first I would like to see the merchandise."

We walked to the back of the truck and Bentepe lifted up the canvas. By the beam from my flashlight, I saw a pile of cloth sacks that were stained by leakage from the opium balls inside. The stains were fresh so there was no doubt that the contents were the real stuff. Two men were sitting there with the cargo, rifles balanced across their laps.

The next time I called Asim's name it would be the signal for our men to close in. But I had to get a little distance from him so I'd have an excuse to call him loudly enough for my men to hear from their hiding place. Casually I took hold of Mehmet Akyar's arm, and telling him I had money in my car to pay him for the load, I led him toward the Chevy where Labernas was waiting.

As I reached the car, I turned around and called out loudly: "Asim!"

He started toward us, and as he did, our people came in.

Asim Bentepe was quick. He pulled out a pistol, a German automatic, and began firing toward the figures of my men looming up in the darkness. His two men in back of the truck leaped up and began shooting, too.

I still had my grip on Akyar's arm. He stiffened with a spasmodic jerk when the firing started but I whirled him up against the car as hard as I could. His head snapped back against the edge of the roof and he went down in a heap. As he groggily tried to rise I brought my knee up into his face and he folded up.

"Galip, Galip!" I yelled at Labernas. "Take care of this one."

Labernas came around the car and straddled Akyar. I turned my attention back to the truck. Bentepe was backed up against it, firing wildly. His two men were shooting and so were my men. It sounded like a small revolution. Then one of his men leaped from the truck and a bullet whistled by my head close enough for me to hear over the uproar. I drew a bead on him and he dropped his rifle, staggered a couple of steps and fell to the ground. Then Bentepe tumbled into the dust and the other man on the truck threw his rifle away and raised both arms in surrender.

It was all over about as quickly as it takes to tell it.

In the lights of the Chevy and the smugglers' truck we took account of the damage. Mehmet Akyar was out cold, his nose bleeding profusely from the knee jab I had given him. Asim Bentepe was stretched on the ground with two bullet holes in his shoulder. He was conscious but he lay there silently. The guard I had lowered on had a jagged wound in his thigh from my .45. The other one had escaped without a scratch.

We gave the prisoners first aid and handcuffed them all together. Herding them into the back of the smugglers' truck, we used their own vehicle to haul them and the evidence to the police station in Kutahya. This was a courtesy extended to the local constabulary. Galip Labernas drove the truck with Ali Eren and one of our men in back to guard the prisoners. The rest of our men followed in the Land Rover.

I took the Chevy and stayed out of sight, waiting outside the town until they could rejoin me. As usual, I wanted the credit to go to the Turkish National Police. Besides, I didn't want to give anybody a free look at me in case I had to work in that area again. Unlike what I'm doing now, while on the job I tried not to put myself in the window.

I didn't even have to testify when we returned to Istanbul with the opium and the four prisoners—they had plenty of evidence, and more than enough police witnesses without me.

Mehmet Akyar, the leader of the group, was sentenced to twenty-five years in prison. So, too, was Asim Bentepe, the negotiator. The two guards drew fifteen years each.

It was a satisfying conclusion. The punishment should fit the crime for those who deal **in the** sale of the living death. Yet, I thought, little wonder **they** fight like tigers before surrendering in Turkey.

CHAPTER 8

Charlie and Mike

WORD CAME that Luciano had made a deal with a Hollywood movie company to film his life story, which seemed a good time to look him up again in Naples, and took me back to Naples once again as Major Mike Cerra. But when I got to the San Francisco Bar and Grill the only one I knew was Frankie (Skeets) Culla, the man who fronted the bar for Luciano. Skeets told me that Charlie Lucky was out of town, had gone to Cinzano with Patty Ryan.

Patty Ryan was an alias of Pasquale Eboli, a brother of the infamous Thomas Eboli, alias Tommy Ryan. Cinzano, in the north of Italy, was the Ebolis' birthplace. Luciano's close association with them was another clear sign of his continuing position of high authority with the syndicate.

Skeets insisted I have dinner with him, and I mentioned I'd read about Luciano having his life story filmed.

"It hasn't been settled but I hear he's been offered $100,000," Skeets said.

"I wonder how much he'd tell."

"Not too much. Hell, even for Charlie that could be trouble."

I told him I hoped it worked out for Charlie and that I was sorry I'd missed him but I had to get back to my base in Turkey.

Skeets suggested I write Luciano care of the San Francisco Bar and he said he thought Charlie would get a big kick out of me sending him a picture of myself and my plane, Charlie being such a speed nut and all. Like I've said, the fewer pictures in my business the better, for obvious reasons. Still, a picture without too much detail of my features might be a big help in really setting my cover with Luciano beyond any question of some possible future doubt—and the risks would be reasonable and worth the game.

My thoughts were interrupted when Skeets Culla asked, "You heard that Luigi Pappagallo went back to New York to see his girl again?"

Pappagallo, the harbor pilot and one of Luciano's closest friends in Naples, was apparently becoming a commuter to the States. I wondered if he was also one of the couriers who brought back Luciano's cut of the action from the States. I told Culla I planned to be in New York soon and if he had an address for Luigi I'd like to look him up. Culla obliged and I jotted down the address. Putting a tail on Pappagallo in New York might pay off, or it might not, but the Bureau didn't like to overlook any possibilities.

Leaving, I told Culla I'd be back again in about two months and that in the meantime I'd send Luciano the picture.

My investigations in Istanbul took up most of my time, but when Charlie Lucky Luciano asks for an autographed picture you make extra time.

I was sitting in the cockpit of a T-33 Air Force jet in Turkey, a flying helmet balanced on the fuselage in front of me, dressed in a flight suit and wearing a parachute harness. Looking at the maze of instruments, I wondered what would happen if I ever tried to take this thing off the ground. My ignorance made me feel embarrassed.

"Hold it, Major," the photographer said, and I put on my best wild-blue-yonder look.

He clicked off a couple of shots and said, "That should do it, Major. Going to send them to your girl?"

"Not exactly."

I had the pictures made up at the base lab and sent one to Naples with a suitable inscription. I got a letter back from Lucky saying that he had framed it and that the picture was hanging on the wall in his apartment.

Two months later, in early June of 1960, I got a chance to see both the picture and the apartment when there was a lull in my Istanbul activities and a coded message instructed me to contact Cusack in Rome, who told me to come to the Embassy annex on the Via Veneto for a meeting with CIA agent Hank Manfredi.

He and Cusack were very curious about Lucky's apartment. They wanted a diagram of the layout, along with information about phone outlets, in case they got a chance to plant a bug and put a tap on the phone. They also wanted me to find out any more that I could about Luciano's movie plans for his life story.

I got a set of travel orders from TUSLOG Detachment 49 (USAFE). They looked terribly official. Once again as Major Michael A. Cerra, I would "proceed to Naples, Italy, for the purpose of ferrying aircraft to the U.S. Upon completion of TDY will return to proper organization. Authority: AFM 67-1. USAFE Manual 30-1 and AFR 34-25 will be complied with before commencing travel."

I didn't have a clue what the jargon meant, but it should impress the hell out of anyone who got nosy enough to check my credentials.

There's an Air Force saying that goes: "There are old pilots and bold pilots. But there are no old, bold pilots." And the same rule goes for undercover men.

When I got to Naples I went directly to the San Francisco Bar and Grill. Skeets Culla was there and I asked him if Luciano was in town.

"He's been sick in bed," Culla told me, "but he's been up and around for a couple of days now." Culla telephoned the California Restaurant and then, much impressed, told me he'd contacted Luciano, who was on his way over to meet me.

Luciano was thinner and sort of pale, and for the first time I noticed the faint trace of a scar on the lower left side of his face— more prominent than before in his features drawn together now in the aftermath of illness.

"Hey, kid, it's good to see you," he said.

"Thanks, Charlie, but what the hell happened to you?" I asked him.

"Nothing, kid. Nothing to get excited about. I just had to take it slow for a while."

We sat down at his balcony table and I took a flyer at what I hoped he'd think was funny, even if true. "Come on, Charlie," I said, and laughed when I said it, "level with me. Is it the clap again?"

He took it as though I'd asked him the time of day.

"No, it's worse than that," he said. And then really gave me the fill-in. "About two years now I've had pains in my chest. They went up my shoulders and down both arms. The doctor told me to quit smoking and I did. But the pain kept getting worse and lasted longer. A month ago they gave me a cardiogram and it showed I got a heart condition. This bum, the doctor, says I gotta stay quiet in bed."

He rubbed his nose in that reflective habit of his. "Well, hell, I got to go to the can and I got to wash. How can I do that in bed? For a month I'm in bed and then I can't stand it any longer. So a couple days ago I tell the doctor I'm getting up and he says if I don't exert myself I can go out couple hours a day."

Luciano grinned wryly. "You know what that bum tells me? No broads or I'm liable to kill myself. I told him when I die I'll have a pussy in my hand."

"Charlie," I said, "you should do what the doctor tells you to do."

"Bullshit! If I have to give up broads I might just as well be dead. . . . But the hell with all that. I'm glad you're here, kid. It's real good to see you." He seemed to mean it.

Our conversation was interrupted when a heavy-set, gray-haired man in his middle 60s, wearing a huge diamond stickpin, approached our table.

"Mike, meet Rosario Vitaletti," Charlie said. "You can call him 'Chink.' He's a friend of mine, from Taormina. Chink lives six months in Taormina and six months at his house in White Plains, New York. Some deal."

"Sounds good to me," I said.

"I had a butcher shop on Avenue U in Brooklyn," Vitaletti said in broken English. "Charlie and I work hard all our life. Now we take it easy."

I had a feeling Vitaletti was more retired than Charlie. Luciano then invited me to have dinner with them at the California Restaurant and on our way asked if I'd been to New York or written Luigi Pappagallo.

"I just haven't had the time," I told him.

"Well, don't," he said. "He got picked up in New York and asked a lot of questions. They might be watching his mail and I don't want them to have your name on record."

Again his concern for me. Charlie was beginning to get to me.

I'd have to watch it. Anyway, our people in New York had obviously been busy after my earlier tip-off.

"Is Luigi all right?" I asked.

"Yeah, it's just that Ass-slinger is doing everything he can to find something on me—even from here. So I don't want him to connect up you and me and get on your tail too."

I told him I appreciated that, but I also valued his friendship. After dinner, Vitaletti said he was going back to the Mediterraneo and Luciano told him to get me a room there.

Luciano took my arm as we got ready to leave. "Kid, you make me feel good. I'm glad you're here. Let's go back to the San Francisco and talk a while."

Talk with Luciano was just what *my* doctor had ordered. I quickly agreed.

Once again that night I was impressed with the range of big shots Luciano knew in Naples, where he was regarded as a combination hero-celebrity. Among the people he introduced me to that night were a Paul H. Topp, former Nazi naval captain who'd been in charge of the German fleet in Naples during World War II and now appropriately a Naples beer distributor, and a Dr. Luigi Derosa—member in very good standing of the Naples *Squadra Mobile,* the police radio car division. When this officer of the law was about to take off, he told me, "If there's ever anything I can do for you, let me know. A friend of Charlie's is the same as a friend of mine."

The next morning, Luciano called me from the lobby of my hotel and said he was downstairs waiting to take me to breakfast at the California Restaurant. When we finished, he asked me if I played gin rummy. I told him I did. Luciano ordered Skeets Culla to bring us a deck of cards and we played about ten games for 100 lire (sixteen cents) per game. I beat him out of thirty-two cents.

Once, when he was undecided about which card to discard, I gave him a friendly needle. "Come on, Charlie, it's only money."

"Kid," he said, "a hundred lire or a million, I like to win—especially at this game." I recalled his indifference about horses, but I guess that kind of betting on pure chance—or the opposite—was too remote for Charlie. He liked contact sport—head to head. Anyway, our low-stakes game was generally relaxed and easy. In later games we'd play for much higher stakes.

Suddenly I had the invitation to Luciano's apartment that Manfredi had hoped for. At about two o'clock Luciano got a telephone call. When he got back to the table, he said, "Let's go, kid. Dinner's ready." That simple.

We drove to his apartment house at Strada Parco Comela Ricci, No. 8, a handsome building set against one of the hills overlooking the harbor. It was one of Naples' newest and most expensive, but the architect had old-fashioned ideas about elevators. The elevator that carried us to the fifth floor required a ten-lire coin (approximately one-and-a-half cents) for each trip. On the left of the elevators was a stairway leading up. You only had to pay for the "up" ride.

In the fifth floor hallway, Luciano led the way to his door, which he opened with a key. Three feet inside the door I spotted a small table with a telephone on it, and was disappointed to see that the number plate had been removed. It was also, of course, an unlisted phone.

As we entered, a very pretty and well-shaped young brunette, about twenty-four, came up and kissed Luciano like it was his right and her duty.

"This is Adrianna," he said casually. "She lives here with me." The resident mistress.

She went back down the interior marble-floored hallway and

Luciano proceeded to take me on a tour of the apartment. It was laid out railroad style, the rooms in a row and leading off from the interior hallway. The first was a den-library approximately twelve feet square with a handsome desk, easy chairs, an old-fashioned rocking chair and a filing cabinet.

No lock, I noted.

Next to the filing cabinet was a bookcase. While Luciano stood looking out over a small balcony serving this one room I saw that in addition to other books his collection included: *Traffic in Narcotics* by Commissioner Anslinger, *Brotherhood of Evil* by Fredrick Sondern, Jr., *Treasury Agent* by Andrey Tully and a paperback edition of *The Luciano Story*. Charlie obviously liked to keep up with the competition.

Luciano opened the balcony door and stepped outside. "Mike," he called from the balcony, "come out and look at this view."

Naples stretched out at our feet, the bay a glistening blue and the Isle of Capri looking like it was standing on stilts in the distance. Several small craft looked like toys darting around below.

"It ain't like New York, but it's the best we got," Luciano said. "Nothing's like New York."

I asked him how long it had been since he'd seen New York, and he didn't answer right away. A hard look came over his face.

"Too damned long," he finally said. "And if I tried to go back that son-of-a-bitch Anslinger would be waiting when I got off the boat."

As an Air Force jet jockey there was no special reason for me to comment about the Commissioner so I let that one pass and changed the subject. "You like to fish, Charlie?" I asked, pointing at the boats below.

He nodded. "But you know something funny? I've never fished since I've been back here. I remember, though, when Frank Costello and me used to take out Capone's yacht and go fishing down around Key West. . . ."

Leading the way back into the library, Luciano pointed to a painting of a slender, dark-haired woman holding a small dog. I stood in front of the painting, admiring it.

"That's Igea," he said. "She was my one love. If all broads were like her, I'd have a hell of a problem. I'd have to chase them all."

He explained that she'd died several years before but that he still had the dog.

"That's all I got to remember her by. She really loved that dog."

I knew from the files that Luciano had never married—at least, we had no record of it—and that this had to be a painting of Igea Lissoni, his favorite mistress.

Turning away, he led me into a living room that was also about twelve feet square. There were four lounging chairs and a piano stood in the corner on the handsome parquet floor. Next came the dining room with a round, polished dinner table, six chairs with high backs spaced around it like sentinels, a huge buffet decorated with a candelabrum, an oversized cut-glass bowl heaped with imitation fruit, and four or five silver bowls. Against one wall hunched a combination radio-record player console.

"This is my bedroom," he told me as we came to the next room.

It was larger than the others, about twelve by eighteen, with a double bed, two straight-backed chairs, a dressing table and in one corner a sewing machine! (I wondered what the hell for but didn't ask. Maybe it was another remembrance. Maybe he was touchy about it. I didn't want to antagonize him.) On one wall was a framed newspaper picture of Luciano going into an Italian court building.

Looking through French doors, I saw that a second balcony extended from the bedroom past the dining and living rooms. A bathroom finished in black-and-pink marble tile connected Luciano's bedroom to one that was even larger. This second bedroom, about twelve by twenty feet, obviously was Adrianna's and was furnished with an outsized double bed, a large bureau, a dressing table and two chairs. It also had its own balcony.

"Come on," Luciano said, leading the way farther down the hallway and pushing through a swinging door into the kitchen.

Three toy Dobermans padded up to him and he reached down to fondle them, giving most of his attention to one he called Bambi and identified as the little dog in the painting of Igea. Adrianna was in the kitchen with the maid, Lidia, a thin, dark-complexioned Sardinian about thirty-five years old. The maid's quarters, I saw through an open door, were behind the kitchen.

Before dinner he fixed me a Scotch and poured some mineral water for himself—he told me it was all the doctor would let him drink. We ate in the dining room, Lidia serving a four-course meal of Sicilian macaroni with meatballs and a heavy sauce, wine, roast beef with potatoes, tossed salad, mixed fruit, coffee and pastry. All during the meal Bambi sat on a chair drawn up next to Luciano's and every so often Luciano would chew a piece of meat, take it from his mouth and feed it to the dog.

"Bambi's eleven years old and the chewing teeth are gone," he said, rubbing the dog's ears affectionately. "He even sleeps with me."

It was a lot to take—the sentimental gangster in mourning for his favorite mistress and in love with her dog.

After dinner Luciano took us to the track, where we were seated with the usual ceremony. Shortly afterward a dapper Italian with a small mustache and a Vandyke beard joined us. Luciano introduced him as a movie producer from Rome and said I was his new bodyguard. I smiled. Luciano turned and winked at me.

Luciano kept up his big loser reputation for the night. On the way back to the city he said the ponies probably cost him more than $30,000 a year but "what the hell, easy come, easy go."

At the California Restaurant we took an outside table and talked.

"That producer," I asked, "is he the one I read about who's going to do your life story for the movies?"

He shook his head. "That's a *Hollywood* Italian. He offered a lousy hundred grand plus ten per cent of the take. Hell, the real Italians offered more. A producer from Rome came to see me here with Broderick Crawford. The guy didn't say so, but I think Crawford wanted to play the part. Crawford ain't my type."

"Who would you like to play the part?"

He said that newspaper guys kept bothering him about this and he told them George Raft, just to keep them quiet. "Actually, he's too old, like me. Maybe ten or fifteen years ago he could have done it. The only actor around now that I'd settle for is Marlon Brando. And they'd probably louse it up like they did the Capone movie."

"I saw the Al Capone story," I told him. "I hope they don't make you look that bad."

Luciano frowned. "That was a shame what they did in that picture. They made Capone look like an ignorant bum. Nobody knew Capone better than me and, believe me, he was no ignorant bum. Everything in that picture was phoney, except maybe how he got rid of the competition."

"You mean the St. Valentine's Day Massacre?" I told him I was too young to remember it and wondered if it really happened like they said.

"It happened, kid, just like they say. Capone ordered it and sent Machine-Gun Jack McGurn to make sure the job got done."

Luciano seemed in a talkative mood—I guess he hadn't had many people around since he was sick—and I decided to risk taking some advantage of it.

"Charlie, tell me something. Is there any such thing as the Mafia?

I heard stories from my grandfather—he was born in Sicily—and naturally I've heard a lot of things, but I have a feeling most of it's dreamed up by reporters and cops."

"I'll tell you something, kid. There's always been a Mafia but it's not like those sons-a-bitches tell it in the newspapers. They blame everything on the Mafia but seventy percent of the guys in jail are niggers and spics. The Mafia's like any other organization except we don't go in for advertising. We're big business, is all."

"I guess the Mafia's been around a long time from what my grandfather said."

"Hundreds of years," he said. "There's a story it started way back when the French were in Sicily. We didn't like it and began knockin' off the French. Then the French tried to get away by pretending they were Italians. So when the Sicilians caught a guy they were suspicious of they'd ask him to pronounce the word 'cicciro.' Sicilians pronounce it 'chi-chi-ro.' The Frenchmen somehow couldn't say that one word right. They said it 'ki-ki-ro.' All they had to do was say 'ki-ki-ro' and they were dead men. We didn't like outsiders then and we don't now. Outside the brotherhood, I mean."

Luciano laughed and I decided to try for the brass ring. "Charlie, I hope we're good friends now, so you'll know it's no sweat to me what you did or who you are. It's also none of my business, but I've read a lot of things and can't help wondering if you really are the head of the Mafia."

His expression didn't change. "No, I'm not, kid. But I'll tell you one thing. Not much is done without my say-so."

"Do you know who he is?" I asked.

"It's no secret. Everybody knows." That much, nothing more. I knew enough not to press it. Except for a sort of half joke, with a surprising response. "I heard it once was a man named Vizzini." Mentioning my real name gave me an uneasy feeling. I had heard that a man named Vizzini had once been head of the Sicilian Mafia, but I'd no proof that I was related to him.

Luciano looked at me. "There *was* a Vizzini, but that was a long time ago. He died couple years ago. I'll tell you something he told me one day. He was over seventy and still had to have a girl every day. He knew what to do with them too. I told him he was about to kill himself. He looked me right in the eye and said 'Todo'—you know, that's Sicilian for Salvatore—'pussy is a million times sweeter than honey and I want it till the day I die.' "

Luciano laughed. "You know something, kid. I agree with him."

I asked him about the alleged Mafia killings.

"Kid, it's no big news for me to tell you it's a tough world to survive in. When somebody goes bad and makes trouble he has to be punished. The first time there's a warning—a slap on the back of the hand. The second time—no warning. It's a matter of survival. That's just common sense."

Luciano paused, then added, "If you fool me once, shame on you. If you fool me twice, shame on me."

I knew he had no use for a yes man so I decided to give him a little argument about taking the law into your own hands.

"Kid, you can't be expected to understand it. In any good organization results count and you got to make your own rules. I can't put up with stupid ignorance or someone making the same mistake more than once.

"Sometimes," he added, "once is enough."

"What do you mean?"

"You haven't seen Momo around, have you kid? I sent his ass back to Palermo and told him to stay there. Nobody pulls a gun on a friend of mine and gets away with it."

I said I didn't think he needed to do that, but secretly I was damn glad I didn't have to keep looking over my shoulder to check on the big ape.

"I told you, you just wouldn't understand," Luciano said. "You were lucky. You were born in America and got an education. You'd be just like me if you came up like me. I was just a squirt when my parents took me to New York. My old man really believed that stuff about the streets paved with gold. Hell, we were starving. I was in the streets, stealing and running penny ante crap games in alleys when your mother was wiping your nose. My old man beat hell out of me every time he got his hands on me. When I was fourteen my old man caught me carrying a pistol. He said he oughta kill me with it but he was too soft-hearted to pull the trigger. I never went back."

I asked him how he'd lived.

"I slept in pool halls and empty houses. I went with a gang. We stole anything we could."

Suddenly Luciano changed the subject and wanted to know how things were with me and how I liked being stationed in Turkey.

"Nothing like it," I said. "If you like belly-dancers."

He laughed and said broads were the same everywhere. I told him the job hadn't changed much. Just the scenery. I was still ferrying military planes from McGuire Air Force Base in New Jersey for delivery to Germany, Italy and Turkey.

"If I can bring you anything back, or take anything over there for you, just let me know," I told him. I was throwing out some bait again, like the first time at the track.

"Kid, you still don't have any trouble with Customs?"

"No trouble at all. I've taken home a diamond or two and some jewelry. I land at a military base. I doubt if anybody besides the Air Force knows I'm coming and going."

"Well, maybe you could do me a favor some day. I'll let you know." Then he stood up and suggested we go to the San Francisco Bar for a while. We played some gin rummy, had a bite to eat and he took me back to my hotel. Once I got to my room I made a detailed sketch of his apartment, as Manfredi had asked, and wrote out a full report of our conversations. It was dangerous to do it then, but I wanted to get it down while it was still fresh in my mind. I didn't dare mail it, though, even to a drop. I'd have to bring it—and me—back alive.

The telephone woke me at nine o'clock the next morning. It was Luciano asking me to come to his apartment again. When I got there he greeted me warmly at the door.

"Come on out on the balcony and we'll have some coffee," he said, and led the way to the living room and through it out onto the largest of the three balconies. While the maid served coffee and rolls, I talked about the great view from his apartment and what a nice place it was.

"You should've seen my place in upstate New York," he said. "I had a place in Highland, just on the other side of Poughkeepsie, that'd make this place look sick. It was big, really big. I paid the local sheriff twice as much as he could steal on the outside to watch the place, and he did me plenty of favors. Every time I think of that place I think of Legs Diamond and Dutch Schultz."

"How's that?"

"One day they came up to my place there to try out a couple of new machine guns. They had a job planned and wanted to see how the guns worked. I wasn't home when they got there but I came in a little later and, would you believe it, I find them shooting at three of my beautiful fig trees I'd been babying. Cut 'em all to hell. I raised hell, told those stupid sons of bitches they should've used the brick wall behind the house, that's what it was there for."

I burst out laughing and he did too.

"It sure is peaceful here, Charlie," I told him, looking out over the bay.

"Yeah," he agreed, "but the world's in a helluva mess, ain't it, kid? Take that son of a bitch Castro. You know, kid, that bastard beat me out of my twenty-five percent of the gambling action in Havana. We had it really going for a while under Battista but Castro tried to get it all for himself once we were out. It didn't do him any good, though. He screwed himself by breaking off with the United States and losing all the tourists. If I was the president I'd cut his goddamned balls off." He shook his head. "Twenty-five percent, down the drain."

I asked him how he came to leave Cuba.

He frowned at the memory of his deportation from Cuba in 1947. "I had the police chief in my pocket—hell, I was stuffing enough money in his. He told me the U.S. kept putting pressure on the Cuban government to run me out. They had Battista over a barrel and I never had a chance. But the chief made it painless as he could for me. They put me on a Turkish ship, the *Bakir,* and the chief told the captain I was a personal friend of his. The trip took twenty-six days and I got treated like a king, let me tell you."

I asked him if the Turkish ship captain knew who he was.

"Sure. He told me he'd read about 'the great Lucky Luciano' and was glad to have me aboard."

It was the first time I'd ever heard Luciano refer to the forbidden nickname "Lucky" and it gave me a chance to ask him personally about it.

"I've never heard anybody call you 'Lucky,' " I said. "I heard you didn't like it—something about reminding you how you almost got killed by some cheap hoods and were lucky to escape. Is that true?"

He grinned and the words seemed to explode from him: "Another bunch of newspaper bullshit! It was the cops who really did it to me. Legs Diamond [at the time a hit man working for Luciano] had killed some guy in New York and there was a big hunt on for him but they couldn't find him. There was a lot of heat on the cops. One day not long afterward I'd been out to the track and just gotten back to my house in the Bronx when it was getting dark. I'd just put the car away and was closing the garage doors when these two big bastards popped out of nowhere. I was pretty sure they was cops the minute I saw them. They pushed me up against the garage doors and frisked me, but I was clean. Then a car with two more guys pulls up to the curb. Each one of 'em takes hold of an arm and they hustle me to their car, throw me in face down on the floor in back and walk all over me getting into the back seat."

As was his habit when upset, he continued to lapse into less precise English, to lose the sort of artificially formal speech he affected at other times, like when I first met him.

"I'm figurin' to turn over and ask them what the hell's going on but these are big guys and they're strong as hell. Before I can say anything they've taped my hands together back of me and put some more over my eyes so I can't see a damned thing. Then they jerk me around so I'm layin' on my back. The car is moving now and they keep askin' about Legs, giving me a few kicks now and then to show they mean business, and I keep tellin' them I don't know nothin'. Finally they give up and paste some tape over my mouth too. After quite a while the car gets into a lot of traffic and then begins startin' and stoppin'. From the sounds, I can tell we're downtown at the ferry and I figure they're takin' me over to the Jersey meadows where they can give me a good workin' over without any interruption. By now I'm sure these got to be cops in plainclothes bustin' their humps tryin' to find Legs 'cause there was a helluva stink in the papers about how the police were so inefficient.

"Anyhow, the cars stopped for a minute, moving in line toward the ferry, and I hear a police whistle right near the car. So I gotta figure some way to attract the cop blowin' the whistle. His friends sure as hell ain't gonna admit who they are to an ordinary traffic

cop and I figured he'd at least have to stop them and get me out—
me saved by a cop, pretty funny. Anyway, before these guys could
stop me I lift my legs from against the door and smash both feet
hard as I can against the side window. It busted out pretty good."

He grinned, briefly admiring his own strategy, then sobered
again. "Maybe the cop with the whistle didn't hear anything in all
the racket down there at the ferry house. There's plenty of it.
Anyhow, not a damn thing happened except that the guys in the
back seat begin knockin' the crap out of me. One of them was
pounding me in the face. He must of had on a big ring or something because he busted my lips under the tape and cut my chin
open and ripped my throat. I could feel blood all over me and I
kinda passed out."

Luciano raised his chin and ran a finger along a thin white scar
across his throat and then fingered the barely visible scar running
down from his lower lip to his chin, the one I'd noticed earlier.
"This is what those bastards gave me."

He didn't give me time to sympathize.

"After a while I feel the car leaving the ferry and I figure we're
in Jersey. The car goes along for a while and then I feel it bouncin'
over a rough road and I figure we're soon gonna be close to some
place where they're gonna start askin' me questions again.

"It don't take long and the car stops and they haul me out, give
me a push so I fall down and then haul me to my feet again. Now
they rip the tape off my mouth and I feel a gun at my head. The
guy who did all the talkin' says I better tell now where they can
find Legs or they're gonna blow my damned brains out. I tell him
he'd better get to it then because I got no goddamned idea where
he is."

Luciano rubbed the scar on his chin. "I got an edge on these
bastards, I know they ain't about to kill me. If it's a mob hit and
they got a gun against your head there ain't gonna be no more

talkin'. They get that close, all you're gonna hear is a bang. And that's the last thing you'll hear.

"Anyhow, they knocked me around some more and finally give up. Somebody gave me a push that sent me face down in the mud and I laid there until I heard their car drive away. After I heard the car leave I started to get myself loose and it took me a helluva while, I'll tell you. Finally I get the tape off my hands and my eyes. It's dark as hell, I see I'm in a little cleared space in the woods and manage to follow the dirt road back to the highway.

"I might as well be in the middle of the ocean. Then I see a car comin' toward me. I hold up my arms and when the car begins to stop I see a young guy and a girl in it. Then the girl starts to scream and I finally understand why. I've got on one of those light brown camel hair topcoats and in the headlights I see the whole front of it is covered with blood and mud, mostly blood. The young guy throws the car in gear and they take off.

"So there I am, wondering what the hell I'm gonna do now when here comes another car. I wave it down and what do you know? Damned if it ain't a police car. Turns out I'm in Staten Island, not Jersey, so I'm under New York jurisdiction. They take me to a hospital and when the word gets out the joint is swamped with newspaper guys. Finally they take me back to the city and the cops want to know who did it. I didn't say nothing. They finally had to let me go and the upshot is that the papers had all that garbage about how lucky I was to get away. I guess that's how it got to be Lucky Luciano. I still don't like it."

I told him I didn't blame him, that there wasn't anything lucky about getting beaten up like that.

Luciano shrugged. "That wasn't the end of it. Those cops must have thought if they kept the pressure on I'd crack or something. Anyhow, about a week later I'm at a crap game down on Fourteenth Street and leave about two A.M. I step out the front door and

I'm standing there for a minute, getting a breath of air, when I see a car down the street that looks to me like the one they worked me over in. I duck back inside, go out the back, circle the block and get up close to the car. There's four of them in the car, all right, and I recognize two of them as the ones who braced me against the garage the night they took me to Staten Island. I didn't know them but I pegged the two others as guys I knew worked on the racket squad.

"The next day I made a few calls. I had some friends in pretty high places in New York. Right up to the top. I spread the word I knew who they were and if they didn't lay off I was personally going to see to it that something damned bad was gonna happen to them. I didn't have no more trouble from them after that."

"That's a helluva story," I said. "Tell me, Charlie, did you have any idea where Legs Diamond was?"

"Hell," he said laughing. "He was right there in my house when they put me against the garage. He got the hell out fast when the news broke about what had happened to me."

Lidia, the maid, came to the balcony and told us dinner was ready. Luciano and I ate alone. Adrianna, he said, had gone to visit friends for the day. Luciano ate enough for two men and after pushing back from the table, said he was beat and wondered would I mind if he lay down for a few minutes.

I was delighted. "Go right ahead," I told him. "I'll get a book and read a little, unless you'd rather call it a day." He said no, please stick around. Then he went into his bedroom and closed the door.

I went up the hallway to the library-den. Like I said, Adrianna was away and Lidia, the maid, was busy in the kitchen rattling dishes.

A real shot to get at that filing cabinet.

I opened the top drawer. There were a half dozen folders full of nothing more interesting than household bills and receipts. Then one thin folder caught my eye. It was labeled "Police."

I opened it and saw two sheets of names written in longhand. It had to be Luciano's own writing because right at the top in bold lettering it said: "Ass-slinger, Washington—head prick," which said it all about how Charlie felt toward the Commissioner. The feeling was mutual.

The other names weren't listed alphabetically or in any particular order as to city or county. Behind some of them—twenty-two to be exact—was scrawled the word "greased"—meaning they were on Luciano's payroll.

I found an unused envelope in the desk and began copying the names of the people on the take. Most were from Naples, some others from Rome, Palermo and even New York.

Down the hall the kitchen door swung open and I heard footsteps coming along the hallway. I eased the filing cabinet drawer closed, slipped the envelope and lists into my inside jacket pocket. One step took me to the bookcase. I took out the first book my hand touched and began to leaf through it.

I knew someone was standing in the doorway watching me. I looked up from the book and saw the maid, Lidia.

"Yes?" I said.

She looked around the room, at the desk and then at the filing cabinet. "Signore, is there something I can get for you?"

"No, thank you," I smiled. "I'm just trying to find a book to read until Charlie gets up."

She nodded her head and walked back down the hall. The swinging door creaked as she went back into the kitchen. Then I looked down at the book in my hand. It was *Alice in Wonderland.*

Jesus.

I put it back in the cabinet as if it was red hot. Then, writing fast as I could, I finished copying the names I wanted on the first sheet and went to the second. I'm not kidding—staring up at me in Luciano's scrawl was my own name. *"Sal Vizzini—N.Y.C."*

So they did have a make on me. Somewhere, somehow, somebody'd put the finger on me even though all of my buys in New York had been under a cover name. And I'd made enough trouble so that someone had relayed my name all the way up to Luciano.

All they needed to go with it was a photograph and I'd be a dead man. I looked at the autographed picture of myself on the wall, the one I had sent Lucky a few weeks before, and was glad it didn't really show my features. Still, it wouldn't do to have too many of them around. I finished copying the names, replaced the papers in the file and got the hell out of there.

When Luciano reappeared half an hour later, rubbing sleep from his eyes, I was out on the balcony with a paperback western in my lap.

I told him it had been a great day but that I had to catch a train to Rome because I was scheduled to fly from Rome's Ciampino Airport back to Turkey the next morning.

He said O.K. but insisted on first taking me to the Londra Hotel, near the port, where he said he had to pick up a letter. When we got there, I offered to go in and get it for him. The desk clerk saw Luciano sitting in the car right in front of the door and handed me the letter without any questions. It was postmarked Hartford, Connecticut, and had a return address that I made a point to memorize.

From the Londra we drove to Luciano's art studio, which he wanted me to see again before I left. When we were back out on the sidewalk, saying good-bye to "Cockeyed Johnny" Raimondo, Luciano's boy who ran it, a street photographer happened to come along. Luciano stopped him and said he wanted to have a picture taken of us together. After the first shot was taken I told him I thought I'd blinked and we had another one taken. As soon as the photographer said he'd need three days to get the prints I suggested I take the film and have it developed in one of our Air Force laboratories where they had top equipment. He asked the photographer how much he wanted for the film and the man told him 3,000 lire, about $4.85.

Luciano handed the man 2,000 lire, about $3.22, and said, "Take it or leave it."

The guy took it.

The by-play irritated me. Here was a man who by all accounts had a fantastic income, threw away thousands betting the races and lived like a king. Yet he frequently asked me to bring him vitamins, cards, toothpaste and other inexpensive items from the PX to save a few pennies, never left any money when he casually lifted a newspaper from an unattended rack, and now was beating an obviously poor street photographer out of a lousy buck sixty-three.

Driving me to the train station, Luciano told me that when I got to New York again I should look up a friend of his.

"Go to the Reno Bar on Second Avenue between 11th and 12th and ask for Butch Salerno. His name's Nick but everybody calls him Butch. Tell him I send him my regards. Now, take care of yourself, kid. I'll see you when you get back."

It shaped up as a successful visit. Manfredi would have his diagram of Luciano's apartment. My conversations with Luciano had been surprisingly informative. The roll of film I carried would go into the classified file. I'd tell Charlie it was overexposed. Butch Salerno was another lead, and some heads were certain to roll as a result of the list of names on the take that I'd managed to copy onto the envelope in my pocket.

All roads don't really lead to Rome, I thought. They lead to Naples.

CHAPTER 9

Gun-Filled Nights in Beirut

THE TURKISH Airlines plane winged in over the sun-bathed Lebanese coast and headed down toward the Beirut airport. This job, I thought as I buckled my seat belt, at least was a change in the action.

This time I was after guns, not narcotics; Arab extremists and mercenaries, not Charlie Lucky and friends.

The ostensible reason for my visit was that Paul Knight, the Narcotics Bureau agent in Beirut, was going on holiday and I was his temporary replacement. Actually, I'd been handed a special undercover job for the CIA. As a narcotics agent I'd have a certain immunity from government surveillance. I'd have a cover within a cover, which was more than you could say for the CIA regulars on the scene.

CIA people are exactly what "Central Intelligence Agency" implies: spies. The trouble is that members of any cloak and dagger outfit never seem to remain completely anonymous for long. Every intelligence group keeps a file on the competition. CIA agents, for example, often have a primary cover as political attachés at various embassies or legations. It's a game in which they, in turn, soon draw twenty-four-hour surveillance by the agents of any country they're assigned to as well as from agents on the other side. It makes it tough, at times, to get a job done. And striped-pants diplomacy is only one method of countering the people on the other side. It's much more effective, for example, if you can knock off arms that the opposition is sending to subversive groups in another country, particularly if nobody but the ones you hijacked finds out about it. What the ambassadors don't know won't strain diplomatic relations at dinner parties.

This job had come through my friend "Napoleon," the CIA chief in Istanbul. He'd heard through channels I was being sent to Beirut and he was in a bind.

"We can't take chances that they might know one of our regular men," he told me. "Our contact in Beirut has a lead on a revolutionary Arab group that has received a major shipment of arms from the other side. The Communists intend to distribute them to troublemakers in various hot spots, but our informant thinks the middlemen might well peddle some of them—skim off some cream for themselves. If we can find the lot, maybe we can confiscate them without anybody being the wiser, then send them along to some of our friends. After all, a Sten gun doesn't give a damn who shoots it, and the game can have two, three or even more players."

The political situation is always jumpy in the Middle East. You try to avoid any overt act that might provoke complications. It was easier for me to pass Lebanese customs and police under my real name. My cover identification, the one that hopefully would get me close to the guns, was waiting for me at the Embassy.

The narcotics post in Beirut was a relatively quiet one. Beirut was the clearing house for labs in the Near East that converted raw opium into morphine base. A lot of stuff moved in and out of that port. The main job was to cooperate with local authorities, keep your ears to the underground and hopefully nail some shipments at the point of origin. For several days I moved around on routine drug business, working into my protective coloration. I checked into the Grand Hotel, not the fanciest in town but tolerable. One thing sure, at twelve bucks a day it knocked hell out of my $16 per diem. Nobody seemed unduly curious about who I was or what I was doing; nobody seemed to be tailing me.

Then the time came to call my CIA contact and he told me to meet him at the Embassy. "There are all the credentials you'll need," he said, handing me a batch of well-prepared cards, licenses and other pieces of identification to help build my cover.

I was "Mike Warner" again, former Air Force officer who'd worked some maybe illegal deals for wildcat oil companies. Flying bootleg dynamite, if anybody asked, had helped me set up a syndicate with unlimited backing. We were after guns for sale elsewhere if the profit was right. Better than right.

"We'll have two agents covering you," he told me, "but maybe you should have a pistol as a backup. Everything we use in the field has a silencer. Or I can give you a .22 with half the normal powder charge. Sounds like a muffled sneeze even at point blank range."

"No gun," I said. "If I get close to what we're after they'll probably shake me down and get suspicious if I'm armed."

He gave me a picture and half of a dollar bill.

"We won't need a code. The informant has the other half of the bill."

Codes are useful if they're clear and simple. Let's say the code is F-C-M. I'd tell the person I was meeting, "I get pretty good mileage on my Ford." He'd say, "I prefer a Cadillac." Then I'd say, "I used to drive a Mercury." It works in any kind of alphabetical sequence previously set up.

The bill was better. He had one half. I had the other. We were the only two who knew what they were for and who had the other half. The picture of the informant showed a man of about thirty with black hair and a nose that went several ways from being broken a couple of times.

"We call him Bittersweet," the agent told me, "because he's always eating those little bittersweet chocolates. He runs a tailor shop and he'll introduce you to the people with the merchandise. Five million dollars' worth of hardware. We need to get our hands on it."

The next day I went to the informant's tailor shop. Bittersweet lived up to his picture. In addition to the broken nose he had a tattoo on his right forearm—a skull with a dagger through it, the point of the dagger coming out of an eye socket. I hoped there wasn't anything prophetic about that tattoo.

"*Ali cum salaam.*" I gave him the Arabic greeting I'd learned back in Turkey which, loosely translated, means "you have the blessing of Allah."

"*Salaam en Ali cum,*" he said, and kept sewing.

Next to his work bench there was a little homemade desk fashioned from orange crates. On it was a box of chocolates and a small pile of papers under a quartz rock paperweight. Also visible from under the rock was half an American dollar bill.

I took the torn half of my bill from my pocket and laid it beside the half under the piece of quartz. He picked them up, matched the two pieces together and checked the serial numbers on both halves. Bittersweet shook hands and proceeded to make us a cup of tea, a relief after all the Turkish coffee I'd been drinking. He even put a couple of those little chocolate drops in his cup.

"I'll tell you what I know," he said in good English. The arms had been bought and smuggled into Lebanon by the Russians but weren't of Russian make. They were French, Belgian, German, Swiss—and even some of American manufacture. They were mostly new and the latest models, including several thousand automatic and semiautomatic. Belgian guns were predominant—the Belgians make the best hand guns. The Russians wanted them distributed to their sympathizers. Working through the local group kept the Russians from direct involvement. But they hadn't counted on their Beirut friends trying to peddle some of the guns. And one friend—Bittersweet—had decided it might be even more profitable to inform the CIA.

"My friend," Bittersweet said, "I am in solid with them. They have delegated me to find a buyer for some of their shipment. The Professor thinks—"

"The Professor?"

"Suliman Abdul Azizi. The man heading this is a professor at the University of Beirut, a few blocks from your embassy. Strongly political, you know." He smiled sardonically. "But I have known the Professor many years. He believes in one thing even more than Marxism—it's called gold." And that's exactly what the Professor wanted, he told me. They weren't interested in paper money or American currency. What they wanted, if the deal could be made, was gold.

Bittersweet impressed me. He had a subtle mind that attended to nuances. I could understand why he had such a reputation with the CIA. If I were caught acting as a spy I'd probably get a trial and, hopefully, be traded out of the country.

If he were caught, he was dead.

I mentioned this, explaining how much we appreciated his help.

"Don't worry about me," he said. "I have grown up here. My father was widely respected as a scholar of Karl Marx. I've developed a reputation as somewhat less political, you might say, one who would be unlikely to permit politics to interfere with a commission." He touched his battered nose. "The Professor knows I did not get this in political science class."

"O.K.," I said, "tell these people that I represent a well-financed syndicate, that you tried to find out who and I said it was none of your damned business. Tell them we've got gold and are interested in weapons—only the very best. Tell them I don't trust you or anybody else."

"That sounds plausible."

"There's one more important piece of bait. Tell them I have my own transportation for getting the guns out of the country."

The suggestion pleased him. First it meant that the gun-runners wouldn't have to worry about moving the guns again, or about smuggling them into any other countries. Secondly it would automatically present them with the pleasing idea of hijacking the guns back from me after they had my gold—or, even better, lifting the gold from me without ever delivering the guns.

Bittersweet, though, had no idea where the guns were stored. "All I do know is that they've moved the cache twice."

"Sounds like they're running scared," I said. "If so, they should be fairly anxious to make a deal and unload."

Bittersweet said he would contact the Professor and see about setting up a meeting. I went back to the Grand Hotel to play my role of well-heeled adventurer with a million in gold to spend for weapons. On my per diem, you grab a couple of checks and you're shot down for the day. There I was, talking about a million in gold and worrying about who'd pay for the drinks.

I waited two days. A lot of the time was spent in my room watching the *muezzin* on the balcony of the minaret across the way calling the hour of prayer for the Mohammedan faithful. Then Bittersweet called and told me to meet him and his friend at two o'clock that afternoon in the lobby of the Hotel International. It gave me time to call the embassy and make sure my two CIA tails would be on the job.

I met Azizi and Bittersweet in the lobby as instructed. The Professor was thick-set, not fat; well-groomed, about fifty, carrying a briefcase and wearing a narrow-brimmed felt hat. He looked like a conservative Madison Avenue ad man, but Bittersweet had told me Azizi never hesitated to prescribe murder when indicated.

"Yes," said the Professor after the introduction, "our mutual friend tells me of you. I have a suite upstairs and—"

"Forget it," I said.

He shrugged and moved reluctantly toward a sofa in the lobby. Actually, I didn't want to leave the lobby and get out of sight of the two agents I hoped were watching from somewhere. Also I'd decided to be blunt with him; independent and seemingly in a hurry.

I went right at him. "I understand you have a product that I might be looking for. My company is shopping. Don't waste my time, I won't waste yours."

"You are very blunt. But then, as you Americans say, time is money. Minutes are golden, but gold comes in many forms—coins, trinkets, ingots. . . ."

"And bars," I interrupted. "Bars six inches long and two inches wide and stamped with the British lion as proof of purity. Don't worry about my gold."

Waiting for me at the Embassy was just such a bar of gold as I described to him. The CIA had it ready in case I had to come up with proof that I owned the means to pay for the guns. I was sure the Professor would insist on such proof.

"First of all," I said, "let's talk about your product."

He nodded, momentarily sidetracked. "The equipment you might be interested in would be—?"

"For one thing, I'm looking for 9mm. automatic pistols," I said.

Bittersweet knew he had those. Then I mentioned some items we didn't think he had, to avoid suspicion that I knew too much about his inventory. "We also want Thompson submachine guns and Singer grease guns and—haven't you got a list?"

The Professor nodded. "We have much equipment, possibly what you have mentioned and perhaps even far better items."

But he had a one-track mind when it came to the gold. He wanted to see it, feel it. "Your bars of gold," he said. "You say they have the British seal?"

"What the hell's eating you?" I asked. "Are we going to nickel and dime each other to death? If you show me one automatic pistol, does it mean you have a thousand? If I show you a bar of gold does it mean I have a van load?"

"Nevertheless," he insisted. "Perhaps a sample?"

I shook my head. "You could steal my gold. I certainly can't steal your guns."

He was adamant. "It is my understanding that acid will not destroy real gold. Is this true?"

He knew damned well it was. And it was obvious he wasn't going to let up.

"O.K., I'll show you a bar of my gold, you show me guns. But how do we work it? Are you going to walk into the lobby with an armload of machine guns?"

He was like a broken record about seeing the gold before showing the guns. He suggested I bring my sample to his suite the following day at noon.

"Let's make it *my* room. Grand Hotel, 204. Noon will be fine."

He finally agreed and left with Bittersweet. I strolled into the hotel bar. After a while one of the CIA agents slid onto the stool beside me. The other was tailing the Professor. To an onlooker, we would appear to be striking up a random conversation. Actually I gave him a quick fill-in and arranged for the gold bar to be delivered to my hotel the next morning. I didn't want it around any longer than necessary—the face value of that gold bar was $1,500, but it was worth three times that on the Beirut black market.

I hoped I wasn't setting myself up for its theft. This gold bar was the only one the CIA had available.

When I got back to my room, the *muezzin* was on the balcony of the minaret calling the faithful to prayer.

Put in a stanza for me, I thought.

The Professor came the next day at 11:30, not noon. He wasn't stupid.

I let him in and after we traded polite greetings I tossed my suitcase onto the bed. I'd put the gold bar in its small felt bag so I'd have an excuse to open the suitcase. I wanted him to see, carefully folded inside out to disclose its pockets, the typical gold smuggler's jacket I'd picked up. But he was too busy with the gold.

With great care he extracted a small glass vial from a pocket case and poured the couple of drops of liquid it contained onto the gold bar. Nothing happened to the bar. The drops rolled off onto the bureau and ate a little hole in the veneer. The gold had passed its acid test.

I didn't have to ask him if he was satisfied. I picked up the bar, put it in its bag. His eyes followed me as I went back and closed the suitcase. He saw the smuggler's jacket then.

"Do you have more of the bars here?" he asked.

Putting the gold bar in a small attaché case this time, I said, "I am a cautious man. I'll put this in the hotel safe while we go and inspect your part of the deal."

A chauffeur-driven limousine waited in front, and the Professor ushered me into the back seat.

"I, too, am a cautious man," he said, handing me a piece of black silk folded several times. "I must ask you to make yourself a blindfold. If you slouch down in your seat a bit and pull down your hat it will attract no attention." I don't like blindfolds. They make me feel so damned helpless.

We rode about fifteen minutes, then pulled into a garage and the doors were closed. I took off the blindfold while we switched to a battered blue sedan. The Professor then asked me to put it on once more, and this time we rode for about a half hour. The diminishing sounds of other traffic finally ended and I guessed we were well out in the desert. When the blindfold came off again we had driven inside a gloomy warehouse.

A large Arab in filthy robes was standing next to the Professor. He had a face like a camel. In the crook of his arm was an old bolt action Springfield, its muzzle pointed directly at me.

"This is Ahmed," the Professor said. "He speaks no English."

Closing the doors through which we had driven were a half dozen more characters. They were a dirty, ragtag crew. One was missing half of his nose. A group of true beauties, and all of them armed.

"Well," I said, "let's get on with it."

Nobody made a move toward a pile of crates stacked in one corner of the warehouse. The Professor took out a pipe, filled it with meticulous care and lighted up. I leaned against a wall and almost gave myself a headache trying to stare down Ahmed the Camel. Nothing. No reaction.

"It seems nobody else is coming," the Professor said finally. "You may inspect the merchandise."

I walked over to the pile of crates and the moment I pulled at the top one I knew it was empty. They were all empty.

The Professor laughed, echoed by his crew. If I'd led the police here on a raid, all they'd have gotten would have been empty boxes, and the Professor's people would have enjoyed some target practice.

"Some joke," I told the Professor. "But if you hadn't done something like this I would have thought you were as stupid as"—I pointed at Ahmed—"he looks."

The Professor laughed again, then spoke to Ahmed in Arabic, who made some guttural reply.

"Ahmed has a rather interesting suggestion," the Professor said. "He says that if we bury you in the sand with only your head showing and I let him work on your eyes with a hot knife, it is quite likely you would tell us where your gold is hidden."

"And all you'd get would be two used eyeballs. My associates obviously will deliver no gold unless I'm there and in one piece."

The Professor understood a standoff. He became downright friendly.

"You know, of course, *effendi,* that it was only a joke. As for bringing you here, I also am a cautious man and wished to be certain."

I told him I appreciated his caution, realizing that in our business one mistake could be a man's last. But, I impressed on him, the time for caution had passed. My patience was getting thin. The time had come for business.

"Tonight," he said.

I agreed. "But if there's a slip-up tonight, Professor, I'm dealing elsewhere tomorrow. And if that old Springfield of your friend's is a sample of what you're trying to peddle, you can forget the whole deal right now."

"No, no," he protested. "Tonight you shall see."

He drove me back to the hotel. Once we got out of the desert, no blindfold. And on the return trip I had a feeling that we almost blew it, because the Professor began to take long and anxious looks into the rearview mirror. There could be only one reason for this. He must have spotted the CIA tail. I'd have to give him the burn-off before the Professor got too suspicious. I lit a cigarette and snapped out the burning match with a sharp flourish of my hand, raising it past my ear and bringing it down with a quick jerk. It only took a couple of seconds, and after a few minutes I felt the Professor relax. The tail apparently had dropped off.

When we got to my hotel, the Professor was still apologizing for the dry run. "We have a great problem. The whole political future of the Arab world is at stake these days. It is difficult to know whom to trust."

Imagine that.

He told me I'd be picked up at nine by his chauffeur; that he would join me later at the right place, and right time.

Back in my room I kept worrying about the amateurish tail who'd allowed the Professor to spot him. When I left the hotel again, I made certain I wasn't being followed. Switching cabs a couple of times, ducking through several arcades and backtracking until I was completely satisfied, I went into a shop and called the CIA at a special embassy number we'd set up. I told them what had happened.

"Hell, Mike," the agent in charge said, "that wasn't one of our men he spotted. It had to be one of the Lebanese agents who follow us on general principles. Our guy shook him and he must have hit on you by accident when we dropped off."

"How come they knew the burn-off signal?"

"I guess we all need a little more imagination in this business. It's a standard kind of signal. Looks like we'll have to change ours."

When I told him about my date with the Professor for that night he was worried that there might be a slip-up. He emphasized that we couldn't have it known that American agents were confiscating guns inside the borders of a foreign country. Rival diplomats love to make noises about this kind of thing.

I told him I'd call the Professor and arrange for another place where I could be picked up and then get back to him. He was to be damn sure the CIA agents lost their tails before they began following us.

The arrangements were made and at nine o'clock I was waiting at the appointed spot. The Professor's chauffeur was right on time. He was alone and silent as he drove. No blindfold. The city lights fell behind. We were in the desert on a narrow, two-lane road. The setup seemed just right. The traffic was perfect. An occasional car. There was no moon to make a tail stand out. I checked the speedometer. We went a good ten miles, then turned off on a road over the sand dunes. The car stopped beside a truck parked at the top of a large dune.

It was the Camel. As I got out he spun me around hard and shook me down, his hands searching me under the arms, around the waist, down the back and along the legs. I was tempted to chop the Adam's Apple out of him. When he moved back, satisfied I wasn't armed, the Professor stepped out of the cab of the truck. The only other person there was the Arab with the chopped-off nose.

The Professor gestured for me to follow him around to the other side of the truck. "I will show you the merchandise now."

We walked around the truck and there, spread out on the tops of a couple of crates, were guns. There was variety, all right, but all I could see were a couple of each kind. My eyes went over them: Belgian Browning automatics, a German burp gun, a British Sten gun, two Mauser 7.92mm. MKB (H) assault rifles, two Colt revolvers and a Swedish rifle. I glanced into the back of the truck. Nothing more inside.

They were still playing games.

"We have a complete list of the total in stock," the Professor told me as if he were a friendly neighborhood hardware dealer.

I was wondering where the rest of the guns were, and how I was going to locate them. But you take what you can get before you demand more. Even in a fixed game you don't throw away the few chips they let you win. So at least I wanted to see the list.

"O.K.," I said, "let me see it."

He handed me a typewritten sheet of paper and a small flashlight. I focused the beam on it and read:

Browning 9mm. hand guns......935

Mauser 7.92mm. MKB (H) assault rifles......1150

Sten guns......200

It went on from there. A very impressive list. I read on down the line, memorizing totals.

Now was the time to go into my act if I was going to get them to take me where they were cached. I handed the Professor the typewritten sheet. "Shove it."

"I am unfamiliar with the phrase."

I got more explicit. If I'm on the level I *have* to be hot about this new delay. So I told him in detail what the phrase meant and what he could do with his list.

"What kind of silly son of a bitch do you think you're dealing with? You show me a couple dozen lousy guns and expect me to make a deal? How in hell do I know this isn't all you have?"

"We will make our deal here," the Professor said in a tone that verified Bittersweet's assurance that he would calmly order somebody's murder.

Ahmed the Camel had been sitting on the runningboard of the truck, looking like one of the reasons Lawrence left Arabia, with that damned old Springfield balanced across his knees. Maybe he couldn't speak English but he read the tone of his master's voice. Jumping to his feet, he jacked a round into the chamber of the rifle.

I turned toward him. "And tell that ugly bastard to stay the hell out of this. I'm damned tired of all this."

A trapped mouse coming on tough at the cats. But this seemed no time to back off. Turning to the Professor, I started in on him again. "You think I'd bring a van of gold out here after seeing this handful of guns? You think I'm going to buy guns I can't see? How do I know they got firing pins? How do I know you're not going to short count me? Look, forget it. Just take me back to Beirut and to hell with the whole thing."

I started walking around the truck toward the car.

"Wait just a moment," the Professor said. "Such anger is bad for the system. As you already know, I am a very cautious man."

"The hell with it." I should have been an actor. Matter of fact, I was.

"You can inspect all the guns tonight if you agree the gold will be delivered tomorrow night."

He put the accent on the "if."

I kept the anger in my voice. "All right, Professor, but this is really it. If you have the guns I'll put the gold wherever you say before midnight tomorrow. Even swap, gold for guns. I'll also bring along some protection."

He looked pained that I should distrust him. "Come," he said, "this time I will let you inspect all of the merchandise."

He said something in Arabic, and his two friends crated the guns and heaved them into the back of the truck. The Professor and I rode in the car with the chauffeur. The two others rode in the truck.

We drove back to the main road and turned in the opposite direction from Beirut. I checked the speedometer again. We'd come ten miles out to this point. Now we drove another nine in silence before the chauffeur wheeled into a barely discernible side road leading into the desert. Three kilometers farther on a building loomed up in the darkness and we stopped behind the truck. It was an old Quonset hut virtually hidden among the dunes. Stepping out of the car my foot hit metal—we were on a long-abandoned airstrip being swallowed by the desert.

The cases were taken from the truck into the Quonset, where there were four more Arabs.

And, finally, the guns. Nearly five hundred cases, I estimated.

The stenciling on the cases had been painted out, so I couldn't tell where they had come from and to whom they had been consigned. It was enough for me that they were here. Choosing cases at random, I had them opened so that I could check the contents. The guns were packed in cosmoline, a protective grease.

"Would it be safe to test fire a couple of them?" I asked the Professor.

"Completely so. No one can hear us here."

Under the Professor's direction the men quick-cleaned a Browning automatic, a Sten gun, an assault rifle and a Mauser. At his command they also produced a few rounds for each weapon.

Before loading the automatic I squeezed off the trigger carefully. To impress someone that you know something about guns, you don't just click it off. You squeeze slowly because at twenty-five yards too quick a pull can throw you off six or eight inches. Satisfied with the pull of the trigger, I loaded it and to test the firing pin unloaded the clip into the hard-packed sand floor in one corner of the building.

Too many cases have gone down the drain because of guns with faulty firing pins. But most of these guns were brand new, with the exception of the Mausers, and in excellent working condition. I was sure of it when I test fired one of the assault rifles in the same manner.

I had another reason for blasting away several times. I'd worried after the first burst that those covering agents (if they were out there as I hoped) might possibly think I was getting shot and break in too soon. At which point I probably *would* get shot. But you only need to kill a guy once, so when they heard repeated firing I hoped they'd figure I was still alive.

"Everything seems O.K." I finally nodded my satisfaction. "What are you asking?"

We started bargaining. At first the Professor said he could sell only two hundred hand guns. His problem obviously was to figure how many he could skim off and still have enough left to hand on to the intended Communist-sympathizer groups. But I kept talking about the gold, and his greed took him over. I knew he'd sell every gun there if he thought I had enough gold.

He wanted $500 each for the hand guns. I bargained him down to $350 each, on condition that I'd take eight hundred. I made a deal for a hundred Sten guns and another hundred Mausers as well as a hundred and fifty assault rifles. It came to more than a million dollars—and me with one bar of gold and over-spent on my per diem.

Through it all, Ahmed the Camel's eyes never left me.

I was holding a Mauser and explaining to the Professor about Kentucky windage, how you compensate for a rifle that shoots off center, when Ahmed said something to him. The Professor smiled at me.

"My primitive friend does not think you really have any gold. Ahmed says he can tell because inside you are nervous and jumpy. He still thinks we should bury you in the sand up to your neck and let him work on your eyeballs with the heated point of a knife."

I figured I'd better get this ESP Arab's mind, as well as the Professor's, on something else. I'd noticed a bottle sitting on a crossbeam at the far end of the building. It was a good fifty yards away and the lighting was bad. A tough shot under the conditions with a gun I'd never fired and which could be well off center. But the situation called for some kind of fast diversion.

Bringing up the Mauser, I took a snap shot at the bottle. It exploded off the crossbeam, glass flying in every direction. Lowering the Mauser, and turning so that the muzzle pointed directly at Ahmed, I grinned at the Professor. "Ask him if he'd like to take a gun into the desert with me and see who is the jumpiest. Or tell him I wonder if he shoots like a camel, too."

The Professor translated. Ahmed said nothing. The six others, who had been watching us silently, stayed silent.

The Professor's mind turned in another direction. He wouldn't easily give up the idea that he might get the gold and manage to keep the guns too. Nobody had to tell him that when they didn't arrive at their intended destination it might provoke some very embarrassing questions by the Russians who had originally paid for and delivered them to him.

"I have been wondering"—he was trying to be very casual—"how you are going to get the guns out the country."

I looked at him. "How did you get them in? And where from? Do I ask you?"

He shrugged. "As I have observed, you are a very cautious man, Mr. Warner."

But still he didn't give up. Riding back to Beirut, he had to make one last try. "You will deliver the gold to the warehouse tomorrow night when you come for the guns?"

"You're really a case, Professor. O.K. I'll tell you what I'll do. I'll bring half the gold when I come for the guns. After my people have taken them safely away, I will personally take you to get the other half."

The Professor sighed and leaned back against the seat.

We went over the details once more. Sixty bars of gold, worth about $270,000 on the Beirut market, would be involved in the first exchange.

Or so he thought.

They dropped me off at the hotel. I waited long enough for the covering agents to get back and make their report. Then I went through the usual tail-shaking ritual and checked in by telephone. It was 3:45 in the morning.

"Do you have the location spotted?" I asked.

"Affirmative."

"Well, it's on this time. The stuff is there. But I wouldn't wait too long getting to it."

"We're ready to move."

I filled him in on the layout of the place, and the fact that they had eight men to deal with. They would need at least two large trucks to carry off the guns. Three would be safer. And they had better come with some guys who knew how to shoot.

"Thanks," he said, and hung up.

I heard later that there was some kind of a shoot-out on the desert shortly after dawn. Two rival gangs of marauders having a tea party on the site of an abandoned air strip, or so the story went.

The Lebanese government never knew what really happened. I doubt if even our ambassador did. The Russians found out, of course, but there was nothing they could do. Well, one thing, maybe. The Professor simply vanished. They had, after all, been sold out. They were appropriately annoyed.

I don't know where the guns went and didn't want to know.

"It worked out fine," Napoleon said when I got back to Istanbul.

And that was all he said.

CHAPTER **10**

Silk Stocking Larceny

THE SITUATION was tense in Turkey and the foreboding was electric in Istanbul. For about a month the city had been under martial law. Rumors were as thick as pigeons in Philadelphia that the Menderez regime was about to fall.

Tanks and soldiers patrolled the streets with trigger-happy vigilance. If anybody acted in a suspicious manner the formality of asking questions was dispensed with. They got shot.

Driving through the city at night was like midnight sightseeing in a cemetery. Nothing moved except the figments of your imagination. I had a special decal for my automobile but after sundown it was more comfortable in the Hilton's rooftop bar. Those itchy-fingered patrols might not see your decal in the darkness. Apologies wouldn't help if you were full of lead.

Still, by day we kept trying to get the job done. It had to lead, though, to eventual complications.

They came when I arranged a large "buy" from a guy named Kemal Kavurmacioglu.

He had agreed to deliver one hundred kilos of opium to my

apartment. Kavurmacioglu set himself up to me as the boss of the operation but I had a nagging feeling that there was someone else in back of him and I wanted this Mr. Big too, if there was one. I also felt that with this much cash on delivery, such a large shot wouldn't be far away. Like they say, there's no trust, or honor, among thieves.

When it came time for the delivery, Ali Eren and Galip Labernas hid out in the bathroom, ready to emerge at the proper moment. Right on time there was a knock on the door. When I opened up, Kavurmacioglu stood there flanked by two other men. They brought in the material and one of the men said something in a low voice to Kavurmacioglu.

My Turkish was getting better all the time and I could piece out that he told my contact he would wait outside in the hall and that Kavurmacioglu should bring the money to him there. It was a command, not a request—this was the boss. He had stepped through the door and closed it behind him before I could make a move.

Swiftly I checked the sacks to make certain they actually had brought the opium. Satisfied, I gave a low whistle which brought Eren and Labernas noiselessly from the bathroom. Their drawn pistols motioned the two opium peddlers to silence. Then I twisted one of Kavurmacioglu's arms up behind his back and piloted him to the door.

"Tell the guy in the hall that we need him and to come in," I ordered.

"That Arab will kill me."

"Take your choice."

I twisted harder on the arm and Kavurmacioglu reached out with his free hand, turned the knob and opened the door.

His fear must have shown in his face because the man waiting in the hallway whirled in the direction of the stairway and took off. I spun Kavurmacioglu back into the room and went after the boss.

My quarry headed straight for the Bazaar, which began a few blocks away and covered several square miles. I knew if he ever got out of sight in that maze we would come up missing one opium peddler. You could lose Ali Baba, the Forty Thieves and half the Turkish army in the labyrinth of the Bazaar without any trouble at all. It stretched block after block in the Suleiman Nazif section of Istanbul, an almost unbelievable rabbit warren of tents and up-turned boxes, of flies and rank odors, of vendors in open stalls hawking every kind of ware conceivable. It was more flea market than market place. You could get your pocket picked in the Bazaar or find yourself sold into slavery. A great place to play hide-and-seek, depending on which side you were on.

I was wearing Italian desert boots, which are good for running, and I dug in. The Arab made a quick turn into the Bazaar and I did a wide-open ninety-degree after him. At this point he had a lead of about thirty yards and he was zig-zagging through the crowd. He shouldered through a knot of people blocking the street, knocking down several of them. I leaped over a couple of prone bodies and pushed some figures aside, drawing a volley of curses in Turkish and Arabic. But I was gaining on him now.

At this point he turned into what soon became a blind alley and came to a frustrated halt. Turning with his back to the wall he brought out a large knife and shouted at me in Arabic.

I heard footsteps behind me but ignored them.

Pulling my pistol, I aimed at his feet and snapped a shot into the dirt between them. Then, very slowly, I advanced closer and raised my revolver until it pointed straight at his nose. The knife dropped from his hand.

Out of the corner of one eye I detected a flurry of motion. Before I could turn, something thudded against my head. Somebody drew the shades and that was the last thing I remembered for a while.

I came out of the blackness with Ali Eren leaning over me, concern etched on his face. Leaving Labernas with the two other dope peddlers, he had taken off after me as the anchor man in a three-way relay race. Hunkered down beside me, he had his pistol pointed at two Arabs backed up against the dead-end wall. Sitting up I could see a detail of stern-faced Turkish soldiers carrying M-1's holding back a curious crowd of bystanders.

One of the Arabs standing against the wall was the man I had been chasing. The knife still lay at his feet and near it was a club that looked like a nightstick. Evidently this was what the other Arab collared by Ali Eren had clouted me with. I had a lump on my head that felt as big as an ostrich egg.

Ali Eren obviously had identified us to the soldiers and, while they offered no assistance, they did not interfere as we led away our two prisoners.

This was the last case I was to make in Turkey for about six months. Because the coup against the government came that night. And when the government fell my whole set-up collapsed.

I got the call from Galip Labernas at two o'clock the next morning, telling me the bad news. It made my headache even worse.

"They have just arrested Ali Eren," he informed me.

"My God! What for?"

It turned out that Ali Eren, being a loyal Turk and a good police officer, had put up minor resistance when the tanks moved up to Police Headquarters. He was now in a cell, along with the Chief of Police and most of his staff.

"I've been temporarily relieved of duty," Labernas said. "They are going to transfer me to the Trabzon."

"Where the hell is that?"

He said it was a long way from Istanbul, on the Black Sea near the Russian frontier. It was a place where they exiled public officials who had fallen out of favor. I told him how sorry I was.

I was even sorrier about my own predicament. In the confusion of the next few days, it was a question whether I would be asked to leave the country. My permit to carry a gun was revoked. All of the men on my Narcotics Suppression Squad were fired or transferred. A whole new cast of characters, from Police Chief on down to desk sergeant, was running Police Headquarters.

One question I asked myself was whether they would open the jails and turn loose the fifty or so opium smugglers I had helped put there. If so, Istanbul could become a mighty unhealthy place for me. Besides washing out a whole year of hard work, it could make me a splash in the Bosporus with a couple of pieces of pig-iron tied to my feet.

Somehow, I told myself, I had to con myself into the good graces of the new boys at Police Headquarters. I needed help, and I got it in a round-about way from a man named Feyzi Saglam.

Shortly after the coup, Feyzi Saglam held up the Turk Bankasi, making off with $175,000. He managed the job with a grease-gun and disguised by a silk stocking pulled down over his head, and by dark glasses. He got away driving a car with the windows sprayed, leaving only a small slit to see through. It was the crime of the year in Istanbul.

The newspapers played it large. The new government naturally became very embarrassed. Here they were, trying to establish themselves, as well as the fact that money was safer in a bank than in coffee cans at home, and somebody walks in and knocks over the biggest bank in Turkey.

The new Governor of Istanbul was outraged. He called in his new Police Chief and gave an ultimatum of find the sonofabitch or you're out. And the pressure went down the line to the department heads.

There was steam in the air the morning I went to Police Headquarters. I was waiting for Major Nazif Oka, the new chief of detectives. When he got back from being chewed out by the boss, he strode to his desk and slammed down the newspaper he was carrying. He ordered everybody out of the room.

I had been trying to get to see him all week, and somehow this didn't seem to be the right time. Still, I hung back after the others left.

"You seem to have a problem, Major," I said.

He grabbed the newspaper off the desk and shoved it at me.

"This is my problem."

It was the story about the bank robbery. I already knew the details. He said he couldn't discuss my situation just then, maybe ever. Everybody was assigned full time to this case. It had top priority and I could please get lost.

"Yes, I know. We have many bank robberies in my country. I've assisted in cleaning up several of them."

I was handing him a line, but it got his attention. I knew the guy was in trouble and desperately looking for help from any direction. I was also well aware that the Turks are extremely proud and that any offer of assistance had to be made with extreme delicacy.

I told him that I was indeed concerned about his problem, that I had a good network of "confidantes," the term for informants in Turkey, and that maybe one of my sources could provide some useful information.

"It is difficult to commit a crime like this without the underworld knowing about it," I went on. "If you will permit me, I will be glad to make inquiries and turn over to you any information I may get."

A shot in the dark, but it worked. He stopped his pacing, actually smiled at me and said he would appreciate anything I might be able to do.

I left Police Headquarters feeling I might be able to get things back on the track after all. I had a contract of sorts to catch a bank robber, which was more rapport than I had had with anyone in authority since the coup. I lost no time getting to work.

Immediately I put my lines out to my string of informants, contacting every thief and con man in Istanbul who was on my payroll, and told them the stakes were double on this job. I wanted every scrap of information that might be related to the bank robbery.

I instructed them to put out feelers for anybody buying or carrying a grease-gun, the weapon used in the hold-up. The underground market in arms was big in Istanbul, but mostly in Thompson submachine-guns, British Stens, German Mausers and M-1's. A grease-gun was something of an oddity. It might well provide a lead in the case.

I also went to Ali Eren. He didn't have a phone, so I stopped by at his place off Taksim Square. Ali had been released from prison and was sitting at home brooding over his dismissal. He was glad to see me.

"Baba, I need help," I told him. "You know that I want to stay in Turkey. I have work to do here. But unless I can convince these people that I am sincere and not political I might just as well leave."

"What can I do?" he asked.

I handed him the newspaper article and said, "You've seen this, about the bank robbery. I've got to find the man who did it."

He looked at me and nodded. The Turks either love you or hate you, and if they love you there's nothing they won't do. Ali Eren was no exception and a genuine fondness had developed between us. He also was a competent police officer, with thirty years' experience, and had a thorough knowledge of the city.

"I will get out right away and see what I can learn," he promised.

I put my hand on his shoulder.

"Be careful, Baba, I don't want anything to happen to you. Things are pretty rough out there right now."

My concern brought the first smile to his face.

"Don't worry. I will."

I left him and stopped off at the Hilton. Chris, the bartender, began shaking up a White Russian the minute I appeared in the doorway. I hadn't seen him in a while.

"How you do, Mike?"

"I'm doing just fine," I told him, climbing on a stool. As far as he knew, I had been out in the interior somewhere flying dynamite. Actually, I was sitting on it here in Istanbul.

A girl called Heide slid onto the next stool and said, "Buy me a drink, Mike."

"Sure, baby."

What the hell, I thought, you couldn't work as an undercover agent twenty-four hours a day. If I had to kill time, I might as well kill it being nice to myself. I bought her three drinks and had four myself.

Within forty-eight hours, reports began filtering back from my informants. One of them concerned a former clearing-house accountant with a previous arrest for procuring, who had been shopping for a grease-gun on the black market recently.

"What's his name?" I asked the informant.

"Feyzi Saglam."

"Where does he live?"

The informant gave me an address but said he hadn't been there for almost a week. Feyzi Saglam had disappeared from all his usual places. I made him my number one suspect, began checking further.

I knew that it was difficult to get arrested for procuring in Turkey. After all, women who get arrested there work off their sentences in a legal whorehouse. That's how they get the money to pay off their fines. There are also high-class illegal call girls, and this was where Feyzi Saglam had taken his fall. He had become involved with one of them and been busted for procuring.

I checked out the girl and found she had disappeared too. I didn't tell the police anything. I decided they should be informed on a need-to-know basis only, but I got the tip to Ali Eren.

The next morning Ali appeared at my apartment.

He looked, as usual, like an undertaker's helper but his news was cheerier than his appearance.

"I found someone who swears Saglam did it and knows where he is staying."

"Good. What do you suggest?"

He suggested surveillance on the place around the clock. He said he had two former police officers who had lost their jobs after the coup and they would work with him. One of them already had a stake-out on the place.

"O.K., let me know whatever it costs."

I told Ali Eren to wait and picked up the phone. The time had come for me to make my big con to Police Headquarters. Getting Major Oka on the line I said, "I've got to see you right away. I have something."

"Is it the robbery?"

"Yes," I told him, and he got so excited he could hardly talk.

He was even more excited by the time I got to Police Headquarters. I told him I knew who pulled the job. One of my confidantes knew him by sight but not by name. Every effort was being made to identify the man, find out where he was and that they would get back to me.

The Major embraced me and took me up to see the Chief of Police. The Chief sat me down with great ceremony and ordered one of his flunkies to serve tea. I had been a pariah for a month, and now was the honored guest.

"Is there anything you need?" he asked.

I told him I would need permission to carry a weapon. In five minutes I had a permit as an Interpol officer to carry a gun. The Chief bowed and smiled and offered me more tea. I told him I would be in touch as soon as I learned anything and that, hopefully, it would be very soon.

I knew I was going to have a tail leaving the place. They didn't trust me that much. So I went down to the American consulate, entered through the front door and slipped out the back. I made sure I had lost the tail before I picked up Ali Eren.

"Anything new?" I asked him.

"Yes," he said. "He is in the place now. I've got two men watching from the outside."

I clapped him on the shoulder.

"You're beautiful, Baba. O.K., let's go."

He took me to the place. It was a German-type building of heavy brownstone. The Germans had a big influence in Istanbul. It sat on a narrow street with brick paving. The building had three stories, and Ali had learned that our man was in a flat on the first floor.

Ali Eren wanted to go in with me but I told him no. I didn't want him to take the rap in case anything went wrong. When he insisted, I agreed to let him cover me from the hall and handed him one of two pistols I had picked up at the Embassy.

I had kicked in doors for years on narcotics raids, and this one presented no problem. But just in case it was the wrong place, I got out a handkerchief and tied it over my face Jesse James style. Then I hit the door and it crashed open.

Feyzi Saglam, asleep on the bed, woke up. He rolled sideways and reached for the grease-gun on a nearby chair. Before he could reach it I was across the room and came down on his head with the barrel of my gun. Saglam went out, colder than frozen haddock.

Ali Eren came in right on my heels and we handcuffed Saglam to the iron bedstead. Everything used in the bank hold-up was there, the silk stocking, the dark glasses and the grease-gun, fully loaded with 9mm. shells. The money was there, too, arranged in neat piles on the table, the bank bags tossed on the floor. We counted it—damn pleasant work. It was all there except for a few thousand *lera*.

We put the money back in the bags and I turned to Eren.

"Have someone go to a phone and call Major Oka. Tell him that Mike wants him right away at this address."

Eren had one of his men make the call. Then he said that he'd better not be around when the police arrived.

"Okay, Baba." I agreed. "No use rubbing their faces in it." He and his men went across the street and down a ways and watched it.

They came in green Fiats, with sirens sounding and little red lights flashing on top. The Major was in the first police car. I met him at the front door.

"He's in there," I said, motioning toward the busted door. "Don't worry. He isn't going anywhere. He's ironed up and ready for delivery. But before you go in I've got to ask you a favor."

"Anything, Mike." He bobbed his head vigorously, dark eyes shining. He would have given me anything he had at that point, including his three wives.

I told him that I couldn't afford the publicity of becoming involved in all this. As usual, I didn't want to be put in the window.

"My people will recall me if they hear I had anything to do with this. It will hurt my career."

I couldn't tell him I wanted him to take all the credit. His pride wouldn't allow him to accept under those conditions. But this way he couldn't very well refuse. As well as remaining undercover, it was part of my plan for getting in solid with the police and reactivating narcotics enforcement in Turkey.

"Don't worry, Mike. I'll take care of that," he said, and then he went into the room where Saglam was tied up. The Major, waxing righteous and furious when he saw the man who had put the entire new department on the spot, began slapping him around and calling him worse names in Turkish than I have ever heard in English.

"Hey, Major," I called to him. "How would you like to give your chief a real surprise?"

He stopped slapping the prisoner and looked at me. I told him about a plan I had cooked up while waiting for the police cars to arrive. He was agreeable. He would have agreed to almost anything at that point. So we put the plan into action. We took the thief down to Police Headquarters and made him dress up the way he was when he hit the bank. We took off the handcuffs outside the Police Chief's office and made Saglam pull the silk stocking down over his head. The dark glasses went on, held in place by a piece of tape, and we handed him the grease-gun. It was unloaded now, of course.

"We want you to walk through that door and hold the gun on the man sitting behind the desk," we instructed him.

Feyzi Saglam wasn't too crazy about the idea, but a few more persuasions from the Major encouraged him to see it our way. We even went through a brief dress rehearsal.

"Does he look all right, Mike?" the Major asked.

"He looks like John Dillinger's second cousin," I said, checking him over.

Then I opened the door and pushed him into the Chief's office.

We could see what happened through the open door.

The Chief let out a squawk and turned pale. He started to get up, then fell back in his chair and just stared.

"Here you are, Chief," Oka said, going in right behind the bandit.

Then I walked in with the bags of money and put them on the Chief's desk. He just sat there staring for a few moments, then finally recovered his poise and leaped to his feet. Things got pretty emotional after that.

The Chief came around his desk in two jumps and grabbed me. He kissed me on both cheeks about a dozen times. He kissed Major Oka. Everybody began kissing everybody else. The only one who didn't get kissed was Feyzi Saglam, who stood there looking like a man from another planet with that silk stocking over his head and those big dark glasses.

The only thing he got, and quickly, was thirty years in jail. They don't fool around in Turkey.

It occurred to me later that my little grandstand play with the Chief might have queered the whole deal for me in Turkey. But it didn't. The next day, when I stopped by the Chief's office to discuss the resumption of narcotics enforcement, he got out the teapot and called in Major Oka.

"Now, what can I do for you?" he asked. "I owe you much, my friend."

I told him that it would be a benefit to him and his country if I were allowed to continue my assignment with the Turkish National Police. I hammered the point that my mission there had nothing to do with politics or with spying, but that I was interested only in the suppression of the illegal opium traffic. I said that the day he proved that I had ever lied to him I would get on a plane and disappear.

He shook my hand with a vise-like grip.

"You have proved yourself to be a friend of ours and of Turkey," the Chief told me. "We would not think of you leaving the country. Actually we will appreciate it greatly if you continue your work."

There was no chance, however, he said, that I would be working with Ali Eren and Galip Labernas or any of their men. Those who had been in control were out and those who had come to power meant to see that it stayed that way. It was the old patronage deal which happens whenever a new faction takes over. They were gone and nothing could be done to bring them back.

But, the Chief advised me, I would be provided with a new team of men who would assist me in any way possible.

The new head of the narcotics squad was a man named Abdulah Pektash. He was tall, about six-foot-three, and had a long face that was heavily pocked. The thin lips under his black mustache rarely smiled. Pektash had been a taxi driver and before the coup an officer in the army. His knowledge of narcotics was minimal but he was extraordinarily proud of his new position.

Naturally the entire business of narcotics enforcement came to a grinding halt in Turkey with the turnover of power. The twenty-nine men under Pektash were as ignorant about narcotics as he was. We didn't make a case against an opium seller from May until November, and all of that time was spent training Pektash and his men.

These guys were tough, as only Turks can be tough, and they were willing. We cleared out one whole squad room at Police Headquarters and I held classes from seven o'clock in the morning until late at night.

We put mats down and I showed them some of the basic tricks of self-defense, how to take a suspect into custody without overly endangering themselves and how to protect themselves against a knife and a gun. I took blows from all of them and handed them back double. Abdulah Pektash was at every training session and I gave him some of the hardest action. He took it without complaint.

Some of the men couldn't write, so I arranged classes in basic writing, enough so that they could sign their names. But most of the training was for the enforcement of narcotics cases: surveillance, moving in for the arrest and obtaining evidence that would hold up in court. Most of them were apprehensive at first. But they got into the spirit of the thing and began competing to see who would become group leaders or supervisors. They became very good. In fact, it wasn't long before the Chief of Police was calling on my squad to work on cases that had nothing to do with narcotics.

They called it "Mike's Squad."

Even Abdulah Pektash, who was the officer in charge, would say to his superior, "If you want Mike's Squad to handle the case, we'd be glad to oblige." We worked on one rape case involving a sixteen-year-old girl in Istanbul and solved it.

But Abdulah Pektash never fully accepted me until we had our first shoot-out with opium smugglers in the interior. I had negotiated for the purchase of five hundred kilos of opium through an informant in Istanbul. The delivery was to be made on a lonely mountain road in the opium-growing belt near Kutahya, close to the area where with my former squad I had nailed four suppliers in a gun fight some months earlier.

I still had that battered 1957 Chevy and the Land Rover and we carried all of our own necessities as well as the usual armament. The only question in my mind, when we made camp that night near the appointed meeting place, was whether Abdulah Pektash and his men would prove reliable. I had worked hard at training them but you never know until the bell rings how men will react. I could only hope that they proved somewhat close in mettle to Ali Eren and Galip Labernas.

The next morning we moved on to the rendezvous spot and cased it by daylight. It was a deserted piece of mountainous terrain about ten miles out of Kutahya where a rocky road crawled through and up out of a deep ravine. The delivery was to be made at dusk one kilometer south of a stone crypt marking some departed Turk's burial place. I checked with Abdulah Pektash on a plan of action.

"Let's pull the Land Rover off the road and hide it," I said. "You and I will sit in the Chevy and wait for them. Your men can cover us from vantage points along the side of the road."

It was a good plan but something went wrong. The opium came in as expected, loaded in sacks on seven donkeys. We could see them approaching in the half-light a quarter mile away just before dark. But apparently they had sent someone ahead to scout the meeting place and found something they didn't like.

There were two quick shots off to one side of us. Immediately the seven donkeys were turned off the road, the three men who were driving them urging them on with whips.

"Let's go," I yelled, starting up the Chevy.

We started up that rocky road, heaving and bouncing. It was almost dark by now. An automatic weapon began chattering close ahead of us and the windshield shattered in front of us, glass flying in all directions. I slammed on the brakes, and before the car stopped moving I rolled out of the car on one side and Pektash rolled out on the other. He had his pistol out and I had my shotgun.

"Stay down," I shouted to him. "Keep under cover but start shooting to hold their attention while I try to circle around them."

He began blasting away to keep them busy. I had to get close enough to make my shotgun effective. I could see the muzzle-flashes of their weapons in the darkness and, hunched over, I ran obliquely to the left before cutting back to the right of their flank.

Suddenly I could see vague shapes in the near darkness about twenty yards in front of me. Their attention was on the Chevy, while Pektash was keeping up a steady fire. Now his four men had joined in the fusillade and it kept the attention of our ambushers off me.

But then, as I went toward them, they were attracted by the motion and several shots whistled past my head.

That's when I cut loose with the shotgun.

The first load of buckshot fired on a dead run tumbled one shape to the ground and the second barrel boomed and took down another. A third figure took off down the slope and was picked off by Pektash and his men.

The two opium smugglers who were riddled with buckshot and died that night were Ferhat Kuk and Mustafa Turhan. The third one, who had tried to run, was only shot in the legs and would live to serve time.

On the long ride back to Istanbul, with almost six hundred kilos of opium, Abdulah Pektash seemed even more morose than usual. Several times he started to speak and then went silent again. Finally he came out with it.

"Mike, you have killed two men," he said slowly. "I am worried that this might make much trouble for you because you are not a member of our police."

I shrugged. "There's nothing we can do about it. They would have killed me if I hadn't killed them. I prefer it this way, my friend."

"There is something we can do, Mike. I will say that I shot them. That way you will not be blamed for their killings."

It's the same the world over. Let a policeman kill a lawbreaker, no matter what he was doing, and somebody is going to start blowing a whistle and screaming about police atrocities and brutalities. They're the types who would have everybody believe that Jack the Ripper really was a misunderstood angel.

I stopped the car and turned to look at him. For the first time I realized the close bond that had formed between us. Turks don't accept you quickly, or easily. It had taken this business to bring us solidly together, and Abdulah's offer touched me.

"Thank you, Abdulah," I said, "I appreciate your offer but if there's going to be any heat I can't let you take it for me."

Perhaps, I thought at first, it would have been better if I had.

The Russian news service made a big thing out of how an American Interpol agent had shot down three "unarmed" Turks driving a donkey caravan.

But it worked out in good fashion, removing any doubts I may have had about my standing with the new regime's police department.

The Chief of Police, along with Abdulah Pektash, visited the Russian news agency offices and made them print a retraction with the true facts. As it came back to me, the Russians were told it was that or immediate deportation—with no guarantees of safe passage out of the country.

CHAPTER **11**

The King Is Dead

THE ORDER to proceed with the Luciano investigation came to me in Istanbul in the Spring of 1961, just after I'd come back from the hilly interior of Turkey with six hundred kilos of opium, and leaving behind two dead men that the Russian news service used to try to make an international incident. I was glad for the change of pace, not to mention the chance for some good Italian food again.

Since the last time I'd seen Charlie Lucky, Major Mike Cerra had been promoted—he was now Lieutenant Colonel Cerra. This had been done to impress Luciano and keep the cover looking legitimate. It also gave me a new reason for contacting him. When I wrote and told him about my new rank he was delighted. "We'll celebrate next time you're in town," he wrote back. I was looking forward to the party.

I got a set of Air Force travel orders from the OSI man in Istanbul that said I would proceed to Naples for ten days TDY (temporary duty). The nature of the duty wasn't specified. I got a plane for Rome, checked into the office for briefing and arrived in Naples by train.

It was almost like coming back home.

Skeets Culla, as usual, was sitting at the bar in the San Francisco looking like a manager. He greeted me and said he'd check to see if Lucky was in town. That was obviously standard procedure—don't bother the boss unless he wants to be bothered.

I told him I was beat and going to check into the Mediterraneo.

The telephone rang almost as soon as I got there. It was Luciano. "Hey, Mike, get the hell over here! I'm waiting for you." He told me he was at the San Francisco and I told him I'd be right over.

When I got there the first thing he noticed was the silver leaves on my shoulders. I didn't always wear my Air Force uniform, and usually brought civvies with me, but I felt this time I had something special to show off.

"Hey, that's great," he said fingering the insignia. "The next time I see you you'll be a damned general." He looked drawn to me, and I wondered if he was still feeling down from the illness he'd had just before my last visit.

We went upstairs to his private table, where we were joined by a husky man with cold brown eyes that he introduced to me as his cousin, Girolamo Salemi. Salemi was a man in his early sixties and from his hard style I wondered if I was going to have to cope with a substitute for Momo. Gerry, as it developed, was a talker, and he told me later that like Luciano he'd been born in the Sicilian town of Lercara Friddi, and that when he was seven his parents took him to New York. He'd been deported in 1927 at the age of twenty-nine.

That made him sixty-three, or a year younger than Luciano, as I found out when I gave Luciano a money clip I'd bought at the Air Force PX in Istanbul. The clip was attached to a U.S. silver dollar dated 1891.

"I picked that date because I thought it was the year you were born," I told him.

"I'm not that old, kid. I was born in 1897."

So he was sixty-four. Anyway, he seemed very pleased with the gift. Pulling out a pack of ten thousand lire notes, he put the money clip around it and stuck it back in his pocket. I told him the clip was the largest size I could find, which was what I knew he'd need to hold his pile.

He smiled, then turned to Salemi and handed him a folded telegram. "Try to get Mike for me again."

Salemi went to the telephone and was quickly back to say he hadn't been able to reach "Mike." Luciano shrugged and turned back to me.

"I hope you can stay a few days and come up to my villa with me. I'm going tomorrow morning to take care of some business."

"I can't say yet, Charlie. I won't know until I call the NATO base."

"Well, give 'em a call right now."

I tried to put him off. "It's almost midnight, Charlie. If I call now it means waking up the Officer of the Day.

"Wake him up. That's what the bastard's there for. Come on."

He led the way to the pay telephone in the restaurant and stood there while I called the NATO base. I was trying to think what I could say to the OD on duty, who certainly wouldn't know me, but before the base answered Luciano, always impatient, turned and walked back to his table. No one was within hearing distance so I asked about a made-up service acquaintance and hung up.

Back at the table I told Luciano I wouldn't have to report in until 9 A.M. the following Monday, and this was only Wednesday.

"Good!" he said. "I'll pick you up at eight tomorrow morning at your hotel." He dropped me off at the Mediterraneo and said good night.

I immediately put in a call to Cusack in Rome. Normally, there's no question that telephone calls are not the ideal method of transmitting information. But I had to check in and let Cusack know where I was going, just in case he needed to contact me. Using careful language—no names—I said a friend was inviting me up to his country place for a few days. That was all he needed. He said he was sure I would enjoy the trip and to get in touch when I got back.

It was exactly eight in the morning when Luciano and his mistress Adrianna picked me up in his new Alfa Romeo Giulia—the same metallic gray as the old one—and we drove to the Hotel Turistico to collect his cousin Salemi. Adrianna held Luciano's favorite toy Doberman in her lap and seemed to be pouting, which seemed surprising since she now wore a diamond studded wedding band on her left hand and on her right a diamond cluster in the center. She also looked a little pregnant.

As we drove north on a winding highway, I asked Luciano what happened to his old car.

"I had to get rid of it because the ash trays were full."

I laughed like a straight man and told him he shouldn't go out with girls who smoked, which I suspect didn't make me popular with Adrianna. I tried to recoup by saying that if I had his money, I'd open an air-conditioned whorehouse.

"That's not my line," he said abruptly, and I remembered suddenly what he'd said about Dewey and being framed on a lousy prostitution rap.

The trip from Naples to his villa at Santa Marinella, thirty-six miles north of Rome, took a little more than three hours, and I wished it had taken longer. As a driver, Luciano hadn't improved a bit. The needle on the dash hovered up around the 120-kilometer mark, and if several other cars hadn't swerved off the highway at critical moments we'd never have made it.

"Charlie, you'd have made a hell of a jet pilot," I told him. He laughed and said, "If you drove like this I'd be a nervous wreck. But when I'm driving, I gotta get where I'm going fast."

We stopped once for gasoline and again for oranges. Luciano was a glutton for any kind of fruit, but he particularly went for oranges. The third time we stopped, it was for a roadblock.

Up ahead, on the bypass outside Rome, there were several Carabinieri and road patrol officers. Luciano saw them signaling for him to stop, and as he slowed down he took out his Beretta and handed it to me in the back seat. Salemi, sitting next to me, had already slipped his 7.65mm. automatic into a seat pocket in front of him.

"Get rid of this for me," Luciano said.

Obviously he didn't want it thrown out the window or he'd have done it himself. Carrying a pistol illegally is a twenty-year rap in Italy, so I could do like Salemi and stick it in the seat pocket. That way, at least, it wasn't on my person. But this was a chance to show Luciano how I could stand up for him. I dropped it in my inside coat pocket.

Luciano slowed the car as we neared the Carabinieri, but they were looking for somebody else and waved us through. Safely past, I asked him if he wanted the pistol back.

"Keep it for me until we get to the farm." A show of trust. Or a test. Or a little of both. . . .

We bypassed Rome on Via Aurelia and, considering Luciano's driving, by some miracle finally came to Santa Marinella and went directly to the villa on the Via Monte Grappa.

The "farm," as Luciano called it, occupied two blocks. The villa was a stucco building with a red tile roof, dominating the main block which was nine hundred feet long by ninety feet deep. In the rear, separated by a narrow dirt road, was another smaller block of property five hundred feet by ninety. On the main block, in addition to the villa, the garage and a garage apartment were well-tended front and rear gardens. On the rear block was another house, some fruit trees, a vegetable garden and a chicken house.

We were met by Luciano's second cousin and namesake, Salvatore Lucania, as well as by Salvatore's wife and twenty-seven-year-old son, Giuseppe, who acted as caretaker. The parents lived in the house on the rear lot. Giuseppe had the two rooms above the garage and these would be shared with Salemi. The villa had a large kitchen, an ample dining room, a main bedroom with a double bed where Luciano and Adrianna slept, a bathroom and a living room that converted into a spare bedroom, where I was to sleep. Along the rear of the villa was a sprawling marble and concrete balcony with cushioned metal furniture, including a sofa, four chairs and a glass-topped table.

Luciano used the villa to relax and for Mafia business. Since he wasn't permitted inside Rome's city limits, the farm served as a rendezvous for people he had to see in the Rome area.

The night we arrived he asked me if I'd like to ride down to the railroad station. He was expecting a visitor from Rome. I said sure. After all, any visitor of his was of special interest to me.

At the station, we met a tall good-looking guy with a lot of black hair—Aniello Napolitano, also called Harry Nap. As purser on the S.S. *Independence* he was also a messenger boy between Luciano and the mob back home. Just like Joe Scozzi, the purser on the S.S. *Dutton,* that I met with Luciano on my first trip to Naples.

Luciano's first question was, "Did you get it?"

Harry Nap nodded and looked at me.

"He's all right," Luciano said. "He's a friend of mine."

We got back into the car and Nap pulled out a thick envelope. "That's from Frank Costello," he said, passing the envelope to Luciano. "You better count it, Charlie. Frank says there's seventy big ones in there."

"I'll count it later because I guess it's there if Frank says so."

Luciano opened the envelope with his thumb and took out a couple of bills. "Here's something for your trouble," he said, but the courier pushed them back.

"Frank took care of me, Charlie."

"OK." Luciano nodded, putting the bills back in the envelope. I could make out twenties and hundreds.

"Now, whatta you hear from Vito and Carlo?" Luciano asked.

"Nothing, Charlie. Not a thing."

Luciano looked at him, but said nothing.

Back at the villa, the two men went into the bedroom. I sat on the balcony with Adrianna in a chair facing the open bedroom window. I could actually see Luciano giving the money a quick count. Then he took it to the bedroom clothes closet, locked the door and put the key in his pocket.

We had steaks that night courtesy of Aniello Napolitano. I complimented Lucky on the meal and he said they'd come right off Harry's ship. "The last time our friend was here he brought two cases of steaks, inch-and-a-half thick, and one whole case of Oklahoma chickens." Harry the provider looked proud.

After dinner Luciano went into one of his black moods. He sat brooding in a chair, his nose pushed over to one side with his thumb.

"Some of those bastards aren't coming up with their payments," he said to nobody in particular, and without another word got up and went off to bed.

Just learning that Luciano was receiving large sums of money was important in itself. It meant that he was still active and still had control, even with a whole ocean between him and the boys in New York.

The name of this courier, like Joe Scozzi of the *Dutton,* would be passed along to the Bureau for further checking, and as evidence that Luciano was still doing business with the likes of Vito Genovese and Carlo Gambino.

Harry Nap left the next day to go back to his ship. Before he did he asked Luciano, "Is there anything else, Charlie? I'll be in New York in two weeks."

Luciano took off his gold watch and diamond tie pin and carefully put them in an envelope, which he sealed and handed to the courier.

"They gave me these when I was run out of the States," he said. "You see that Vito and Carlo get them. Tell them to hock these things for me. I'm running a little short."

Harry said nothing, picked up the envelope and pocketed it.

It was Luciano's very effective way, I realized, of telling them, "you sons-of-bitches haven't paid your installment."

Later I heard from an informant, who said he'd talked to Harry Nap, just how effective Luciano's message was. It got through so well that Vito and Carlo made their apologies by having Harry return the pin and watch, plus retroactive payments and two more in advance. An expensive way of saying a transatlantic "We're sorry."

As soon as the courier left Luciano seemed to relax. He got me out onto the pink marble balcony for a session of his favorite form of masochism—gin rummy, which proved to be a game he loved to relax by, was insatiable for, and got lousier at the more we played. He just couldn't or wouldn't master it, although he acted as though he took it seriously. During the four days I stayed at the villa we had a set routine of gin in the morning until two o'clock lunch (before which he'd take his big red "football" pill that was prescribed to absorb excess fat in his blood), then after lunch gin again until about five, followed by his nap from five to seven, when we'd drive to Civitavecchia some six miles for the evening papers. There'd be another session after dinner.

This Thursday, after Harry Nap had gone with the "message" for the delinquent Vito and Carlo, Luciano stripped for action, which meant he took off his shirt, shoes, socks, and rolled his trousers up above his knees. He was really decorated—a large tattoo of a naked girl on the left inside forearm, another of an Italian sailor on his right outside forearm, and on the inside of his right forearm a heart with an inscription I couldn't make out. There was also a scar on his left shin. While I shuffled the cards he told the maid to bring him a pan of hot salt water because his corns were hurting. Not exactly your classic picture of one of the most feared—and rightly so—gangsters in the history of the underworld.

The game started at ten cents a point, quickly went to a dollar, and pretty soon he wanted to go double or nothing. Eventually he was into me for two million dollars, and it was like Monopoly with play money. I knew I'd never get paid, but it was a good, relaxed atmosphere for me to risk some more questions in.

The most obvious at the moment was how he got the scar on his shin.

"I had it since I was fourteen," he said. "I had a pistol and was showing it off to a friend of mine. The dumb bastard accidentally pulled the trigger."

"Was that the only time you ever stopped a bullet?" I asked.

"Yeah, but like I told you, I put a few of them in other people."

I decided to change the subject and asked him what was happening with the movie he'd told me they wanted to make of his life.

"Hell, I cooperated all the way with them for a while," he said. "I even arranged through a contact in Rome for them to pick up a copy of the whole damn Interpol file on me. They paid a grand for it. I was sort of curious myself to see what kind of junk they had in it. You know what they came up with? A mug shot, fingerprints, my arrest record and some stuff about me still being the head man."

I wasn't surprised they'd come up empty. I'd checked that file myself. "But what about the movie? You said there was a hundred thousand or more in it for you. That's a lot of money, Charlie."

"Yeah, I know, but when I read the script I told them no. They wanted to phoney it up, just like they did with Capone. The real story's better, but they probably wouldn't believe it if they heard it. Not that they're going to. Anyway, I don't need the money that bad."

The next morning after his usual breakfast of two soft-boiled eggs, biscuits and tea, Luciano had me back out in the sun on the balcony playing gin for Rockefeller stakes, with the usual results. After several losing games he slammed his cards down on the glass-topped table and said, "Mike, if you could fly airplanes like you play this game you wouldn't need wings."

"I win a game once in a while," I said modestly.

His cousin Salemi came out and joined us. "Mike called," he said. "He'll be here tonight."

Luciano nodded, seemed pleased. I was looking forward to the arrival of the mysterious other Mike.

But close as I'd come to Luciano, and for all his confidences to me, it was obvious that this Mike was going to be off limits. That Friday evening, around nine, Luciano asked me if I'd ride into Civitavecchia with Giuseppe, the caretaker, and pick up the papers for him. Naturally, I went along.

When we got back to the villa, there was a Dolphin Alfa Romeo in the driveway, license tag Roma 354208—Mike's car, I suspected, and it turned out I was right. I memorized the tag numbers to be checked out later by the office to get a make if possible on the owner. Later, as I did so many times in my thirteen years undercover, I would jot down the figures in Japanese—that language school training paid off many times. Looking, memorizing, recording and passing on information was the guts of what I did. It wasn't all glamorous shoot-outs and playing house with Luciano's friends from the Snake Pit.

Shortly after I got back from town another car pulled up, and two men went inside while a driver sat waiting in the car. Luciano came out briefly to meet them, called one of them Todo and went back inside with them. He waved to me and said he had some business to discuss. I took the hint.

But I also decided to take a stroll for myself. In the covering darkness I worked my way around the house to the dinning room window. Even the shutters had been closed but I put an ear up against a crack. The voices were muted and I couldn't make out the words of the man who was talking, but then Luciano's voice broke in.

"No. Leave him alone."

The other voice again, still low but by now I could make out a couple of names, including a Joe Bruno. I could visualize Luciano sitting there, thumb pressing his nose back, considering and judging.

Then: "O.K.," I heard Luciano say, "Tell them to go ahead. He's been warned."

The back of my neck was tight. The Mafia court with its one-man judge and jury was in session, and verdicts had been given. There would be no reprieve for the condemned men—or for a snooper like myself if I got caught.

There was a light in the garage at the end of the villa and I was distracted by the sound of the caretaker putting away some tools. The light went off and I could hear footsteps approaching. I froze against the side of the house, trying to take some cover behind a shrub. Giuseppe passed within a few yards of me and went off into the darkness. Close. Too close, but I had to risk hearing more.

Their talk had now switched to other business—local connections and delivery schedules, and I caught the names of Giuseppe Corso from Milan and Pietro Davi in Rome. There were some other names that came through garbled, but I already had more than I could remember without taking notes. I pulled away from the window, and using the light from it to find my way I strolled around the corner of the villa and found the gardener talking to the driver of one of the cars.

"Just took a walk up the road," I told them. "It's a nice night." I said it casually. I hoped it sounded that way.

Two of the names I'd heard designated for hits that night were very familiar. Both were guys I'd busted on narcotics charges and turned into informants. Their days of informing would be over fast if I didn't get away from the villa and manage to warn them.

The next morning, Saturday, this seemed even more urgent when I saw that both cars of the previous night were gone. Gone about their business, no doubt. I asked Luciano if his friend Mike had been there and if everything was all right.

"All right? Hell, better than that," he said. "That was a big guy in the government down in Rome."

"You know some important people, Charlie."

"Are you kidding? He works for me."

I told him I thought I'd go in to Rome for the day to take in the Vatican. I said it was strange but I'd never had time to see it before and this looked like my best chance before the next Monday when I had to report back for duty in Naples. As a matter of fact, I wasn't lying—I hadn't seen the Vatican and I would have liked to pay it a visit. But that wasn't the first on my agenda when I got to Rome. John T. Cusack was.

Luciano said he understood and wished he could go with me, but that he couldn't get into Rome without being bothered. I was glad of that. Having him along was the last thing I wanted.

Earlier that morning, after I'd packed to leave, I'd noticed a developed roll of 35mm. film in a tray on the dining room table. I held it up to the light from a window and saw it included photographs of Luciano, Adrianna, Salemi and Giuseppe. I knew our files had no pictures of Salemi and Giuseppe so I took the roll of film and stuffed it between the cushions of the living room couch. Adrianna had an English setter puppy she kept at the villa that she was always blaming for taking things. I hoped she'd blame him again this time.

She did, after she'd noticed at breakfast that the film was missing. She also cuffed him with a slipper and complained to Luciano that he was always taking things and chewing them up and hiding them. Luciano ignored her. Just before we were to leave for the station I told him I'd forgotten my damn comb and brush in the bathroom—which I'd purposely left there—and went back into the house to pick them up. I also picked up the roll of film.

Once we were in the car he asked to see my wallet. That had become a sort of ritual with him each time I left. If the wallet looked low on cash he'd try to put some in it, and I wouldn't let him. I'd tell him I carried my money in my pocket and that I was O.K. Then he'd ask to see it and I'd have to show him. This time I told him I had a couple of hundred, which seemed to satisfy him.

And then he said, "I've got something else for you," and handed me a pair of gold cuff links with four different colored stones. He insisted I take them as a gift to celebrate my promotion to lieutenant colonel. I didn't see how I could possibly refuse them and so I didn't.

When he dropped me off at the station, he tapped me on the shoulder. "Take care of yourself, kid."

That was the last time I ever saw him.

Charlie Lucky Luciano was a murderer, drug dealer, at one time even a stool pigeon. I'd have shot him without a moment's hesitation if I'd had to, especially if he ever pulled that Beretta on me He was also a cool, in-charge guy. He had a sense of humor, except about himself and the rotten deals he felt he'd been given. He'd "buried 100 guys" and waxed sentimental over a picture of his lost love and her surviving dog. He was a simple man and I think a complex one at the same time. I'm not going to lose any sleep over him, but I'm also not going to forget him.

The consequences that flowed from my infiltration of Luciano's set-up in exile didn't stop with his death a few months later, on January 26, 1962, when he staggered and fell at Capodicchino Airport in Naples. Other agents followed down the name leads I'd gotten from Salemi and overheard during the secret session at Luciano's villa. As soon as I got to Rome and saw Cusack, I passed along the information about the two informants with the death sentences over them. One was gotten to in time by our people. The other informant, I'm afraid, wasn't nearly so lucky. Word was late getting to him, and they found his body in the trunk of a car in New York with seven bullets in it. Luciano was still calling the shots, literally.

As for me, I had Luciano's personal calling card to people such as Trigger Mike Coppola, Patsy Erra, Peanuts Tronaloni and Johnny Royale—all names Luciano had talked about during my visits and told me to look up. I'd told him I would, and I did my best to keep my word.

There are a couple of theories about how and why Luciano died. The official report said heart attack, and we know he'd had a history of heart trouble. I'd personally seen the effects of it—espe-

cially during my last two visits. Some others think the mob may
not have believed him when he said he wasn't going to have the
movie of his life made and were afraid he'd talk too much. Maybe
they managed to have him poisoned, although no autopsy ever
provided evidence for this.

In 1968, two years after I'd retired to South Miami, Florida's
then Governor Kirk asked me to do something about the flow of
narcotics into the port of South Miami. That assignment took me
back to Italy, and while I was there I checked in with Cockeyed
Johnny Raimondo. I asked him what he thought about Luciano's
death. He said he thought it was a heart attack, and nothing more.
But he also said that if anybody poisoned Luciano it would probably have been Adrianna, who was mad as hell at him for his
carrying on with the ladies.

Personally, like Raimondo, I believe Luciano died of natural
causes. He insisted on what he felt was due him, but he really wasn't
in anybody's way. They listened to him and he had a reputation
for settling fights, not making them within the underworld. He was
a peacemaker, although sometimes his brand of peace meant death
for people who got out of line. But most of all, I just don't believe
anybody had the balls to kill him. If he'd been in the States some
ambitious punk might have tried to make a reputation by shooting
him. But in Naples, operating as he was . . . I don't believe it.

Like I said, Luciano is a hard man to forget. I know I won't
forget the thump I felt seeing his death notice in the Miami *Herald*
over my morning coffee. I was wearing his gold cuff links at
the time.

CHAPTER 12

The "Mongo" Connection

THE SATCHEL with the explosives was getting heavy. Sweat poured down my face and neck. My clothes clung to me in the steaming jungle heat and the mosquitoes seemed to be eating me alive.

I'd walked more than three miles along a dirt road from the Thai village. Now I was looking for my landmark in the ghostly light of a half moon. My watch showed me it was three o'clock in the morning. Plenty of time before daylight. Still, I couldn't waste too much of it finding that tree I'd spotted on my one previous trip. The spot where my guide had turned off on a concealed path to the river.

This time I had no guide.

I was alone with the satchel full of explosives and the jungle knife and the .45 automatic at my waist. None of these would help much if I was caught. For I was illegally crossing the river which was the border between Thailand and the puppet state of Mongo.

Colonel Woo Fong and his private Chinese Army were over on the other side. Sound asleep, I hoped. If they weren't, and I was captured, they'd make short work of me. Short work if I was lucky;

these bandits have intriguing methods of disposing of an enemy in a manner that prolongs their entertainment.

Where was that damned tree? I had to locate it to turn down to the river and wade across at the right spot to reach their clearing another mile back in the Mongo jungle. And I had to get there. For in that clearing in the middle of their village was a two-story factory.

Inside the factory was more than forty tons of heroin, opium and morphine base destined for illegal sale in the United States. Enough to send every user in the country on several trips. One hundred million dollars worth of junk. And I meant to send it sky high.

It was a fifty-fifty chance, I figured, whether I'd get in and get out again. Right now getting in and setting those charges was my main thought. I'd worry about getting out later. But I was sweating, on the verge of panic at not being able to find that damned tree which was my landmark. I told myself to take it easy; it had to be up ahead somewhere close by.

Suddenly there it was, right in front of me. Leaving the road, I plunged into the jungle and stumbled as cautiously as possible along the barely discernible path.

It was only a half mile to the riverbank but it seemed an interminable journey. Branches lashed at my face, tugged at my clothing and tore at the satchel in my hand. I was panting heavily when I reached the river.

The last time, following Colonel Woo's guide, we had been challenged by a guard on the other side. But he had accompanied us back to the village, so I had to hope that this time there would be no guard on the other bank. Or, if there was one, that he would be sound asleep.

I'll soon find out, I thought, as I tied my shoes to the satchel and stepped into the warm, sluggish water.

It was a hell of a lot different from the kind of water where all this had started a couple of months earlier. Back then, my fishing boat had been riding the three-foot swells of the Gulf Stream, thirty-five feet of white-hulled teak and mahogany called the *Arabian Hawk,* cutting through the glistening blue-green waters of the Atlantic. The sky was cloudless and the salt air was an exhilarating tonic.

The outriggers dipped gently and the two needle-nosed ballyhoo live baits strung from them skipped over the crests of the waves some forty feet astern with a dancing motion calculated to raise a sailfish if there was one down here. Miami was a distant smudge on the horizon and the peaceful quiet was broken only by the faint creakings you hear on any boat and the muffled throb of the motor.

I had gotten back from Turkey via Naples with a few scars, a bellyful of Atabrine for recurrent malaria and what I considered a diabolically clever plan. I would take my boat, turn off the ship-to-shore radio and hide out in the Gulfstream for a few days.

Nobody would know I was playing hookey. I wouldn't have anybody on board with me except Pierre, my Turkish retriever, and he wouldn't talk.

But the plan didn't work.

I'd been trolling only a couple of hours when a Coast Guard helicopter skimmed toward me like a homing pigeon. It circled overhead and I could see one of the men in the bubble checking out my registration numbers with binoculars. Slowly the chopper settled, hovering down low over me, its fans flattening out the gentle waves. Then a slate was lowered on a light line. Scrawled on it in chalk were four words:

"Call your office. Emergency."

I waved acknowledgment. The copter soared upward and went its way while, resignedly, I trolled back to port.

When I docked, the word was to call Washington immediately.

I did so, and listened patiently while the Boss chewed me out for the delay.

"Radio trouble," I told him.

He said, "How quickly can you be in Washington?"

"I'm on my way," I replied. "What's up?"

"You're going on a trip."

"What direction and how long?"

He hesitated. The Boss never liked to make disclosures over a telephone. Finally he said: "Far East. Who knows how long. I'll give you the details when you get here."

It was top secret, and no wonder. At this time, Customs had jurisdiction over narcotics outside the United States everywhere except for Europe, where the Narcotics Bureau had control. Now Customs wanted to open an office in Bangkok. The Boss intended me to be the instrument to euchre Customs out of the Far East and add that to the Bureau's command.

"No Narcotics Bureau agent has ever been in the Far East except on surveys for the United Nations," he told me. "The trouble is that Customs has been sitting on its tail over there and hasn't made a case in years."

For one thing, as he pointed out, it wasn't their specialty. They kept a few men out there, in places like Singapore and Tokyo, but they were concerned mainly with things like furniture coming into the country, and excise tax, and requests to bring canary birds back to the States. So, with nothing being done, things were in a hell of a mess.

The drug problem in Thailand was tremendous. An awful lot of hard stuff was coming in from Burma and Laos and other neighboring countries, and uncounted numbers of servicemen were becoming addicted. When they bought a pack of cigarettes for seventy-five cents, instead of getting a quarter change from their dollar they were being given a heroin pill. And they took it—what the hell, and **why** not. The same thing happened when they shopped in stores or paid a check in a Bangkok night club. Soon they were hooked.

"Customs would gripe if you went in there as a regular agent," the Boss said. "So you'll go in to Bangkok as an army officer sent over there to educate military personnel on the evils of drug addiction."

I pointed out that that wouldn't give me much of a cover for working underground against dope peddlers.

"That will be your cover against Customs—your reason for being there, in case anybody gets nosy. Work up your own cover within a cover."

"We can reactivate 'Major Michael Cerra' of the Air Force," I said.

"Fine. But let's give him his full clout. We raised him to the rank of Colonel."

"I almost forgot. Thanks for the promotion."

My instructions were to work closely with the Thai police. I was to make undercover approaches as an Air Force officer who wasn't averse to picking up a fast buck on the side. The dodge was that with my rank I could send packages home to the States in military aircraft. Thus I'd set up the seizures, but I'd let the Thai police move in, make the arrests and take the credit.

"What we're after most of all are the guys moving those Communist morphine bricks stamped '999,' " the Boss said. "They smuggle them into Thailand from a small puppet state called Mongo. The morphine is converted to heroin and then it's finding its way into the United States. So there's double jeopardy—it's causing addiction among servicemen and also being moved into the States in large amounts."

He paused and then added: "Pull this off, Sal, and we'll get the green light on Far East jurisdiction and take over from

Customs. Then we'll really get the job done." He said, with emphasis, "I'm not going to tell you any more. Do what you have to do."

Flying into Bangkok you wonder just where they're going to set the plane down. This is the rice bowl of the world and the whole countryside for miles around looks like one big flooded rice paddy. But suddenly you're over the city and the airport materializes.

It's a different world, although Bangkok is a relatively modern city with the accent on fantastically beautiful Buddhist temples which keep the Thais chained to the past. The outskirts of the city are interlaced with canals called klongs, along which sit tiny houses built on stilts to raise them well above the monsoon floods. The klongs are arterial waterways, heavily traveled by boats, and the people wash their clothes in them and fish right off the front porch.

The city itself is much like any other Far Eastern city with good hotels and everything which goes with big city life. I checked into a hotel on Suriwongse Road by the name of the Kings Hotel. Then I checked in with the police.

Captain Paul Vanigbandhu, who I called Captain Paul, was Chief of the Narcotics Division. A short, sturdily built Thai with a smooth, smiling face, he listened attentively and courteously while I presented my real credentials and explained my mission. I sized him up, added what I already knew about him, and liked the result. I didn't pull any punches.

I told him the Narcotics Bureau knew that the job wasn't being done, and that he wasn't getting any help from our people. I said, "We don't want any of the credit, that belongs to you; but we do think we can help you do the job to everyone's benefit."

He was, he said, "extremely delighted" to obtain our assistance.

We set it up so that I'd arrange contacts, turn the information over to him and he'd make any arrests without my being put in the window.

He told me that the local police were hampered by a loophole in the law—it only prohibited the sale of "white heroin." So, to get around this, the makers mixed in some purple dye and sold pellets of purple heroin.

He took me to the window and pointed to the city. "You can buy it anywhere out there," he said. "It comes all packaged and labeled, with trade names like Lucky Strike, Flying Horse and Five-Five-Five, which is five American dollars a bag for a handful of pills."

He also said the "999" Communist morphine bricks were plentiful. "We have trouble gathering evidence because we're known. But that is why you are here."

Meanwhile, "Colonel Cerra's" mission had been well greased. The military authorities accepted me at face value and they began working out a schedule to fly me to the various bases and outposts to deliver my lecture on narcotics.

Captain Paul was right about the "999" blocks, which are stamped with those numbers because they're supposed to be the purest percentage of morphine you can get. The first buy fell right into my lap.

He was a cab driver, waiting in front of the Kings Hotel for a fare, a little man who was yellow all over. He had a yellow shirt that seemed to melt right into his yellow skin. Even his teeth were yellow. He spoke precise English and told me his name was "Tak."

Cab drivers in almost any city can get you just about anything you want. They know all the angles and all the answers. I hired him for the sightseeing tour and he took me on a round of the various temples.

"That one," he pointed to a building near the palace, "was Miss Anna's house—you know, Miss Anna and the King?"

"Oh, sure," I said. "It's a shame I can't take that home with me. I can get just about *anything* back into the States."

He placed his arm on the back of the seat and turned around to look directly at me. "Anything? Maybe you want to shop for souvenirs?"

I didn't want to rush him if he was a lead. So I told him I wasn't interested in souvenirs at the moment. "But I sure want to go out tonight and see some of the night clubs."

"I take you if you desire," he said, and I told him to come for me that evening. When I left, I tipped him generously. Tak would be there.

He was. And he took me on a tour of the night clubs Bangkok had to offer. There was no doubt that the Boss had the right dope. In two places I paid for a pack of cigarettes with a dollar bill. My change came without explanation or discussion in the form of a heroin pill.

As the evening wore on, I pretended to get successively more drunk at each stop. Every time I returned to the waiting cab, I slurred my words a bit more. Finally I figured I looked drunk enough to make it sound legitimate when I made my pitch to Tak.

"Helluva place," I grumbled, sprawling on the back seat. "I can't seem to find any stuff to buy."

"Stuff?" he asked, not moving the cab.

"Sure, stuff," I mumbled. "Stuff, horse, H or just plain damned heroin. I gotta get me some stuff to send home. I know some guys'll pay me a fortune for getting 'em some stuff."

"Colonel, sir," he turned around to face me in the semidarkness. "If it could be arranged, how much of this stuff maybe you would like to buy?"

"All I can get. I have some big people back home."

He was trying to see me clearly in the faint light of the neon in front of the night club where we were parked. "Colonel, sir, would you perhaps be interested in morphine blocks?"

"Damned right," I said hiccupping. "Damned right. But I gotta see a sample first. A good sample. I don't wanna buy no junk that isn't any good."

He turned around and started the motor. When I got out at the Kings Hotel, tipping him lavishly, he bobbed his head. "Colonel, sir, I will come to the hotel for you at noon tomorrow. I think that I can have the sample you desire."

Tak was as good as his word. Sharply at noon there was a rap on my door. When I opened up, he was standing there with that yellow smile. He also had a package which he handed to me.

In it were eleven morphine blocks. They were the ones we were after—on each of them was stamped the legend "999."

They certainly hadn't stinted on their sample.

"This will do just fine," I told him.

"Colonel, sir, I have advised my people that you are a good man seeking much material. I will be around here whenever you are ready for our much hoped-for business. You will find the price what you call right."

I told Tak that I had a terrible hangover from my activities of the previous night and intended to remain in my room but that I would get back to him within a couple of days. Later I got off one of the blocks to the Boss in Washington, along with a report of my progress.

The remaining ten blocks I took to Captain Paul, who clearly showed his surprise when I dumped them on his desk. And his elation was clearly evident when I provided him with Tak's description and the number of his taxicab.

Captain Paul didn't waste any time. "We'll put him under immediate surveillance. It will be no problem to tail him to where the bricks are kept."

So I lost a good driver. The next day Tak led them to a hideout —a warehouse on the edge of town where they found morphine blocks stacked like cordwood. There he and four others were apprehended. It was quite a haul. More than three hundred kilos —half a ton of potential misery.

Captain Paul was extremely grateful. It made a big splash in the local papers, and it looked great on his record. He was so appreciative that he sent a copy of his official report to the Bureau in Washington, adding, for their eyes alone, a glowing account of my part in the seizure.

Immediately after making this case, I began giving my antinarcotics lectures at various military installations in the immediate Bangkok area. Through new contacts thus developed, I was able to make several more cases, which resulted in half a dozen other seizures. One of them amounted to three hundred kilos of morphine base—about a third of a ton. One case that brought Captain Paul a great deal of publicity came when he and two of his men trailed me and an informant by canoe. We traveled almost an hour through a maze of klongs to a laboratory where an elderly Chinese had been chained to a metal peg for years—slave labor in a heroin lab. The newspapers made much of it.

Captain Paul took the public credit because of my insistence that my cover must not be broken. However, he continued sending the Bureau his highly complimentary reports.

It provided the ammunition the Boss needed in Washington. He took the reports to Treasury, which was over both Narcotics and Customs, and laid them on the line. He showed what one narcotics agent had done in a few short weeks after years of Customs' inactivity. He pointed out that all those seized narcotics had been destined for the United States.

The Boss won. Treasury issued a directive making the Bureau of Narcotics responsible for all enforcement world-wide. Customs retained only the job of guarding against smuggling across U.S. borders.

Great job, the Boss cabled me. *A real feather in our hat. Keep up the good work.*

I figured I'd accomplished the job I'd been sent to do and looked forward to returning home. But Captain Paul cabled the Bureau and asked them to keep me on duty in Thailand to help them a bit longer. The Boss approved, and I decided that if I was ever going to get back stateside I'd have to nail the main Thai source.

The Mongo connection.

It didn't take long to put the finger on Colonel Woo Fong. Authorities in the Far East are not restricted by kid glove methods when it comes to interrogation. Captain Paul could be even more persuasive than most. He knew the territory and the routes by which heroin and morphine base were smuggled into the country. Very little was being produced in Thailand itself. It came in by truck and mule-back from Burma and the Shan States to the west, from Red China and Laos to the north and east, and was floated down the Menam by sampan to Bangkok. Within a span of several days he had the information I wanted.

"There is a remote village at Tiklak," he told me. "Across the river, which is the border of Thailand, is the so-called state of Mongo. It has been set up by one Colonel Woo Fong. He was down here with the old KMT 93rd Chinese Battalion during World War II."

Captain Paul paused and shrugged. "After the war, he set himself up in the manner of the old Chinese war lords. He has simply taken the territory and created his own state. He has his own army of over a thousand men. Up to now none of the surrounding governments has found it necessary, or expedient, to challenge him. It is easier to walk around the thorn bush than to uproot it.

"But," Captain Paul added, "it is through Mongo that most of the 999 morphine blocks, the opium and the heroin are coming."

It posed an apparently insoluble problem. There were no diplomatic relations between Thailand and Mongo, which made legal entry and re-entry impossible. The bridge across the river at Tiklak was heavily guarded, by Thai troops on our side and by Colonel Woo's heavily armed forces on the other. This was the Berlin Wall in spades. Nobody crossed.

"Well," I told Captain Paul, "I think I'll just take a trip up there and look around. Maybe something will develop."

There was a military base near Tiklak. I flew up there and gave my antinarcotics lecture. Captain Paul had arranged for me to stay with a family in Tiklak and it was no trick at all, through them, to spread the word in the village that the American Air Force Colonel was privately trying to buy a large quantity of narcotics.

The bait hardly hit the water.

After all, Colonel Woo Fong had nothing to fear. The Thais had no desire to start a war with him and he was safe in his own bailiwick. So I wasn't surprised when a man in native garb, obviously Chinese, appeared at the house asking for me.

He spoke in halting English. His message was that Colonel Woo would like to meet with the American colonel. Arrangements would have to be made for me to visit Mongo. Would it be convenient for me to be ready for a visit the next day?

The Chinese are gung ho on protocol. So I told him to convey my deepest respects to Colonel Woo Fong. "Be pleased to tell him that it will be a great honor for this humble person to have the pleasure of meeting with him."

He did a double take. And not just because of the formality of my reply—I'd answered him in the Cantonese dialect. From my days as a Marine in China during World War II, I had a working knowledge of that as well as Mandarin, enough to get by without an interpreter.

He bowed respectfully and left. But he was back the next day before noon and asked me to follow him. It was a long, hot trip.

We followed that dusty road under the hot sun for more than three miles. The guide rejected all my attempts to strike up a conversation so I, too, lapsed into silence. It was just as well. I wanted to memorize every inch of the route we traveled.

At last we reached a curiously twisted tree shouldering itself above the others at the roadside. My guide led the way through a screen of bushes and we came onto a faint trail which we followed a good half mile to the river. Telling me to remove my shoes, he took off his sandals and led the way across the river. At its deepest, the water was only waist high. When we reached the opposite bank, now inside Mongo, a flat-faced Chinese outpost stepped from behind a tree and confronted us. His rifle had a fixed bayonet and was pointed directly at us.

"I am bringing the American under Colonel Woo's orders," the guide said impatiently in sing-song Cantonese. "You should have been told."

The guard shrugged and slung his rifle on his shoulder by its leather loop.

"Please to take off your clothing," the guide said, beginning to strip himself.

He didn't have to tell my why. I saw that he was covered with leeches from the waist down, and I set a world's record shedding my own clothes.

The guard meanwhile lighted cigarettes and handed one to each of us. The leeches dropped off like magic as the guide touched them with the lighted tip of the cigarette and I hastily performed the same operation.

He offered to do my back and I did his. The guard just watched.

Back in our clothes, we all three started up the trail leading from the riverbank, moving through a forest of banana trees with birds and monkeys chattering. We had traveled about a mile when we broke out of the jungle into a large clearing. Around the sides were the customary little houses on stilts. And in the center was a large, two-story building, also elevated on pilings to a height of about four feet, with a wide set of steps leading up to a broad veranda. It was a good two hundred feet square, constructed of wood and bamboo, with a rusty tin roof.

There were soldiers all over the place. But what took my eye was the figure standing straddle-legged at the top of the steps of the main building.

It was Colonel Woo Fong and he was something straight out of Ghengis Khan. He wasn't big. He was massive. Only about five foot ten inches tall, I guessed, but he had to weigh close to three hundred pounds. He wore a Chinese army uniform with a chest full of decorations and hanging at his side was a sword which obviously wasn't ceremonial. Despite his bulk, the face was like one you see in those ancestor prints, flat and granite-planed, with a thin black mustache that came down along the corners of his mouth. The brown eyes were flinty and did not look at me with kindness.

"I am Colonel Michael Cerra," I said in Mandarin, the language of the Chinese upper classes. I bowed formally. "It is an indescribable pleasure to meet you, Colonel."

He didn't move or invite me up the steps. Instead he stood there towering over me, and there was not even a trace of pretended politeness in his opening remark.

He gave it to me in Cantonese: "Just how long have you been a colonel?"

I was taken aback for a moment. Now, I know that "face" is all important to the Chinese. A man does not display his emotions publicly. So I restrained my temper, and kept my face blank and my tone polite as I replied in the Cantonese dialect he had used: "About a year, sir."

"Good," he said arrogantly. "I outrank you by a year. So you will remember that, and also that I expect you to salute me in front of my soldiers."

I wanted to haul him down off of those steps and knock some of that pomposity out of him. Instead I snapped him a stiff salute. "As you wish, Colonel."

There was a sneer under that thin black mustache as he peremptorily waved me up the steps. "Come, we will talk."

He heaved his bulk onto an oversized bamboo chair in one shady corner of the veranda and beckoned me to a crude bench.

"I understand you are in the market for a large quantity of my material."

"Yes, I am," I said. "And I have ways of getting it flown back to the United States. But I want to be sure it's good stuff and worth all the trouble."

He gave me that overbearing smile and the chair creaked as he shoved up out of it. "Come, I will show you."

Just inside the door was a small partitioned area with one door leading off to the left and another to the rear of the building. What immediately took my eye in this small anteroom were four battered display cases. The glass tops were long since gone but laid out in the cases were samples of all Colonel Woo's "products." There were those "999" morphine bricks and all the other items Captain Paul had desribed plus more—raw smoking opium in containers, little one-pound balls of gum opium wrapped in leaves, and small packets of heroin in stapled plastic bags with the trademarks showing through: "Red Monkey," "Flying Horse," "Lucky Strike" and "Five-Five-Five." The heroin was in grain form and also in pellets. The kind being sold to the servicemen.

I pretended to be surprised at seeing purple heroin.

"It is only dye and does not affect the product." He gave me that Fu Manchu smile. "The Thais are stupid. This allows us to operate until they think of passing another law outlawing all heroin."

The colonel picked up a "999" brick and showed it to me, then he broke open a ball of opium. He reminded me of a shopper in a market place—squeeze the tomatoes, finger the melons, pluck a grape.

"My quarters are in there," he said, nodding to the door on the left. "Come, I will show you my factory."

We passed through the door into the rear of the building. Along the corridor we passed several rooms with bunks which he said were for his most valued workers. I counted beds for at least a dozen people. Then we came out into a large area which encompassed the entire rear of the building.

I was dumb-struck.

This was the factory and it was an unbelievable sight. There were twenty men at work, cooking opium, pressing the "999" blocks, processing heroin, making pellets and packaging the various products. There was so much of it stacked up that it occupied one whole wall.

The sight of all that junk sent cold chills up my back.

"I'm very impressed with your operation, Colonel," I said to Woo Fong, and I wasn't lying. There had to be forty tons of opium and five or six hundred kilo bags of heroin all ready for "market."

A mountain of misery. A hundred million dollars worth of narcotics on the stateside market!

We ate dinner under a huge tree in the rear of the factory with Colonel Woo's newest "wife." She was a tiny, brown-skinned little thing with wide childish eyes which she had every right to have— after all, she was only twelve years old. The main course was roast dog. Up there, the hill tribes raise pigs but they don't eat pork. They trade the pigs for dogs and eat the dogs. But there was also chicken, which came chopped up, bones and all. And, of course, there was rice and tea.

While we ate, Colonel Woo explained that he would deliver any amount of narcotics I wanted to the Thai border.

"How you get it across is your affair," he said. "I will not deliver into Thailand and I will not set foot across the border myself. But I will give you the best price you can obtain anywhere. I need money for guns."

After that I was only half listening to him because it sounded as if I was stymied. Here I was, sitting on what could well be the largest collection of illegal narcotics in the whole damned world, and there didn't seem to be anything I could do about it.

Yet something just had to be done. Because sure as hell all of this stuff was going to wind up in the United States sooner or later.

My eyes followed a chicken as it scratched and pecked its way amid the pilings which elevated the factory a good four feet off the ground. I remembered the Boss's parting words back in Washington: *Do what you have to do.* Then it came to me what that was: I was going to come back and blow this damned cesspool out of existence. I'd be on my own, of course, if anything backfired. Nobody would lift a finger to help me. But I had to take the chance.

Taking my leave with the guide, I told the Colonel I'd be in touch with him as soon as I worked out a way to get the stuff across the border. We retraced our route to that little Thai village of Tiklak, stopping once again to remove the leeches after we had forded the river going back. And when we reached the road I made particular note of that curiously twisted tree which was to be my landmark when I returned.

It certainly can come as no surprise to anyone that we have governmental agencies which deal in what, for intentional lack of more explicit explanation, may be called direct action. They are a kind of peacetime OSS.

I went to one such in Bangkok and explained my plan. The man in charge took it in stride. You gear yourself to be matter-of-fact or you don't last in a business such as ours.

"Draw me a diagram of the place," he said. "Come back tomorrow and I'll have what you need."

As promised, he had it all ready. He gave me four charges. Each one had a pull detonator—a cord with a T-handle at the end. He instructed me on how to attach them at the places he had marked on my diagram.

"When you pull the detonator cord you'll hear a small 'pop.' After you pull the first one," he cautioned, "you've got forty-five minutes to get the hell out of there."

He stowed them gently in the satchel and wished me luck.

I didn't tell Captain Paul or anybody else my plan. I didn't want him involved; nor did I want anybody able to put the finger on me.

Flying back into the interior, I made my way from the military base to Tiklak at two o'clock in the morning when the village was asleep. It was imperative that nobody should see me—with my height I stood out like a lighthouse among the shorter-statured Thais. Word would be certain to get around. So I circled the village to get to the dirt road.

It was a long walk and my nerves were as tight as violin strings.

The satchel seemed to weigh a ton. Sweat poured off me and the mosquitoes were sheer murder.

My watch showed three o'clock before I located the tree and made my way down the path to the riverbank. As soon as I got into the water I hunched down until only my head was exposed— my head, and one arm holding the satchel, my rubber-soled shoes and .45 high out to keep them dry. The bottom was muddy, and as I inched my way across the seventy yards to the other shore I could imagine those leeches fastening on me by the hundreds, feasting on my blood.

Cautiously I crawled up the bank, listening to make sure I hadn't been observed, then I peeled off my clothes. It was the same as last time. My body was plastered with leeches—big, fat and slimy. This time I wouldn't have dared light a cigarette if I had one. I stood there ten minutes in the darkness, feeling for them and picking them off. They're so soft they come apart like little blobs of Jello if you don't get at them just right. Finally I figured I had them all off, at least I hoped so. I had to get on with the job.

I got back into my clothes, strapped on the knife and the .45 and picked up the satchel of explosives. Then I started up the trail to Colonel Woo's village in hopes of blowing to hell his heroin factory, along with anyone unlucky enough to be sleeping inside.

Just enough moon was out to keep the night from being totally black. In my jacket I had a hooded lamp with a red bulb that cast a faint glow at my feet when I pressed the button. It couldn't be seen for more than a yard or two in any direction, and it helped me get through that banana jungle. Several times I strayed from the path and disturbed birds that screamed their displeasure. Each time I froze, sweating, until they settled down again.

When I reached the compound I stopped for a long minute, looking and listening. No guard. . . . But I'd given thanks too soon. For right at the edge of the clearing one of Colonel Woo's soldiers stood motionless, leaning sleepily on his rifle.

You do what you have to do. Putting down the satchel, I drew my jungle knife and came up noiselessly behind him. With my hand over his mouth he never made a sound and I eased his body to the ground. I jabbed the knife in the ground to clean it.

Retrieving the satchel, I gained a thicket on the edge of the darkened clearing and looked around for more guards. None was in sight so I had to take my chances. Crouching low, I ran across the clearing and ducked in under the building.

From overhead, as I worked my way to the back of the building, a cacophony of snores came to my ears. Sleep tight, you bastards.

I'd memorized the spots on the diagram that the man in Bangkok had marked for most effective placement of the explosives. Two toward the rear to make certain that the factory and the storeroom got the brunt of it. One toward the middle, and one up front.

That forty tons of junk had to go. So did the Colonel who was behind it all and would keep right on doing it if he wasn't stopped.

I set the two charges in place under the factory and storeroom. I pulled one of those T-handled cords, ducked back to the other charge and gave its cord a yank. "Pop." "Pop."

I still had two charges to place. Forty-five minutes to set them and get back across the river. But they sure as hell couldn't stop me now, even if they caught me this minute. This place was going to go even if I had to go with it.

Sweat dripped into my eyes, burning them. I groped for the satchel, found the handle and started toward the center of the building when my foot struck something soft and yielding.

"Oink!"

I'd stepped on a pig asleep under the building. I jerked to a halt, the blood pounding in my ears. But there was no other sound. The pig grunted and apparently went back to sleep. No alarm.

Circling well around him, I felt my way to the middle of the building and attached the third charge. There was another soft "pop" as I pulled the detonator. Three down, one to go.

On the last one I changed the placement, attaching the charge a bit away from center so that it was more directly under the sleeping Colonel Woo.

"Try that for size, you bastard," I whispered up to him as I pulled the cord and heard that final "pop."

Now I had to get out. A look at the faintly luminous dial of my watch told me that I had thirty-five minutes before the fireworks started. The whole thing—setting the charges and my encounter with the pig—had eaten up ten minutes.

I got ready for a dash across the clearing, and then it looked as if my luck finally had run out. Two guards emerged from opposite sides of the clearing, rifles slung on their shoulders, and converged on the center of the compound squarely between me and the path to the river. They rested their rifles on the ground, lighted cigarettes and began talking in low tones.

Five minutes passed. They each lit another cigarette. Ten minutes passed. Crouched down out of sight behind one of the pilings, I really began to sweat.

Twenty-five minutes left and those charges were going to go boom. I had to get out—not only across the clearing but a mile down to the river.

Twenty-four minutes. Twenty-three minutes. Twenty-two minutes.

There was only one thing to do. I'd have to wait until there were only a couple of minutes left before the charges exploded and then make a break for it, taking out those two with my .45 at a dead run. I couldn't risk waking up the compound and having Colonel Woo escape the blast. The factory had to go, but he had to go with it.

Eighteen minutes. Seventeen. Sixteen.

Then luck started running for me again. The guards shouldered their rifles and each of them strolled back the way he had come. I waited another minute after they disappeared to make sure they were gone.

Then I took off across the clearing and, once outside the compound and under cover of the jungle, stopped to listen for any alarm. None.

Thirteen minutes.

I held myself to a cautious walk for a couple of hundred yards. Then I took off down the trail as if Satan himself were after me. Twice I slammed into trees and knocked myself flat. Once I tripped over a protruding root and went sprawling on my face. I spat out a mouthful of dirt.

Finally I stood on the riverbank. My heart pounded like a kettle-drum and my lungs fought for air. Sweat poured off me. A cloud of mosquitoes hummed around my head.

Four minutes.

Even that muddy, turgid water felt good as I eased myself into it without a splash and made for the other shore. The safe side. Thailand.

I was standing naked on the bank, pulling off those damned leeches, when it blew.

Even from this distance the roar was ear-splitting. The ground shook as if from a tremendous earthquake and the sky lighted up back in the direction of the factory. I stood there enjoying every second of it.

"So long, Colonel Woo Fong, you bastard," I said. I put on my clothes and, sore, bruised and utterly exhausted, I began that lonely walk to the base.

Back in Bangkok in my hotel room late the next day I counted eighty-seven red splotches where those damned blood-sucking leeches had fastened themselves to various parts of my body.

A telephone call from Captain Paul interrupted me. He said he had good news for me—I could make plans to return home.

"How's that?" I asked.

"Well, I think everything will be under control for a while, anyhow." He sounded elated. "We had a fantastic stroke of luck," he said. "Would you believe it, that place in Mongo where all the junk has been coming from—well, it caught fire and blew up."

"No!"

"Sure did. And they think that Chinese colonel was killed inside when it went. I sure hope he was."

I didn't answer. I was thinking about the Colonel's bride, hoping that they'd had a fight that night, that. . . .

While I packed I began thinking of that clean, clear, blue-green water of the Gulf Stream.

No leeches there.

CHAPTER **13**

Queer Money

BOB MANPELL was too big and too tough to forget. I hadn't seen him in ten years, but I recognized him the instant I saw him in the security office at the American Embassy in Bangkok. He was sitting in a chair large enough for most people, but not for him.

He must have gone 235, none of it fat. When he stood up he topped off at about six-foot-three, a big good-looking fellow with dark hair and a clear complexion. He should have been on the roster as tackle for the Green Bay Packers. He had plenty of reason to remember me after what I did to him ten years before, but I could see that he didn't.

"It's been a long time," I said.

He uncoiled that huge frame and stood up, wearing an I've-seen-you-before-but-can't-place-the-name look.

"Your face is familiar," he said.

Well, if he didn't know, I'd keep him guessing for a while.

Bob Manpell and I had attended the Treasury Academy training school in Washington, D.C., at the same time. We had engaged in a lot of acrobatics and traded some pretty good blows in hand-to-hand combat and judo courses. And we were partners in exercises such as Hare-and-Hounds, where you are graded on how well you slip a tail or follow someone else.

Recruits from all branches of the Treasury Department—the Alcohol and Tax Division, U.S. Customs, Secret Service and the Bureau of Narcotics—were required to put in a few months there. Manpell was with Secret Service and I was with the Narcotics Bureau.

One day, in the hand-to-hand combat course, he'd gotten a hold on me by grabbing my shirt at the neck and pushing his forefinger into my throat. It was a very painful hold.

I was supposed to get out of it by twisting his hand over and falling down. But he outsmarted me. As I went down he went down with me and pushed even harder. He practically broke my windpipe. He had very strong hands. But I got even.

Later, while practicing the karate chop, I had to hold the board for him while he tried to break it in two. The idea was to follow through with lots of force, and he did it with gusto. Well, I turned the board up on end as he was coming down and he couldn't stop. It almost broke his hand.

Now, standing before him in the Embassy security office, I reached for his right hand. Then instead of shaking it I turned it gently and inspected it.

"This hand looks all right now," I said casually.

Recognition. "Sal Vizzini! Well I'll be damned!"

After a few more I'll-be-damneds and How-the-hell-are-yous, he said that that was a lousy trick I had pulled on him back in Washington. I told him that maybe I'd be able to make it up to him.

I knew that a Secret Service agent was coming to Bangkok to investigate counterfeit U.S. $20 and $100 bills that were finding their way on the market. I had heard from one of my informants, a Chinese national named T. K. Hang (alias Robert Mack), that he could lead me to the plates as well as the counterfeiters.

The matter wasn't in my field as a narcotics agent, but I passed the information along to Jim Brown, the security officer for the State Department at the Embassy, and he bucked it along to Washington.

Meanwhile, he instructed me to keep my informant warm, just in case I would be asked to cooperate. It wasn't unusual for an undercover man from one federal agency to be loaned out to another on a special assignment. I had already done stints for Customs, the C.I.A. and the Justice Department, as well as Secret Service. Bob Manpell had flown in from Honolulu, his permanent base, to take charge of the case.

We were in Brown's office at the Embassy, and he got a little impatient when we started reminiscing about old school revels at the Academy.

"Knock off the old home week," Brown said from behind his desk. "Let's get on with what we're here for."

I briefed Manpell on what I knew. The twenties that had shown up in the PX and other places were passable, the hundreds rather poor quality. The informant seemed pretty certain that he could lead me to the plates, which was more important in a counterfeit case than just getting bogus bills or their passers.

The government would spend $15,000 or $20,000 on a buy of counterfeit money if it would lead to the plates. But it wouldn't waste $1,000 to buy $10,000 worth of bills if the plates were still out. They could always print up that much more tomorrow. Information leading to seizure of the plates also upped the price of informants.

"How reliable is this informant?" Manpell asked.

"Grade A," I told him. "I've used T. K. Hang on a number of

cases. He's hungry and anxious to get back to Taiwan with some cash."

"Who will be the UC on this?"

I told him I'd work undercover for him, partly for old times' sake and partly because there wasn't another UC in that part of the world that he could count on. He smiled and rubbed the heel of his right hand.

Manpell was what was called a "covering agent," one who didn't work undercover. He covered the UC man, supplied the funds, gave orders and stayed out of sight until some muscle was needed. In a country like Thailand, where people come in small packages, Manpell would have been about as conspicuous in an undercover role as Goliath at a midgets' convention—even if he had been trained for it.

"I won't try to tell you what to do undercover," he said. "That's your job. But I'll hang close."

Jim Brown suggested that we use his home in the American compound as a meeting place. Nobody could follow us past the guards at the gate. I would meet Manpell there once a day to brief him on progress. Manpell insisted on giving me "partner protection," just as we learned to do at the Academy.

I talked him out of it. "I'll let you know when to get in the act," I said, and left the Embassy to contact T. K. Hang.

T. K. Hang didn't speak any English, only Chinese. Luckily my Chinese was equal to it.

I was registered at the King's Hotel in Bangkok under the name of Theodore Warner, and I had plenty of credentials to prove it. As far as T. K. Hang knew, I was an ex-Air Force pilot who'd hung around the China-India-Burma area after the war doing flying jobs that were slightly mysterious and probably illegal. That was all he had to know.

I told him that I was flying up to the interior for a day and would like to meet the people with the bogus twenties when I got back. "Set up the deal and you can be on your way to Taiwan with a stack of real twenties in your pocket. Enough for a hello to Chiang Kai-Shek."

That wasn't the exact content of what I said because it comes out different in Chinese, but he got the general idea. He agreed to bring his friends in for a look-see at noon the next day. We would meet at my hotel.

I was a half-hour late on purpose. They would have to wait in the lobby if my room didn't answer, and I wanted a look at them before they got a look at me. I strolled in wearing a flier's cap and carrying a flight bag—enough to appear like a pilot just back from a trip.

T. K. Hang was there, sitting off in a corner of the lobby with two guys as Chinese as himself. One of them was slight and thin. He wore sharply-creased Western clothes and a bland Oriental expression. The other guy was half again as high and twice as wide. He looked as though he had been carrying a grudge against the world since he was a baby. Obviously, the large one was the muscle. The little guy was the boss.

Hang introduced the little guy as Wan Chi Pitrakoon.

"So delighted to make your acquaintance," Pitrakoon said in almost perfect English. He was wearing a mirthless smile—the kind of a smile he would doubtless keep right on wearing when he cut your throat. His manner was oily and his handshake dry.

I opened my bag to get a pack of cigarettes, and left it unzipped on a chair next to Pitrakoon while I went to the desk for the key. Out of the corner of my eye I could see him giving it a quick frisk. Good luck, buddy, I thought to myself. He would find an extra shirt, a pair of socks, a flight log, a couple of pictures of broads and some shaving gear, items that any cargo pilot would have.

I invited them up to my room and after some Chinese hanky-panky about "mutual trust" and "flowering relationship" I told him to please cut out the crap and get to the point.

Pitrakoon leaned forward, still with that smile, and said, "I understand you are interested in some of my merchandise."

"If the merchandise is of good quality. Do you have any samples?"

He said that he did and took out three twenties and one hundred. I looked at them and told him they weren't what I expected.

Actually, the twenties were pretty good except for some lines in Jackson's forehead that weren't clear. The edge of the seal was also faulty. The $100 bill was very bad and I looked at it with disgust. The color was off and Ben Franklin's own mother would never have recognized him from the picture on the face of it.

"Is this the best you can do?" I said. "It looks like play money."

"They are really quite good, Mr. Warner. And the price is reasonable. Only twenty-five cents on the dollar."

I gave him an outraged look, as though I hadn't heard properly.

Anybody but a tourist knows that the going price on counterfeit bills is fifteen cents on the dollar, maybe twenty if the quality is excellent and you have a ready outlet such as a gambling casino. And in Bangkok nobody would go above ten cents on the dollar.

Even if I were interested, I told him, I'd still have the expense and trouble of getting it out of the country, going to Hong Kong or Singapore, spreading a little here and a little there. I started to put the three sample twenties in my shirt pocket.

Pitrakoon smiled politely and said, "I'm sorry but you can't have them." Then he reached over and picked them out of my shirt.

"You must be in bad shape if you can't spare three phoney bills as samples," I told him. "What kind of a penny-ante game are you playing?"

"Not penny-ante," he said. "Quite frankly, my friend, I don't trust you."

"Well, that makes us even. I don't trust you either."

What else could I say? Then I complimented him, saying that by being cautious he was protecting me as well as himself, and that I wouldn't do business with anybody who trusted me. I told him that I would be interested in seeing more of his hundreds, but if they were as bad as these to forget it.

He still wouldn't let me have the three twenties. I couldn't tell whether he was buying my story or not. He left with T. K. Hang and the bodyguard, saying he would be in touch with me.

After they left I got in touch with Captain Paul Vanigbandhu, my friend with the Thai police, and asked him to run a check on Pitrakoon. The report came back that he was a Chinese refugee from Kweichow province, the kind you find in every city in the East, often arrested, never convicted, on the fringe of everything from dope to murder. Pitrakoon was also known by the name of Jeffco, an unlikely alias for an Oriental.

That night I met briefly with Manpell at Jim Brown's house in the compound and reported that I had made contact.

"He's hinky," I said. "I don't know what made him suspicious. All I can do now is wait."

I waited for three days and was about to give up. I spent the time kicking around Bangkok bistros at night, doing things a loose-ends pilot would do. Sometimes I felt a tail but never saw one. You never know in that part of the world. I avoided the Embassy. I passed on "Nothing to report" bulletins to Manpell by phone.

On the fourth day Pitrakoon called. "Would it be possible for us to meet today?" he said in his low unctuous voice.

I tried to make mine sound matter of fact.

"Sure. C'mon up. Around three."

"No," he said. "I would prefer that you came to my room. At noon. I am in Room 310 at the Grand Hotel."

The Grand Hotel was one of the better hotels in town. It was where Marlon Brando stayed when he was there filming "The Ugly American." The lobby was large and busy. I moved through it and took the elevator to the third floor, found Room 310 and knocked on the door. It opened a few inches, then the gap widened and a voice told me to enter.

"Come in and be quiet," it commanded, and I did exactly what it said. I was looking into the business end of what seemed to be a 9mm. Browning automatic.

"What's this all about?" I said to Pitrakoon, who was standing in the darkened room holding the gun. He remained silent and impassive while his bodyguard closed the door. Then, moving quickly, the bodyguard grabbed my arm and twisted it behind my back with such force that I almost cried out. I thought about using some of those guaranteed escape techniques I had learned, but knew that would ultimately get me in more trouble. I resisted just enough to keep him from breaking my arm.

"If you're thinking about robbing me, you're crazy," I said to Pitrakoon. "I don't carry any real money on me. And if this is the way you do business, I sure as hell don't want to deal. I thought I came here to negotiate with a businessman."

"You work for the police," Pitrakoon said.

"You're out of your mind," I said. "Now get this ape off my back and put away that gun."

"You work for the police," he repeated. "If you do not admit the truth, we will kill you."

I had heard about the Chinese water torture and other artful methods the Orientals have for making people talk. But the one they used that day was more direct. At Pitrakoon's command, his muscle man steered me toward an open closet in the hotel room and inserted my left hand between the door and the jamb.

He closed the door just enough to let me know what more pressure would bring.

"Now, the truth, Mr. Warner," Pitrakoon said, then went over to a radio on the bed table and turned it up full volume.

The truth, I knew, would make me a dead man. If I could fake it, I might end up with no worse than a broken hand. I tried talking.

"I will tell you anything you want to hear, whether it's truth or not. But if you keep this up, you might as well kill me."

At a nod from Pitrakoon, the other man pressed harder against the door. The edge cut into the back of my hand, sending a blinding flash of pain up my arm. The man was grinning, actually enjoying it.

When I tried to break loose the flat of his huge hand landed along the side of my head.

"Tell us you work for the police," Pitrakoon's voice said, as the door closed harder against my hand.

Then, in impatience or desperation or pleasure—maybe all three —the other man leaned all his weight against the door. I heard myself scream and mercifully passed out from the pain. . . .

I was lying on the bed when I came to. My left hand was on fire. Looking down, I saw a knife-like slash across the back of it. The cut was deep and ugly but I was surprised to see that there was very little blood.

Pitrakoon stood there watching me, the pistol dangling at his side while his friend returned from the bathroom with a bucket of ice water. Suddenly, it occurred to me that this whole routine had been well planned. I plunged my hand into the ice water. The coldness numbed the pain but I was feeling very sick to my stomach.

"This was necessary," I heard Pitrakoon's voice say. "You must understand why we had to do this. A police agent would have cracked and revealed himself. Now we know we can trust you."

"Sure, sure," I said, slowly getting to my feet. "My best and trusted friends always break my hand when I'm dealing for queer."

I asked if I could go now, and Pitrakoon seemed actually solicitous.

"By all means. You must have your hand attended to at once. And please understand, Mr. Warner, that what we had to do was necessary."

I got a towel, put some ice in it, wrapped the cold compress around my hand and stuck it inside my shirt. I didn't look back leaving the room. Walking through the hotel lobby, with my hand stuck inside my shirt, I wondered if anybody would think I was stealing something.

You're getting punchy, I told myself. Nobody but a law officer would think that way, and I couldn't afford to think like a cop. I had to think like a criminal. Think like a criminal, maybe catch a criminal. Also those plates, which by now I had a personal stake in.

The doorman got me a cab and I told the driver to take me to the American hospital. In the emergency room I explained to the medical officer on duty that I'd had an accident working on my plane. He ordered X-rays and found three broken bones in my hand and a fractured knuckle on my index finger. By now the hand was swollen up like a grapefruit.

They gave me a shot and a supply of pain pills that I lived on for a week. I left the hospital with a bad headache and a dull pain that went all the way up the arm to the shoulder.

My feelings about getting even with Pitrakoon and Company had gone out of focus temporarily, but I called Paul Vanigbandhu at Police Headquarters and gave him a brief description of what had happened. He was all for lowering the boom on the target then and there.

"No Paul," I argued. "That will only blow the case. I'll take care of Pitrakoon in my own way, but I will need a little time. Besides, if we don't get the plates, all we have is two Chinese hoodlums."

He agreed reluctantly.

That evening I checked in with Bob Manpell at the compound, and laughed weakly when I showed him the hand. Some joke, eh?

I told him that this made us even for what I did to him back in Washington, D.C. He didn't think it was so funny. He came up out of his chair, his eyes blazing, and wanted to take my Chinese friend apart immediately.

"The plates, Bob," I told him. "You want those plates. You'll blow it right out the window if you don't calm down. Besides, Pitrakoon belongs to me. This is one I want to settle personally."

Manpell didn't calm down easily. "Okay, Sal, but I'd really like a piece of the action when we make the hit."

"You'll get it."

The next day, and the day after that, Pitrakoon called me and left call-back messages. I didn't return them. I had left word with the switchboard operator at the hotel that I wasn't taking any calls, only messages. My hand was hurting like hell and I didn't really trust myself to think clearly.

The third day Pitrakoon phoned twice more, and after the second time I called back.

"We would like to meet with you, my friend," he said softly.

"After what you did to me?"

"I have already told you that what we did was necessary, Mr. Warner. I had to make certain that I could trust you. Now we can both trust one another. I assure you it was nothing personal."

I told him that it was personal with me, that my hand was broken in four places, and that I had a dim view of him, and all of his ancestors too. It wasn't difficult for me to play the role of an outraged victim. I was one.

"Perhaps I can make it up to you, my friend," he said. He explained that he had $20,000 in choice twenties on hand, and could deliver another batch worth $100,000 within a week. Was I interested in that quantity and could I come up with the necessary payment?

"Don't worry about my finances," I said. "I have good backing."

I told him I could use the twenties, but that he could light his old cigar butts with the hundreds I had seen. They wouldn't fool a blind man. We agreed on a price of fifteen cents for each dollar's worth of phoney bills.

"O.K.," I told him. "I'll meet you at the Grand Hotel tomorrow at three, but this time you come to my room. I'll have my partner with me."

Pitrakoon made no objection.

"I would be delighted to meet with you and your partner, Mr. Warner. I have, as I said, no doubts about you now."

After he hung up I called Paul Vanigbandhu and told him we had our fish back on the line. He wanted to know what he could do.

I told him that I would need connecting rooms at the Grand, on the third floor if possible, one in my name and one under somebody else's. I would also need him and two other men to cover us upstairs and a surveillance team staked out in the lobby.

He called back almost immediately to say that we had 322 and 324, just down the hall from Pitrakoon.

"Good," I said, and called Pitrakoon to tell him where to meet me.

That night I contacted Manpell and brought him up to date. He again asked to be in on the proceedings but I convinced him that we were still working undercover and that this should be left to me and the local professionals.

Shortly after noon the following day, two of Vanigbandhu's men checked into 324 at the Grand. They had instructions to keep the connecting door to 322 unlocked and slightly ajar. Paul and I moved into 322 about an hour later and settled down to wait.

We had rehearsed our part of the script. All we needed to complete the cast was Pitrakoon and his muscular friend.

They arrived about 3:15. There was a knock on the door and I told them to come in and be quiet. I had received those identical instructions a few days before on the same floor of this same hotel. I wasn't likely to forget for some time. The rest of our plan called for a slight variation of their original theme.

The bodyguard came in first and found Paul's gun leveled at his belly. I reached out quickly with my good hand and grabbed Pitrakoon by the throat. They call it the "muffler hold," a paralyzing grip involving the thumb and forefinger on either side of the windpipe.

I found myself wishing he would try to fidget or squirm, because then I would be forced in good conscience to squeeze harder. But he stood there tense and still, his tongue out and those slant eyes round as half dollars. I told Paul to frisk the other man and take him in the bathroom.

"Close the door and keep him there a while," I said.

Without realizing it, I found myself squeezing harder on Pitrakoon's throat. It didn't really bother me. A busted windpipe for a broken hand seemed a fair and reasonable exchange.

Then I saw his face turn a splotchy purple and felt his body begin to go limp. I released my hold and gave him a chop under the ear. It knocked him against the wall and he collapsed on the floor.

I stood over him for a moment, then looked at my bandaged hand. I felt no pity at all.

"Okay, Paul," I said. "Bring the other bastard out now."

The bathroom door opened and the huge fellow shambled in, covered by Paul Vanigbandhu's gun. He lost some of his Oriental composure when he saw his boss lying still on the floor.

I looked at Paul and asked him in Chinese, "What shall we do with this one?"

"Let's kill him."

I thought about that for a while. Then I said, "O.K., but let's give him a choice. Ask him which way he wants to die."

Police brutality? I guess you could call it that. But at the moment

I preferred to think of it as justifiable retribution. Besides, to be technical we weren't policemen yet. As far as anybody in the room knew I was still a money-pushing flier named Ted Warner and Paul was my sidekick. And we were still negotiating for a buy of queer money.

Paul explained to the large Chinaman that I was a very important man, that he had made a grievous error in mutilating my hand, and that he must pay for this mistake with his life. Which way did he want to die?

The man looked at the crumpled figure on the floor. Sweat gathered on his forehead. "But I only work for him. I did what he ordered. Please, I will do anything to make up for what I did."

"Would you kill him?" Paul asked, pointing to Pitrakoon.

"Yes," he said, nodding his large head. "I will kill him right now if you ask me to."

I walked over to Pitrakoon who was making gagging noises and beginning to regain consciousness. I nudged him with the tip of my shoe.

"Your big mistake was not killing me when you put my hand in that door," I said to him, shoving my bandaged hand down under his nose. "Take a good look at it because it may be the last thing you ever see."

Pitrakoon wasn't the type to win medals for bravery. He began coughing and whimpering. But he hadn't lost his skill as a negotiator. He began talking about making amends for the pain and inconvenience he had caused me. He talked about giving me a handsome gift, if only I would listen.

"Get up, you bastard," I said, acting undecided. "Maybe there is something we can work out."

He crawled to the edge of the bed and pulled himself up onto it. The other man was still standing against the wall in a kind of stupor. Paul had his gun out in case either one showed unusual revival signs.

"All right," I said, as though I had arrived at a decision. "My hand is worth at least $10,000 of your phoney twenties. The trouble you have put me to is worth another $10,000. I want $20,000 in payment for what you have done or neither of you leaves this room alive."

He agreed, nodding his head eagerly up and down. The windpipe treatment had left him with a little difficulty talking.

"I will go and get the money immediately," he promised hoarsely.

I shook my head slowly. "How do I know you'll come back?"

"You can keep him as a hostage," Pitrakoon suggested quickly, pointing toward his protector.

"Let's just kill them," Paul said impatiently.

I walked over to the big man, who was wearing a locket-type triangular piece of gold on a chain around his neck. I lifted the locket and chain from around his neck and studied it. Many Buddhists wear this type of amulet. It contains the ashes of their ancestors and is highly prized by its owner. It's supposed to be a good-luck charm, capable of warding off evil spirits and even stopping bullets.

"I'll keep this until you get back," I said. "You will go get the money, instead of your boss. He will give you instructions about where to find it, if you don't know already. If you are not back within two hours, I will blow his head off. Then I will start looking for you. You won't be able to run far enough that I won't find you."

Pitrakoon gave him detailed instructions. The money, he said, was in a suitcase in the basement of a house on the other side of town. He told his man to get the money and come straight back.

I dropped the amulet in my coat pocket. Then I told Paul Vanigbandhu that I would watch Pitrakoon and for him to do what he had to do. According to our prearranged plan, he left and alerted the two men in the next room and the two others he'd stationed downstairs in the lobby.

There was no way for Pitrakoon's boy to get out of their sight. From the moment he left the hotel, two surveillance teams followed him in separate cars. Besides, he was too shaken up to think of looking for tails.

The big guy went directly to the house and was inside only a short while. He arrived back at the hotel room, breathing hard, shortly before the deadline. He carried a paper bag holding $20,000 in twenties.

With the appearance of the money a sudden transformation came over Wan Chi Pitrakoon. He changed from a sniveler to a counterfeiter looking for ways to move his merchandise.

"Ah, you see?" he said, once again self-assured and confident. "Pitrakoon keeps his word. Now we can trust each other again. We will do business now."

"Sure," I said, not trusting my stomach or Pitrakoon either. "I'll be in touch with you."

That night I met Bob Manpell and informed him that my job as undercover man on the case had been completed. I gave him the $20,000 in counterfeit twenties and an address where he could find the plates and the printing press.

He hit Pitrakoon's place the next day and got close to half a million in bad hundreds and passable twenties. He also got the plates, which had been engraved in Japan.

The counterfeiters, who got seven to ten, never suspected that I had anything to do with putting them away. As far as they ever knew, I was a larcenous pilot who was pushing the last batch of queer off their press.

As the UC man, I was happy about not being put in the window.

As the covering agent, Bob Manpell had two sets of plates and a hell of a lot of queer money to ship off to Washington.

"How's the hand, kid?" he asked solemnly, as we said good-by at the Embassy. It was the same line I had given him when we parted ten years before.

CHAPTER 14

A Cellmate
Is Not A Playmate

ONE PARTICULAR stewardess, a brunette with a full lower lip, had large dark eyes that seemed to say she knew what you were thinking and it was all right with her. My interest was academic. I wasn't going anywhere, except to prison, so I sat quietly handcuffed to the two federal marshals taking me there.

Nobody else on the plane knew I was handcuffed. They put a chain from the cuffs to your belt. The belt is turned around with the buckle in the back so you won't get any ideas about unfastening it. They put a topcoat over the cuffs to hide them.

"Would you care for a magazine, sir?" she asked.

"No, thank you," I said. No use reaching up. Handcuffs make a bad first impression.

They had certainly made a bad first impression on me. I was not used to helplessness. You learn fast. Get out of line and you get leg shackles too.

The stewardess leaned way over to talk to a kid across the aisle. I wished she wouldn't do that. Well, Tony Tivoli, I said to myself, you see, crime really doesn't pay. I tried to delay thinking too much about the stark facts of my situation, but there wasn't much to do but think. I had been doing a lot of it since we left New York.

The federal marshals with me weren't hired for their charming conversation. They just put me in a seat and hunkered down along-side. It was like sitting next to two fire hydrants. Anyhow, what's to say? You're taking a turkey to market, and you don't chat with a trussed-up bird.

These U.S. marshals knew all they needed to know about me. I was Tony Tivoli, alias Swift Tony, headed for the Atlanta Federal Penitentiary on an armed robbery rap for a seven-to-ten stretch. They had picked me up earlier that day at the West Street holding cell for federal prisoners. "Convicted and awaiting transportation," said my papers, prepared at F.B.I. headquarters on Broadway.

I stopped being Sal Vizzini somewhere between F.B.I. head-quarters and the West Street cell, where I stayed overnight. The marshals picked up Tony Tivoli.

One of them cuffed my wrist to his waist. When we got to the airport they turned my belt around and fixed up the chain arrange-ment. Carrying your coat over the cuffs eliminates a lot of conver-sation with people who are thrilled at the sight of a real live criminal. Also, airlines aren't really happy about prisoners showing a lot of obvious hardware. . . .

"Please fasten your seat belts and observe the no smoking sign." We were coming to Atlanta.

The landing was smooth. The stewardesses stood at the exit as we left, with those stewardess smiles, all bright-eyed and bushy-tailed.

Plainclothes prison guards met us. I was handcuffed to one at the airport. The marshals rode with us to Atlanta penitentiary, a grim, square fortress. From inside, the walls look twice as high. Inside at the "reception room," the prison authorities receipted for me.

The sack of laundry had been delivered.

Processing-in took hours. At first, you are impatient with the waiting. There were time gaps between physical exams and filling out forms and the rote questions on allergies and the like.

And suddenly it hit me. Impatient for what? In this place time wraps you like a clammy sheet. There's nothing to hurry for. There's no way to lighten the heaviness of time; no way to shake it.

I remembered that during Marine Corps physicals there always had been a lot of good-natured griping and bitching.

In prison, you keep your trap shut.

"Do I get the job?" I said, after filling out one long form.

The guard looked at me, no expression. It gave me an empty feeling where my stomach had been. Right then I knew my other enemy, the one that comes with doing time. The big-mouth label. Silence is the only armor in prison. I shut up.

"Strip!"

I took off my clothes.

"Strip!"

I had forgotten to take off my ring and watch.

I removed the gold cross I wore around my neck on a chain. Everything went into a basket.

They threw me a pair of boxer shorts and a T-shirt, one pair of gray pants, one pair of heavy "boondocker" shoes, and a shirt-jacket. The shirt had a white patch on the pocket with a number. I'll never forget that number. It was 20886710.

As long as I was there I would be known by the last four digits of that number. Nobody has a name in a federal penitentiary.

A guard with a billyclub and a blank face marched me through the echoing corridor until we came to cell block K. Finally, we stopped at an empty cubicle. It was about the size of four telephone booths and had four bunks, all of them empty.

I started to ask where everybody was but never finished.

The billyclub slammed against the bars. The guard stood there, tapping the club on the palm of his hand and waiting for me to go on. I didn't. The grilled door clicked shut.

Number 6710, alias Tony Tivoli, was home.

The deputy commissioner had warned me. "It's going to be tough," he said, leaning back in his swivel chair at Bureau Headquarters. "You're going to be another con. No protection because nobody will know who you are except the warden, and he'll be too far away to help if something goes wrong."

All the necessary papers had been quietly prepared. The purpose was to gain the confidence of Big Al Cicceroni, a rackets guy who had been involved in the theft of a million-plus in negotiable government bonds. One of four suspects in the case had been murdered, and Cicceroni was doing time in Atlanta on another charge. They wanted me to find out from Big Al where the bonds were. Simple.

Leaning forward in his chair, the deputy commissioner tossed a bunch of photographs on the desk.

"Take a good look at your man."

Big Al Cicceroni came through in pictures like two different guys, neither very friendly. The official mug shots made him look like a professional goon: heavy brows, no neck, nose squashed over on one side of his craggy face. He'd be the heavy no matter where he performed.

In other pictures he came through like a gangland fashionplate. He wore expensive, pin-striped suits with wide lapels, enough jewelry to start a hock shop, and a flop-brimmed hat that looked like it was left over from the St. Valentine's Day massacre. One old newspaper shot showed him with a girl draped over each shoulder. Big Al liked the broads. All photographs showed him radiating arrogance and violence.

I had heard of Cicceroni. Torpedo and button man. He'd worked his way up in the loan-shark racket and wasn't fussy about operating in other areas. As far as was known, he had no narcotics record. Lately, he had moved into hot stocks and bonds.

"Now let's go over this one more time," the deputy commissioner said. "You will be treated like a prisoner. You will be subject to the same restrictions as other prisoners. It's safer that way. Not even the guards will know you are a federal agent."

So that's the way it was.

I don't think I'll ever forget my first night in that place.

At nine o'clock, the lights go out and the big bolt slides into place, sealing off an entire block of cells. A tomb-like silence is broken only by the footsteps of the guards making their rounds.

There is no talking after lights-out. Talking will get you a bang on the head or time in the hole. If you want to talk, you have to get right down and whisper in somebody's ear. I wasn't feeling like talking anyhow.

I lay there in an upper bunk, waiting for something to happen. I didn't know if the other three cons in the cell were planning to jump me or not. I knew, of course, that there is a lot of homosexuality in prison, and sometimes a prisoner is discovered very dead with a knife between the ribs. Whatever was coming, it wouldn't catch me asleep.

My cellmates were beauties. The short fat one—he kept cracking his knuckles—was in for transporting stolen vehicles across state lines. He had also knocked over a bank. Another one, who kept humming under his breath all the time, had been caught peddling dope. I never found out what the third guy was in for.

What mattered most was the guy in a two-bunk cell directly across from mine. That was where they kept Big Al Cicceroni.

The next morning I went to the warden's office. It was strictly routine. Every prisoner coming in and going out gets to talk with the warden, and sometimes in between if he puts in a special request.

For a while the warden gave no indication that I was anybody but just another prisoner. He asked routine questions and I gave routine answers. If he didn't bring the matter up, I sure as hell wouldn't. Then I began to wonder if he knew who I was.

Holy Christ, I thought to myself, maybe somebody forgot to tell him. Then an assistant left the room and he said, "OK, we can talk now. But make it fast."

"Yes, sir," I said, greatly relieved.

He asked me what I wanted. Did I want to be put in the same cell with Cicceroni?

"No," I told him. "That might make him suspicious. But you can put me to work wherever he's working."

"Anything else?" he asked. "I can't give you more time than I give the other prisoners. It wouldn't look good. News travels fast on the prison grapevine."

"So I've been told," I said. "There's just one other thing."

Quickly, we worked out a signal that I could use in an emergency. But it would have to be a real emergency. He would look my way each day when he reviewed the prisoners in the yard and if I blew my nose it meant I had to see him in a hurry.

The interview ended and shortly afterward I was assigned to work in the prison laundry—Big Al's domain. He was foreman of the prison gang that washed sheets, pillow cases, blankets, the inmates' clothes. He had about a dozen cons in his gang, and the guards didn't interfere as long as he kept order and got the wash out. Big Al ran things his way.

"Hey, here's a new one for you," the guard said when he turned me over to Cicceroni.

Big Al looked me over. He was sweating, although it wasn't hot in there. He had tufts of hair sticking out of his ears and tufts of hair bristling up off his back. He had long, hairy arms and a barrel chest.

"What's your name?" he asked.

"Tony," I told him.

"Okay, Tony, you start at the bottom and work up. Maybe someday you get my job, eh?"

I didn't like the way he said it.

"You start bleaching," he said, and took me over to a large tub where they had jugs of bleaching solution. "This is how much you put in, and don't put in too much, because that will louse up the works. And if things get loused up we lose privileges, and if we lose privileges on account of you, you sonofabitch, I'll nail your ass to the wall."

Bleaching was the worst job in the laundry room. The bleach splashes on you. It gets on your skin and clothes and leaves blotches, and the other cons call you leper or zebra. A rotten job. But there was no complaint department.

Every two hours, there was a ten-minute break and everybody lit up for "smoke-time." You can talk as long as you keep it low. The guard gives everybody a cigarette. One guy gets a light from the guard and goes around and lights up everybody else. They don't let you carry cigarettes in your pocket. No matches, either.

I stood there waiting my turn to light up. The light never came. What came was Big Al's hand that shot out and took the cigarette from my lips.

He shredded the cigarette between his fingers, threw what was left of it on the floor and looked at me.

"What's the matter, Tony?"

I said nothing. I was the new boy on the block.

"Understand this," he said. "When you get your cigarette and candy ration, you bring them to me. Maybe I give you half, maybe I don't."

For a moment I was a bit of a wise guy and asked him if this was prison policy.

"It's my policy. Don't be a wise guy, because you belong to me."

I went back to my bleaching vat. This job was going to be even tougher than I thought.

"Take it easy," said a little guy at the next tub. "He's just testing you." I calmed down and mixed the bleach.

Just before chow time, the guards blew a whistle and everybody lined up. We showed the guard our hands and got a quick frisk all the way down to see if we had kept anything, like a stirring utensil. You could file one of those things down and kill somebody with it. We marched swiftly, in that eerie silence you find nowhere but in prison, to the mess hall. Two whistles and everybody sits down. Three whistles and you start to eat. Big Al was right across the table from me.

My next demonstration came almost immediately. I reached for the biscuits and Big Al whacked my hand with his spoon. There are no knives and no forks. I dropped the biscuit on the table.

"Don't eat until he tells you," the con next to me said.

"Listen to him, Tony," Al said.

Just before the whistle signaled chow time was over, he said "Okay, Tony, you can eat now."

I chewed a little meat but let the biscuit lie there. I never ate another biscuit as long as I was there.

Sometime soon I intended to make my move. But I would pick the time and the place. Obviously the mess hall wasn't the right place. Neither was the laundry room. It turned out to be the "yard." The right time was the following afternoon.

The yard is the only place where prisoners are permitted to

mingle in large groups. And yard-time is very important to them. Except for visiting days, it's their only connection with the outside. They can actually see large patches of blue sky, even if they are hemmed in by high walls with towers manned by sharpshooting guards behind .30 caliber machine guns.

In the yard you play ball, sit in the sun, pitch horseshoes or just stand around and talk. I never really liked being in the yard. Plenty of times I would rather have gone to my cell—just to be alone. But the rules say you go to the yard at four o'clock, or to some other place like the library or the sick bay. You go by the rules.

Another thing I didn't like about the yard was the way the inmates split up the territory and fought over it. Each group had its own patch of ground, with imaginary boundaries, and no one dared step into another group's territory. Cross that imaginary line and somebody challenges . . . "Hey, move your toe back. You're two inches in."

Cellblock K had its own corner in the farthest part of the yard. When we went there the next afternoon I could see about fifteen inmates lined up in a semicircle. They had their arms folded and their backs to the corner. They were setting up a screen so the guards couldn't see what was happening—Big Al was waiting behind the screen.

"You got grievances?" he demanded. "You don't like the way I run things here?"

I started to answer but in midsentence he slugged me. He really flattened me, and as I lay in the dirt with my lip bleeding, looking up at Big Al and that semicircle of guys, I knew the time had come.

"Don't worry about them," he said, nodding at the semicircle of inmates. "This is between you and me."

I got up on my hands and knees and crawled toward him like I couldn't make it up any further. Then Big Al made a big mistake.

He clenched that big ham of a fist and leaned over to give me another belt. When he did, and while he was still leaning forward, I brought my head up under his chin.

It was a solid crack. His head snapped back and hit the wall. Then I went to work on him. I gave him about eight in the gut, just below the second button of his jacket. The breath came out of him in hooting gasps. I could practically feel him throwing up, and I was enjoying it.

Finally, his head sagged forward and my right knee came up under his chin. He went out cold.

I turned and walked straight toward the semicircle of cons. I moved two of them aside and said, "Excuse me." They let me through.

I left Big Al lying in the dirt, the back of his head and lips bleeding pretty badly. I heard later it took eighteen stitches to close him up. But he never blew the whistle. He said he slipped in the laundry and cut his head.

The guards never let on that anything had happened. They get bored and don't mind seeing the inmates work each other over once in a while, as long as they keep it orderly.

I wasn't sure how the fight would affect my future with Big Al. "He'll kill you," predicted my knuckle-cracking cellmate, and I brooded on this for a while. One sharpened spoon would do it, I thought. If they want you, they get you. I figured it would happen in the laundry room, where Al was completely in control.

I looked over toward his cell and saw he wasn't there. They were probably still sewing him up or keeping him in the infirmary. I didn't sleep very well that night, but I was getting used to this by now. At least, things between us couldn't be much worse than they had been.

He ignored me at breakfast next morning, sitting there like some kind of wounded gorilla. He kept tapping his spoon on the table. Okay, I thought, we'll see what happens in the laundry room.

Nothing much happened at all until the first cigarette break. I worked with my bleach and he stayed in the background. Then the laundry gang all went to a corner for a smoke. One con got a light from the guard and went around lighting the rest. Just before he got to me, Big Al shouldered his way forward.

I measured the distance and tried to decide where to kick him first. It was an instinctive reaction. Big Al pushed the other con aside and offered me a light from his cigarette.

"You're all right," he said through a stitched lip. "You're a stand-up guy."

I lit up and smiled. He put a heavy arm around my shoulder and smiled too. I didn't know what we were smiling at, two puffy-lipped guineas who weren't going anywhere smiling it up in the federal pen.

"You don't take no crap from nobody, eh, Tony?" he said.

"Well, my Sicilian grandmother brought me up, and she told me never to take any crap. Not from anybody."

He laughed, and the guard gave a warning rap.

"Your grandmother was right. Where you from, Tony?"

I told him Chicago.

He said we'd talk later.

Big Al wanted to make peace, so we made peace. Still, I wasn't buying it all the way. Guys who made that kind of a mistake have been found folded up in trunks of automobiles, or at the bottom of the East River. If they want to get you, they get you, and being in prison just makes it easier.

I hadn't been in a week yet, but it seemed like a year, like a big piece of forever. Sometimes I woke up in a cold sweat and would think I was coming out of a nightmare. Then I would look around and the nightmare was still there—the bars, the hard bunk, the lousy little commode with the dirty sink, the other cons snoring and wheezing. It was real, all right.

There would be sweat as cold as ice-water under my arms. I could never remember the really frightening part of this recurrent nightmare, but it had something to do with being recognized.

In daylight I could handle the logical worry that some dope pusher I had busted would recognize me from somewhere. I could handle the idea that the next con I met might whisper, "Hey, Sal, what the hell are you doing in here?" And I would have to turn him around with some fast talk. I had done it before. But at night, well, my subconscious wasn't handled so easily.

At night, I thought the hell with this; I'll take my football and go home. I can't win this game. Next day, I would blow my nose for the warden and have him get me out of here. But things always seemed to look better in the morning.

Then I got the break, the one I had hoped for. Big Al Cicceroni asked me if I'd like to be his cellmate. He came up to me in the yard and said, "How'd you like to bunk with me?"

I didn't want to appear too anxious. I shrugged and said, "Well, two don't snore as loud as four."

I don't know how he swung it. A federal penitentiary is relatively fix-proof. But hundred-dollar bills talk pretty loud, especially if it's for a small favor, and I knew that Big Al had a supply of C-notes stashed around somewhere. It gave him a certain leverage, like being alone in a four-man cell.

Anyhow, when the whistles blew that afternoon and our gray line lock-stepped back to the cells, I found myself in a new home.

"Hey, you," the guard ordered when I started to go into my old cell, "Not there. Over here."

I did an about-face and entered Big Al's cell. He sat on the lower bunk grinning up at me.

It makes a difference how you get into a place, I thought. If you want to get into the lion's cage, it's better to be invited in than tossed in, although sitting there on the edge of the bed my new bunkie looked more like a hairy gorilla than a lion.

I wondered what kind of psychology worked on gorillas. Well, I thought, we'd play some games and find out.

We did a lot of talking, Big Al and myself. We talked during the regular "talk time," and again after they killed the lights and set the long bolt for the night. This is when you listen for the guard's footsteps and have about twelve minutes to whisper before you hear them coming again. He wanted to know everything about me, and I made him work for what he got. I was using the old ploy of pumping him by letting him pump me.

It wouldn't be easy getting him to tell me where he had put a million-plus in government bonds.

In bits and pieces I gave him the story of the bank job I was supposed to have pulled in Chicago. I embroidered it a little for dramatic effect: one man on the door, two to grab the money, and the guy in the car outside who finked out and left us holding the bag. We had to shoot our way clear, and we would have made it clean if the driver hadn't talked to the police. Even so, I managed to put away my share before they ran us down. It would be waiting for me when I got out.

He gave me a patronizing smile when I mentioned that my share was forty G's.

I told him that this wasn't all I had. I had worked other jobs before. "I got damned near twice that waiting for me when I get out, and it's where nobody will find it. I got about eighty big ones."

He said I was amateur night, but I could see that I was getting to him. Big Al had to be bigger and tougher and smarter than anybody else. Big Al wore his vanity like a neon sign. He had to be the *numero uno,* the number one biggest shot wherever he was.

One night after lights-out I could hear him stirring and breathing heavily and I could almost guess what he was going to say before he said it.

"Hey, Tony," he whispered.

"Yeah?"

"Where'd you stash it?"

"Stash what?"

"Your eighty big ones."

I leaned toward him. "Hey, you crazy or somethin'? You think I'm gonna tell anybody where I stashed eighty grand?"

"Forget it," he said, "I was just curious." But in the dim light I could see him smiling.

I brought up the subject of money again several nights later. There wasn't much else to talk about except money and women.

"With my stash, I got some great propositions when I get out," I told him. I went on about using maybe twenty thousand to finance a parole and having sixty left over for a deal I had in mind.

We were playing checkers on a lower bunk and he grabbed my arm. "Stop talking about your lousy eighty grand," he said. "Start talking a million and I'll listen."

I shrugged off his hand and moved a red checker. It was beginning to look like I had him hooked. Ever see one actor trying to upstage another ham? Well, that's the way he was acting. I slipped him the needle about talk being cheap and waited.

"I've got a million waiting for me when I get out."

"Sure you have. And I'm John D. Rockefeller and you're the King of France."

"Don't be a wise guy, Tony."

"Okay," I said. "So you got a million."

"A million and a half."

"In cash?"

"In something just as good," he said. "Government bonds."

"Are they safe?"

"Safer than a church. I've got them in a bank."

"Okay. I'll play you the next game of checkers for the million. That is, if you really have it."

That brought him up off the bunk breathing hard. I shrugged him off and looked down at the board.

"It's your move, Al."

So the bonds were in a bank. From what I'd been told, the government had looked just about everywhere else for them. Agents had been over every inch of Big Al's apartment, his mother's house, the residence of every woman he shacked up with and all the joints he frequented.

They had put out feelers offering a deal for information leading to the recovery of the bonds. Absolutely no dice. If it was in a bank the search had been narrowed down considerably. The question now was what bank.

How long it took me to get the answer to that one would determine how long I had to sweat it out here in prison. So I went to work on Big Al's other soft spot—his weakness for women.

Whenever he got through bragging about what a big man he was with the women, how they fought over him, he always got back to the one he described as "my woman." Her name was Maria, and they had a couple of kids, even though they hadn't gone through the procedure of getting married.

Al told me they just never had gotten around to seeing a preacher but that she was a good woman. He said that when he came home after being out with some broad his conscience would hurt, he would get down on his knees and ask forgiveness and she always forgave him.

I couldn't quite picture this ape down on his knees asking forgiveness from anybody, but I didn't say so. What I said was, "I
hope to God you didn't tell her where you hid the bonds."

He came up off the bunk. "Don't you say anything against her.
Nobody says anything against her."

"I'm not saying anything against her, it's just . . . well,
you know how women talk and all that. . . ."

I thought he was going to come after me.

"Look, you know her . . . I don't. But don't hate me for
thinking. I mean . . . hell . . . a million bucks."

"A million and a half," he said, correcting me again.

"For that kind of money I'd circumcise an elephant in Times
Square," I said, and that got him to laughing.

He stomped around the cell, pounding a massive fist into his
palm. Suddenly he stopped and came over to my bunk.

"You see," he said, "I've got a little insurance going for me.
Maria's uncle is president of the bank. He's in this thing up to his
eyeballs. I got so much on him he don't sneeze unless I give him
the okay."

I tapped my forehead with my finger, indicating that I thought
he was a very smart cookie. I could have kissed him, almost. He
had just given me my reprieve from prison.

The next afternoon, when the warden made his inspection tour
of the yard, as arranged I blew my nose when he looked at me. I
was on my way to his office, on some pretext or other, before I
got back to my cell.

"Your people have been worried about you," the warden said.
"Not a word in three weeks. Are you okay?"

"I won't be if you keep on wasting time."

"What's up?"

I told him to get pencil and paper, and he took notes while I talked . . . the bonds they wanted were in a New York bank . . . I didn't know the name of the bank . . . but they could narrow down the search by checking out Cicceroni's common-law wife . . . first name Maria . . . last name unknown . . . her uncle is an officer of the bank where the bonds are being held . . . she only has so many uncles and only so many of them work in banks . . . get moving.

The rest of it was up to the agents on the outside. They'd move with wire taps, surveillance teams and search warrants. If they didn't have the bonds within twenty-four hours, they'd be doing a lousy job. And now I decided I'd better get back to my cell before somebody got hinky.

I'd still be prisoner No. 6710 one more day.

Leaving the warden's office I told him, "I'd like to get out of this hotel by tomorrow." He said he would try to arrange it.

My last night in Cellblock K was no better and no worse than the others. I had another nightmare, slightly different this time. I could see Big Al coming at me with those hairy hands, and woke up in a cold sweat. It wasn't worth going back to sleep, so I lay there listening to the reassuring snores from the other bunk.

In the laundry room next day, where Big Al had promoted me from bleacher to folder, time went more slowly than ever. The cigarette didn't taste good at smoke-time. I kept checking the other cons to see if any of them acted strangely. They were as bored and hang-dog as ever. The whistles blew and we marched back to the cell.

Finally a guard appeared. "Get your gear together, 6710."

"What the hell!" I said, acting as if I was surprised.

"You're being transferred."

Big Al rolled out of his bunk and asked, "What's this all about? You in more trouble?"

"Damned if I know."

The guard banged his billyclub against the bars and told me to get moving.

"Hey, keep in touch," I said to Big Al as I left.

As far as I know, Al Cicceroni never associated me with the seizure of the bonds. I was a con named Tony Tivoli who had been transferred to another prison.

The bonds were found in the false bottom of a desk drawer at the bank. In fact, the desk belonged to the president of the bank, who eventually shot himself after getting out of jail on parole. The bank changed ownership, which took one bank away from the mob's control.

On leaving Cellblock K I was escorted to the reception room where I put on my own clothes and got my gold cross back. I was glad to have a neck to hang it around. Two federal marshals signed me out, telling the warden I was to be delivered to F.B.I. headquarters in New York. As far as they still knew I was a hood named Tony Tivoli.

I was recuffed to my belt with the buckle turned around in the back. I held my topcoat over my wrists and we were off to the airport.

On the plane I looked around for the brunette stewardess with the full lips. She wasn't there, but a redhead with long hair was a wonderful substitute. Travel always made me feel good. So did the idea of being almost free.

CHAPTER 15

Pot, Hash—Surrender on the Installment Plan

IN THE hold of the freighter *Constantine* it was as dark as the inside of a tomb. And almost as quiet, except for the eternal creaking noises any ship makes as it wallows against the mooring lines that hold it helpless to its dock.

It was four o'clock in the morning and the entire ship's crew was asleep, even the watch I had ghosted past at the head of the gangplank. If he had challenged me, I'd have played just another drunken sailor returning to the ship until close enough to poleaxe him. But he never stirred and my rubber-soled shoes carried me noiselessly to the open forward hatch, where I went hand-over-hand down a rope into the inky blackness.

The small flashlight I took from my pocket cut through the darkness as I sent its finger of brightness probing over the cargo. What I was after I found stacked behind an array of machinery, the wooden crates stencilled for delivery in Cairo. But I had to be certain these were the right crates.

From the knapsack on my back I took a cold chisel and a folded piece of heavy cloth. Propping the flashlight so its light was riveted on one corner of the nearest crate, I jammed the chisel under the corner slat, covered it with the cloth to deaden any noise, and slowly pried up the holding nail. It came out with barely more than a whisper and revealed burlap sacking underneath. The chisel went back into the knapsack and my pocketknife snicked open and made quick work of the burlap.

It was just as the informer Kemal Mustafa had said when he came to me in Istanbul: "There is a large shipment of hashish going out of Izmir on the freighter *Constantine,* bound for Egypt. I thought you would like to know."

Izmir is a port south of Istanbul, and I knew that any substantial shipment meant that ultimately a high percentage probably would find its way into the United States.

"How much is a large shipment?" I asked him.

"Three hundred tons."

Three hundred tons *was* a tremendous amount, and after it was processed properly, it was a good bet that most of it would wind up being imported by the U.S. as hand-painted dishes, pitchers and other such innocent items.

Innocent until the paint was carefully scraped away and the so-called pottery was broken down and pulverized into marketable hashish—the most concentrated form of marijuana.

On my assignment in Turkey marijuana was not my bag. After all, most of the marijuana used in the States was either homegrown or smuggled in from Mexico. Still, I couldn't turn my back on it, so whenever I came on a field, and they had them a couple of miles square, with the grassy stalks waving in the breeze, I'd get to windward and with a few well-placed matches manage a respectable brush fire. . . .

I get a little sick to my stomach when I hear people preach that marijuana should be legalized. First of all, I don't believe that tobacco cigarettes should be legal either. Juveniles at least aren't supposed to be able to buy tobacco; why then make it legal for them to buy marijuana—especially in view of the documented reports of its disorienting effects, including loss of memory and deterioration in intellectual and psychomotor performance. Marijuana isn't harmless. The answer lies in treatment and education, not in legalization.

On a personal note, I have known too many hard-core addicts who started on "harmless" marijuana. This is not to say that every marijuana cigarette leads to use of more lethal drugs, but every heroin addict I've known started out smoking pot. It's a stepping stone. There are uncounted case histories of people under its influence throwing victims off bridges, cutting them with a knife or shooting them dead. Possibly they would have committed the same crimes under the influence of alcohol. But the record indicates that proportionately more violence is associated with marijuana than with alcohol. Again, it's also my personal experience, and I suppose I have a fairly broad range of first-hand evidence in these areas.

On this issue I *may* be prejudiced, but I think less than most— after all, narcotics has been my business. And I am convinced that legalizing the use of marijuana would be surrender on the installment plan. Hashish is the end product of marijuana. And there is historic reason why hashish is an Arabic word meaning "assassin." Through the centuries, the sultans who wanted someone taken out of circulation would load up their killer with hashish. Under its influence he reached a euphoric stage in which he would carry out a slaying even knowing it was going to cost him his own life.

In those earlier days, the dried stalks of the marijuana were heaped in a damp room and flayed with sticks, making the dust rise and cling to the walls and ceiling. The finest dust rose the highest, was the most concentrated and the most highly prized for its effectiveness. The dust then was scraped from the ceilings and walls and punishment for anyone who dared steal it was quick and severe—the thief's head was cut off.

Today there are other methods of obtaining this most concentrated and purest form of marijuana, a brown powder more coarse than talcum that's easily compressed into bricks or shaped into pottery for illegal importation into other countries.

On delivery to the customer it's scraped into a loose powder once again and smoked by being mixed with tobacco or marijuana. Other users mix it into a preferred liquid and drink it. It also is sniffed or tucked under the lower lip like snuff. The negative effects are the same no matter which method is used.

While the growing of marijuana in the mid-East was practically of no consequence so far as illegal importation to the United States was concerned, a vast shipment of hashish was another matter. As I've said, when compressed into what appears to be pottery and shipped into the States it has been in increasing demand on the illicit drug market. . . .

Three hundred tons of it was a blockbuster.

"Are you sure there's that much on board the *Constantine?*" I'd asked Kemal Mustafa.

"My brother serves on the ship. He helped load it into the forward hold. The bricks are packed in burlap inside wooden crates."

"When does she sail?"

"After two more days. There is some delay for another cargo."

I paid him liberally for his information. Then I drove to the port at Izmir and located the *Constantine*. She was a small freighter and, which is unusual in those ports, well-painted and clean. There wasn't too much activity aboard, and Kemal had told me that most of the small crew had been given shore leave.

With only a skeleton crew, I didn't anticipate too much difficulty getting aboard and carrying out my plan. I left the dock to get ready.

What I needed cost me less than fifteen dollars: cold chisel, small flashlight, strips of fabric, two large glass jugs, enough oil and gasoline to fill them with a mix of both liquids, and the backpack to carry it all. A paper match booklet and a cigarette should take care of the rest. I went to an inn near the waterfront, had an early dinner, took a room and slept like a baby until three A.M.

The streets were empty when, with my pack on my back, I strolled down to the docks and approached the gangplank. As I'd anticipated, there was no challenge from the sleeping watch and within a few minutes I was standing over the cases of hashish.

Kemal Mustafa had given it to me straight. After prying off the lid with the chisel I slashed open several of the crated burlap sacks and in each found those brown bricks of hashish. Working cautiously, I arranged the crates in a close-order square, sweating in the closeness of the hold.

Propping the flashlight, I sprinkled the gasoline-oil mixture from one of the jugs over the crates. Then I put the other jug in the nest of crates, soaked a strip of the fabric in the highly flammable mixture and plugged it into the mouth of the jug that still was filled with oil and gasoline. To the trailing end I attached the book of paper matches.

What I had was a kind of Molotov cocktail, a sort of poor man's napalm bomb. You don't want to be around when the thing goes off and I didn't intend to be. Which was the reason for the book of paper matches.

When the fuse burned up to the liquid in the bottle the jug would erupt. There was a reason for the mixture of oil and gasoline. When the bottle exploded, the gasoline would burn fiercely but briefly, particularly without the flames being fanned by wind, and it was as still as death in the hold. But the oil, fed by the gasoline flame, would burn steadily and the crates and their contents would be certain to go up in the smoky fire. The book of matches and a cigarette were the time fuse that would give me the grace period I needed to get off the ship.

The chisel went into the backpack and I shrugged my shoulders into the straps. Then, kneeling beside the full jug with its fabric fuse, I lit a cigarette, tucked the unlighted end into the top of the match cover and fastened the flap of the match book so that the cigarette stuck out as far as possible and yet was held securely with the unlighted end against the match heads.

I had maybe three minutes before the cigarette burned down to the sulphur heads of the matches. At that point the matches would burst into flame, the fire would streak up the fabric fuse and that jug would explode, setting fire to the whole mass of crates.

I didn't waste any time once I closed the cover of the match book over the cigarette and checked out the set-up.

Scrambling for the rope by which I'd slid down into the hold, I barked my shins on the machinery, picked out the rope in the tiny beam of my light, reached over my shoulder and stuffed the light into my backpack and went up that rope like a runaway monkey.

And I didn't waste any time on deck, although I slowed my rush from the ship when I neared the head of the gangplank. But the watch still was nowhere to be seen as I scrambled ashore and headed back up the pier away from the ship. Reaching the corner of a ramshackle warehouse, I ducked around into a heavier darkness and stood there, waiting.

It took no more than a few moments.

There wasn't much of a noise, a faint thump, because I had planted the bottle deep in its nest of crates. But peering around the corner of the warehouse I could see a cherry red glow from the forward hatch cutting through the blackness of the night, a fiery glare that quickly mushroomed.

Several figures appeared on deck, flitting back and forth in the reflected glare of the fire, but from what I could see nobody was doing much of anything to stop what I'd set off.

I waited long enough to be sure the fire had done the job, that whatever was left when they finally did get the blaze under control wasn't going to be worth much of anything to anybody. Then I walked back to my car with the inner satisfaction of a man who feels he's done a good piece of work, and headed home to Istanbul.

Maybe it was only a small shot this time, but it was part of the big picture—and that was one load of hashish that wasn't going to make its own assassins.

CHAPTER 16

A Croupier
Vs. "Castro's Mafia"

"NINE'S THE point, forty-five, the gun that killed Jesse James," I rattled off, running the number one crap table smooth and easy, like I didn't know they were hating my guts. "Nine right back, fifty-four, Little Nina from Pasadena—man lets it ride. New point, ten . . . Big Dick, the Ladies Home Companion . . . seven, he shoots, and out."

I was in San Juan, Puerto Rico, passing as Vincent M. Vento, a hot-shot croupier from Reno and Las Vegas, and they were buying my cover. In fact, the promotions were coming so fast that they were damn near doing me in.

The first night at La Concha they set me to work at the black-jack table. Any six-year-old kid could have done it. It's sort of a ladies' favorite, and required nothing more from me than a fast patter and an ability to add. It's always been a big winner for the house at casinos, and my first night at the blackjack table was to prove no exception.

The second night too I subbed as a blackjack dealer and, finally, all within a period of four days, I was put up on the box in charge of the number one crap table. The other guys were burned. It was a real prestige spot.

Pagan, the casino manager, liked the way I called the numbers in English. The other guys were all Puerto Rican except for a few Cubans and they couldn't handle the vernacular. In English, it came out sounding like a Speedy Gonzales routine. Maybe that's why I got the job. Anyhow, I was giving it the old college try.

"Four's the point," I called. "Little Joe, the way the train went through the trestle . . . Toot-toot . . . seven right back; two rolls and no coffee. Next shooter."

Break time, the pit boss signaled. The work schedule at La Concha called for one hour on and a half-hour off, but you weren't allowed to leave the premises on breaks. I turned my stick over to the man relieving me and went downstairs to the croupier's lounge.

It was hot in the lounge. I climbed out of my powder-blue casino jacket and got a cigarette from the employee's tray. We were issued cigarettes on breaks because there were no pockets in the casino uniforms. The chips used in the casino were almost as negotiable as money and no pockets made them harder to steal, or so the theory went.

Not another man on the shift was speaking to me. They were sitting around playing checkers, talking and watching TV, just like I wasn't there. I was the intruder in the ranks, the cat from the States, the guy who had walked in and copped one of their coveted spots. They resented my presence and were taking no trouble to conceal the fact.

The hell with them, I thought. I hadn't come to Puerto Rico to worry about the feelings of my fellow croupiers. I was there on an assignment which, for the previous man on the case, had terminated in a pine box. They found him with twenty-seven knife wounds.

All I had to do was infiltrate the Cuban Mafia, which was a little like playing Russian roulette with two guns instead of one. Large shipments of cocaine from Bolivia and heroin from Mexico were being brought into Puerto Rico by way of Cuba. There was reason to believe that the operation was being carried on with the knowledge of Fidel Castro, that his supporters were running it, and that the profits were getting back to shore up the dictator's shaky government.

None of the people involved was squeamish about killing. It wasn't the kind of assignment you break both legs rushing to get, and you move slow once you're on it.

I had been down in the Keys on a long weekend, trolling for marlin and whatever else would bite, when the ship-to-shore cut in with a message to get my tail back to Miami. Something urgent had come up, and since Washington was on the other end of the line, it looked like something out of the country.

Back in Miami on the second floor of the Post Office Building, I used the office hot line to get back to Washington.

"Vizzini in Miami," I said to the deputy commissioner. "I got word that you called."

He asked me how the weather was; I said fine. Whenever they start off giving you the routine about weather or family you know you bought it.

"Where to this time?" I asked.

"Puerto Rico. They're having a hassle down there that they can't handle locally. They've already lost one man on it. The government has asked we send one of our best men to help out. Your name came up."

I could have told him flattery would get him nowhere, but I wasn't wasting the breath. Besides, there were only two or three of us in the Bureau available for special UC duty, and he told me the Commissioner himself had hand picked me for the job.

"You will report to José Nuñez Barber, head of the Narcotics Division in Puerto Rico, and plan on staying a minimum of three months. More likely you'll be there for six. We will send you a teletype on what we have on the case, but you'll get a better briefing from Nuñez once you get there. And, Sal, pick an air-tight cover. We don't want to lose you. We want you back."

The teletype arrived within an hour. It contained a few hard facts and a lot of unconfirmed rumor. The Bureau had known for some time that Havana was a clearing house for drugs coming from Latin America and that the stuff was being funneled into the U.S. through Puerto Rico.

Once on Puerto Rican soil, which is technically part of the U.S., the problem of moving the stuff on to Miami or New York for further distribution was greatly reduced.

I smiled when I read that cocaine, in particular, was coming through the San Juan gateway in large quantities. This was a feedback of a report I had sent in myself six months before after busting a large supplier of cocaine in Lauderdale.

Kilo for kilo, this crystal-white product of the coca leaf was worth more than heroin. It was in demand, not only by addicts, but by people looking for that extra kick. The Bureau had reports about cocaine being passed out in appetizer dishes at swinging parties, just like peanuts, and I had busted a few celebrities myself who got their highs going this route.

When sniffed, cocaine has a hallucinatory effect. It can also be mixed with heroin and shot intravenously. For strung-out junkies who can afford it this is supposed to be the ultimate. They say it makes them feel as though they can walk down any street and look into a seven-story window.

The best cocaine came from labs in Bolivia. The Bureau was aware that trafficking in the stuff was centered in this hemisphere. They could even pinpoint the location of some of the labs. What they suspected, but didn't know for sure, was that Castro and his boys were secretly involved in the smuggling.

This, I learned from reading the teletype, would be part of my job.

The sheet also contained the names of two expatriated Cubans, known to be Castro henchmen, who were operating in San Juan. One was Caesar Vega and the other Luis Valdez. The Puerto Rican authorities had been trying for months, but hadn't been able to lay a glove on them. They would be my two prime targets.

Then there was a character named Jesus Rolon, alias the Sultan, also known as Boxer. If anything big was going on, the Sultan would be involved. As the top gangster in Puerto Rico, he dealt in everything from drugs to murder.

I made a mental note to look up Jesus Rolon. He would be a potential target. But, hell, so would every two-bit hood in the San Juan underworld. You don't usually start at the top on an assignment like this. You start at the bottom and work your way up, and one mistake along the way is usually one too many.

The orders I had received earlier were confirmed at the bottom of the sheet. I would proceed to San Juan and contact Puerto Rican narcotics division boss Jose Nuñez Barber. Picking a cover would be left to my discretion. After all, it was my neck.

I left Miami with credentials saying I was Vincent M. Vento. The name wasn't important. Any one would do, as long as I remembered to respond to it when someone paged me. I had used the name Vento before and felt safe with it. Selecting a suitable cover, I decided, was something else.

In the past, I had posed as an Air Force pilot without being able to fly a plane and a ship's captain without knowing step one about navigation. I'd also faked being a lot of other things. But the circumstances of this assignment could force me to play a role I couldn't fake. At least, not a hundred percent.

In San Juan I didn't call Jose Nuñez Barber right away. I rented an efficiency apartment at the Capital Hotel, familiarized myself with the city and swung like a tourist for three days. Then I made my telephone call.

"This is a friend from Miami," I said.

There was a short pause on the other end, and then Jose Nuñez Barber said, "Yes, I have been expecting you. When can I talk with you?"

"Tonight, but it will have to be my way."

I asked him what kind of a car he was driving and he said a black Olds 88. I told him to be at the Caribe Hilton parking lot at eight o'clock and I would join him when I was sure neither of us was being followed.

Nuñez Barber was on time. I waited between cars until I was sure there were no tails. There were two men in the Olds, one heavy-set and the other slim. I rapped on the window, got a nod and climbed in the back seat.

The slim one introduced himself as Nuñez Barber. His companion, he said, was Lieutenant Ortiz Reyes of the San Juan Narcotics Squad. "Lieutenant Reyes will be your contact while you are here. He will supply you with funds and whatever else you need. You will keep him informed of your progress and turn over whatever evidence you gather in the course of your investigation."

We agreed that the steam room at the San Jeronimo Hilton would be a good meeting place.

I listened while they briefed me on the local situation. Nuñez Barber spoke almost perfect English. I could speak Spanish almost as well, which was one thing I had going for me on this job. I told them that I would need a fool-proof cover, even if it meant going to some trouble, and that becoming a croupier in a casino seemed to be the best.

"But that takes a skill all its own," Nuñez Barber said.

"It has its advantages," I told him. "It's acceptable but on the fringe. It gives me an excuse for being out late, hanging around bars and bistros after work. And nobody would ever suspect a working croupier of being a government agent."

"You will be required to pass an examination."

"I learn fast," I said.

And I did.

Legalized casino gambling is part of the scene in Puerto Rico. There are dozens of casinos over on The Strip, where most of the big hotels furnish roulette along with room service, and a few over in Old San Juan.

I made all of them, buying chips and playing, but mostly watching. I watched stickmen and dealers, observing everything from their general attitude to tiny subtle movements. Each night I would come back to my efficiency with a few more chips and practice in front of the mirror.

Of course I wasn't starting from scratch. You don't grow up in the Marines without learning what makes a blackjack game tick, or to roll dice only if the other guy bucks them off a backstop. I was a good alley crap shooter and a fair country card player.

Learning to handle chips was the hard part. In a gambling casino, chips aren't counted out individually. Instead the tableman "tops them off" with a deft and accurate maneuver, matching a pile of chips on the table with an equal pile—or pushing with uncanny speed thirty-six chips at you when you hit a number at roulette.

Watch a croupier and you'll notice that even as he is keeping the bets straight, talking with customers, or whatever else, his hand is moving swiftly in this "topping off" action as if it had a separate intelligence. It takes practice.

Alone before the mirror, I stood there topping off hour after hour, watching myself, looking for a clumsy or amateurish move. My legs got so tired they ached. I kept practicing the deal and the pay-off. I did this every night for weeks. And Vincent Vento got pretty good.

No croupier school ever taught a tableman or card dealer any faster or better. When I walked in to take the government exam, I had the moves and the lingo down cold.

Humberto Pagan, who ran the casino at the La Concha Hotel, was an observer when the test was given to a group of applicants. He didn't do it out of the goodness of his heart. His reason for being there was to skim off the best of the applicants at the source, and he got interested in me because I spoke Spanish as well as English.

"You've got a job with me if you want it, Vento," he said. "Where did you say you worked before?"

"Around. Just around."

He gave me a look which said he didn't give a damn where I had worked before. He needed a Spanish-English-speaking croupier, and I was it.

That afternoon I was outfitted with a tuxedo. There were three different colored jackets: powder-blue, white, and black. A name plate saying Vincent Vento was made up. I would wear it on the jacket where the breast pocket would have been, if there had been pockets. That night I was assigned to the blackjack table.

The dress rehearsal was over. This was curtain time. Strangely enough, I felt even more nervous than when I sat down at my first gin rummy game with Luciano. In this game I had better win. Within minutes I had two ugly drunks and a female exhibitionist among my customers.

The drunks heckled me. I ignored them and kept the table going. When one of them got particularly hairy I looked through him politely. Everybody was "sir" to Vincent Vento. The stacked brunette at the end of the table kept leaning over, showing a lot of bosom through her low-cut dress. She got the middle-distance stare from Vincent Vento.

Another test came the second night while I was subbing at the blackjack table. Coming back from the second break, I saw that a Secret Service man I knew from Miami was playing. He looked at me as I dealt cards out of the shoe and I looked at him. Neither of us showed any recognition. I hit his fourteen with a queen on the first hand and he drifted away. He wasn't a gambler.

He had his job, I had mine.

The real trouble came the third night. Pagan had been acting pretty friendly, giving me a compliment here and there, and the best way to get off to a lousy start with the other croupiers was to get too many compliments from the boss.

It came to a head on the second shift break when I went down to the lounge for a smoke. I hung my jacket on the rack in the next room. When it was time to get back up on the floor again, I went to get my jacket and it wasn't there. The others were looking back over their shoulders as they left. They knew something I didn't know.

Well, you couldn't show on the floor in your shirt sleeves, so I started looking. Working through all the lockers, I finally found the jacket rolled up in a ball and stuffed in a dirty, unused locker. I tried to straighten out the wrinkles and got back to my table twenty minutes late. Pagan gave me a black look. I didn't explain. No use to whine.

They'd had their fun. Now it was my turn.

I waited until the next night. While the others were in the lounge on a break, I scooped all of their jackets off the pipe-rack in the next room. I put the coats in a locker, bolted the door with a large padlock I'd gotten that day and went up to the kitchen for a sandwich and a cup of coffee.

I was back at my table on time but nobody else on the shift was. After about twenty minutes, the croupiers still on the floor began to get nervous. Pagan put an assistant in charge and hurried downstairs to see what was wrong.

When he came back up he called me into his office.

"What do you know about the jackets?"

"I'm having some trouble keeping track of my own," I told him. "Matter of fact, I keep it **on even** though it's damn hot down there."

"Yes, I know."

Pagan was nobody's fool. I could have gotten fired then and there, wasting a whole month of work establishing my cover. No other casino would have hired me. I was taking that chance, and I got away with it. But it really raised hell with the whole croupier staff.

They had to call in a maintenance crew with a crowbar to break the lock. That took an hour. When they finally located the jackets nobody could wear them, at least not right away. I had sprinkled them with orange soda pop before stuffing them in the locker.

They made me work the rest of the evening without a break. When tablemen and dealers were relieved, the ones going off duty gave up their jackets to those replacing them. In the confusion, there was a lot of milling around trying to find jackets that would fit. And later, after the roulette table had closed down and the dice had stopped rolling, it took quite a while to get the coats sorted out. I didn't stay around to watch.

The coat-switching deal seemed to break the ice. The other croupiers accepted me after that. All but one, that is. I was forced to give him one more treatment, and the treatment was physical.

The one who needed more convincing was a big Puerto Rican named José Perez. He was bigger than I was and had an equally big mouth. He kept sounding off, making himself obnoxious. I listened for two nights and did nothing. Then he made the mistake of following me into the men's room and spinning me around.

That was as far as he got. I gave him one in the gut, about one inch below the navel, and brought my knee up aginst his jaw as he went down. He fell hard.

I left him lying there on the floor, but said to one of the others on the way out, "Your friend needs some help."

A couple of the other croupiers went in and got him, and Pagan came down. José Perez never did tell them that I hit him. He said that he slipped and hit his head against the side of the john. So they sent him home. He was out two or three days.

The strange thing about it was that Perez didn't show any anger when he came back. He wanted to be my friend. He wanted to buy me drinks after work. That was all right with me. You make use of everything you can in this business.

"Come have a drink with me at the Farandula Club," José said, as we were closing the casino one night. "I have friends you will like. I have told them of the, what do you say, 'very tough guy' from Las Vegas."

"Hell, José, I'm not so tough." I grinned. "I just hate to get my jacket all wrinkled."

The Farandula Club was located on Fernandez Juncos Avenue, one of the main drags of Santurce, about five minutes' walk from my apartment and about the same distance from the casino. It was a dimly lit joint with a juke box, tables and a dance floor way back. Even at this hour, with dawn not far off, it had its collection of local hoods.

José introduced me to the bartender as his "amigo." He bought a drink and I bought one. I could tell the moment I walked in that I had come to the right place.

An undercover agent has a built-in sensor that sends out a little hum when he's making contact. You go into a town cold, you do what you can, you meet who you can, you play it by hell and by hunch . . . and then, if you're in luck, the little hum starts.

The Farandula Club was where the action was. You name it, they had it; booze, dope, girls, perhaps murder. The bartender said as much after José vouched for me and told me to come back often.

I said I would.

That's where I met Carlos Serra, the man who would introduce me to Caesar Vega and Luis Valdez. He also introduced me to all the rugged action I would have in Puerto Rico.

CHAPTER 17

Finale in San Juan

I'D HAD this strangely empty feeling coming to Puerto Rico and it came back after I met Carlos Serra. You couldn't call it fear; Carlos Serra wasn't the kind of fellow you're likely to be afraid of. I put it down to osmosis, or whatever else the experts call a strange foreboding of disaster. It was a gambler's hunch that after all these years of rolling sevens the dice were about to come up snake-eyes. I had the feeling my luck was running out.

In this business you count on luck to keep you alive. Without it you don't go far, and I had used up enough for a dozen lifetimes.

Since moving into my pad at the Capital Hotel Apartments, I'd awakened several times from a dream I couldn't explain. Usually, it was the same dream. I was standing with my back to a boarded-up storefront, holding a three-foot piece of chain. Shadowy figures I couldn't identify were coming at me from out of the darkness.

I couldn't place the scene. And I never found out what happened because I always woke up, sweating, before an attack actually happened.

Rays of sunshine would be leaking in around the edges of the drawn curtains. Because of my schedule I usually got to bed about the time the rest of San Juan was having its morning cup of coffee, and slept until noon or later. I'd get up, light a cigarette and tell myself to stop being a fool. There was my three-foot length of chain on the doorknob, just where I had left it. I always felt better with that piece of chain around. It weighed only a pound or two and had shiny steel links. I had brought it with me from Miami and wore it around my waist hidden under my croupier's cummerbund. Carrying a gun wasn't practical, and the chain put the house odds a little more in my favor. I could unhitch it and have it ready for action in seconds.

I met Carlos Serra at the Farandula Club a few nights after I'd first been taken there by José Perez. The bartender introduced us. Even in the dismal light of the place, Serra was wearing smoked sunglasses. He was youngish, in his thirties, and had a clammy handshake.

In the report I typed up later I described him as "five-foot-ten, 185 pounds, shaven head, blond mustache, black horn-rimmed glasses, a native of the Dominican Republic."

"I used to own this place," he said glumly. "That bitch I'm married to made me sell out."

I nodded sympathetically.

"She keeps the law on me so I'm always tight for cash."

Carlos Serra was a whiner and part of my job was to be a good listener. I'd heard more sad stories than Dear Abby.

I asked him who bought the place.

"Vega," he said. "A man named Caesar Vega."

That interested me. Vega was one of the main reasons for my being on this assignment, but I was careful not to show too much right then.

I decided that Carlos Serra might be very useful, that he would bear checking out. Next day I got in touch with my contact, Lt. Ortiz Reyes.

I hadn't spoken to him since our original meeting in the parking lot. I assumed he knew where I was working and what I was doing. If he didn't, he wasn't much of a cop. We met in the steam room of the San Jeronimo, with towels wrapped around our middles, and I asked him for a run-down on Serra.

I got the expected: small-time hood, pusher, pimp, bully-boy, in with the local mob.

"Has he ever worked with the police?" I asked.

"No."

"Any arrests?"

"He's done time for assault. He's vicious and has a big mouth. But he has connections."

"Shall I be friendly?"

"Go ahead. Do anything he wants. But don't tip him that you're working with us."

"That will take bread. He's short on money."

The Puerto Rican authorities had agreed to furnish "buy" money for the job, which included cultivating sources, and I told him I needed an advance of a thousand. He didn't quibble. I signed a receipt and got it in twenties and fifties.

I told Ortiz Reyes that I would be in touch when I had something to report.

After finishing up at the casino, I loosened my croupier's tie and strolled down the deserted streets toward the Farandula. I was the tired pro from Vegas, but my bankroll was all action.

Carlos Serra was sitting where I had left him twenty-four hours before. For all I knew, he had never moved. I showed a fifty and ordered us a drink.

After a second drink he glanced over one shoulder and then the other—as if anybody cared in a dump like that—and pulled out a handsome gold watch. Even in the dim light I could see that it was Swiss-made and expensive.

"Could you loan me two hundred on this?" he said, pushing the watch across the table.

"Sure," I said. "But, hell, Carlos, that's penny-ante stuff. A man with your reputation and background. Look, you need more than two hundred."

"Well, if it won't run you short."

"Make the loan three hundred," I said, peeling off two extra fifties. "A man like you should operate in style."

He took the cash and I took the watch. Then I said, "C'mon, Serra, you don't really think I'm here to work for peanuts in a gambling casino. I'm out to score big and you can cut in on it."

I let him know my real purpose for being in Puerto Rico was to establish sources for buying cocaine and heroin. I was setting up business back in Miami and wanted to talk to people here who were reliable and could provide a steady supply.

One of the first things I did was buy an ounce of cocaine from him, wrapped in a piece of tin foil. That way I had him tied up. Buy an ounce of cocaine from a guy and he's as guilty as if he sold you a carload. I would meet with my contact in the steam room at the San Jeronimo Hilton and turn over the evidence. I would initial it and he would initial a receipt. That way we maintained a continuity of evidence for the hit later, after we had bagged the big guys.

Carlos Serra vouched for me at the Farandula, where I negotiated for samples in the men's room, and at the Ali Baba Club, a place where the real trash gathered. It seemed as though every second whore in San Juan showed at the Ali Baba, and there were more sellers of hard drugs than there were buyers.

I made fourteen buys in less than two weeks. I made a buy from a pusher named Rego Berto; $270 worth of heroin. I bought cocaine from Hector (Erto) Oromi Bilboa, beating him down from an asking price of $100 a gram to $30 . . . and got four packs, tinfoil-wrapped.

They buzzed around me like bees over clover.

"Hey, you buying?" said a regular at the Parada Club. He came running like there was a sale on switchblade knives. "I'll let you have this for $350."

Inside the brown paper bag he held out was a Mason jar, like the kind Grandma used for strawberry preserves. And inside the jar, wrapped in wax paper, was junk.

Things were moving fast. Almost too fast. I was making so many trips to the steam room with evidence that I was beginning to lose weight. And I hadn't seen a hair of Vega or Valdez.

Carlos Serra's need for cash never was satisfied. He came to me one day wanting three hundred dollars, and when I asked him for collateral he handed me the keys to his yellow Triumph convertible. I kept the keys and the car. At least I would have wheels to get places until he paid off.

The arrangement didn't last long.

I was sitting at the typewriter in my apartment doing reports when the knock came.

"Who is it?" I called out.

"Carlos," the answer came, and his voice sounded shrill, excited.

I was already going through a maneuver I had practiced many times before. It took exactly eighteen seconds. In case I was interrupted doing reports, or somebody searched my room, one glance at that official Bureau stationery would have blown my cover wide open. So I found a hiding place.

Beneath the sink in the kitchen was a half-refrigerator, about the size of a dishwasher. I took it out and removed the screws from the fiberglass top. Under it was a space large enough for my paper work. The lid fit back perfectly on top of the papers.

Only my district supervisor in Atlanta knew about the hiding place, and I kept the reports up to the minute. If I was going to meet Carlos Serra, I would tell him so in a message, timed and dated. That way, if something happened and they found me in a canal, they would know the last person I was with.

"Just a minute," I called, removing the evidence.

There was more banging on the door, and when I opened it Carlos Serra stood there looking upset even behind his dark glasses.

"I want my car," he shouted, "I want my car. I'm not doing any more business with you."

I couldn't figure what was eating him. Maybe he'd been sampling some of his own junk. Maybe he had suspicions I wasn't what I was supposed to be. Whatever the reason, I couldn't afford to go on the defensive.

"Hey," I said. "You come up with the bread and I give you back your car. Don't play any games with me."

Things got pretty active after that.

"I'll cut your damned heart out," he yelled, and came at me with a knife.

It was a large knife with a silver handle and a blade big enough to carve a forty-pound turkey. He held it low, which showed he knew how to use it. I sucked in my stomach as the blade grazed my shirt and reached for the length of steel chain I kept hanging on the doorknob.

"Get away, Serra." I warned him once. Then I swung the chain.

The chain whipped out and coiled around the top of his shaven head. It was the closest thing to a halo that Carlos Serra would ever wear. The knife popped up in the air and his glasses went flying. I swung again and missed, catching him on the shoulder.

He staggered toward the door, his head bleeding, and I let him go. He made it out of the building and collapsed on the sidewalk, but not before telling the manager downstairs that I had tried to kill him. At least, that's the story I got when the telephone rang a few minues later.

"We've called an ambulance," the manager said. "He says you tried to kill him and he's going to the police."

I put the phone down. There wasn't anything to do but wait. I needed cop trouble like a broken leg, but that was what I was going to get . . . unless I had Carlos Serra pegged wrong.

They arrived within an hour—three plainclothesmen from homicide. "Vincent Vento?" one of them asked. I nodded.

"We have a warrant for your arrest," he said, and pushed his way through the door.

The other two followed and began looking around the apartment. One of them opened a closet door and began snooping around inside.

"Does the warrant say you can look in my closet?"

"What are you, a wise guy?"

"No," I answered. "I just wanted to know."

I was playing the hard guy they expected. As far as they were concerned, I was a blacklisted croupier who had to leave Vegas for reasons unknown. The regular police in San Juan hadn't been filled in on who I was or what I was doing there.

They acted like cops act most everywhere. They slapped the cuffs on me, not too gently, and hauled me off to a waiting prowl car. On the way downtown, I sat in the back between two of them and got a series of elbow jabs that jarred my teeth. I took it. What else?

At headquarters I was told by the detective lieutenant that I was being booked on charges of assault with intent to commit murder.

"We don't know much about you, except that you've been passing post office money orders," he said. "We have places to put people like you."

He was right about the money orders. Except for walking-around money, I kept my funds in post office money orders and hinted to guys I dealt with that they were forgeries picked up at a discount. It helped my image with the criminal element.

They hadn't booked me yet so I said to the lieutenant, "Do I have the right to call an attorney?"

He shoved the phone at me. "It won't do you any good but go ahead."

Ortiz Reyes had given me his private number with instructions to call him if I was in trouble. I dialed the number and gave the prearranged signal when a woman answered.

"This is Vincent Vento. Tell the attorney that I'm at the jail and need his help."

"Si, Señor Vento," the voice said.

They rousted me around for another ten minutes until a call came through for the lieutenant. He looked puzzled when he hung up.

"The chief says you're a two-bit hood, that I'm supposed to let you go. But don't let me see you back this way. Not ever."

The lieutenant also gave me a backhand across the mouth.

"Mucho gracias," I said, trying to grin, and got out fast.

On the cab ride back to my apartment I was in no mood to appreciate the old-world charm of San Juan, or the neat rows of palms out by the big hotels, or any of the other brochure items that make it a tourist haven. I was too busy taking inventory.

Where had I gone wrong? Who besides Carlos Serra wanted to stick a knife into Vincent M. Vento? Had I blown my cover?

At the Capital Hotel Apartments I reclaimed a package I had stowed in the hotel safe. It contained a Colt Cobra .38 and several clips of ammunition. Upstairs, I loaded it and checked the action. I put in a call for Ortiz Reyes. The message I left said to meet me at 5:30, same place. Then I buckled on the length of chain, covered it with a sash and set out on a tour of familiar bars.

The bartender at the Farandula gave a friendly nod and took my order. No sweat there, I decided. Vincent Vento was still in good standing. I moved on to El Chico and the Dona Lola.

At two of the three places I was approached by pushers. "Sure, sure," I said to them. "I'll see ya tomorrow."

But the atmosphere was different at the Ali Baba Club. I knew it the minute I walked in the door. It's something you sense. The bartender was the tip-off. His eyes avoided me. He seemed uneasy taking my order.

I dropped my money clip on the floor and used it as an excuse to give the place a closer look. At a table in the rear, sitting with two men, was Jorge Velez, a pock-faced hood that I had negotiated with for an ounce of heroin.

His companions were two Cubans. One was Rigoberto Rodriguez Rosal, also called Blanco, and Hector Jaca Flores, who went by the name of Yaya. Yaya came over to me at the bar and there was no friendly greeting.

"Blanco want to talk to you."

I nodded and followed Yaya to the table where the others were sitting. Their coats were unbuttoned and I could see they were wearing guns in their belts. I brushed my coat pocket to reassure myself mine was there.

"You want to talk to me?"

"Yes," Blanco said, getting up from the table. "Out back."

I followed them through the kitchen and into the alley. It looked like alleys behind bars everywhere, piles of trash, broken bottles, a mongrel dog foraging in a garbage can.

Blanco turned to me and his face was tight.

"We heard you was with Angel Gonzalez yesterday before he got picked up."

"Yeah, so what?"

"So we're going to kill you, Vento. We think you're a cop."

I was ready for them. Before they could reach for their guns I had my hand out of my side pocket. It held a .38 Cobra and they were looking down the muzzle.

I took their guns away and tossed them over a fence. Then I said to them, politely, "Now what's this all about?"

"You've been making a lot of buys around here," Jorge Velez said. "And you was with Gonzalez before the cops got him. You knew about Gonzalez and the stamp collection."

Sure, I knew about Angel Gonzalez. He was one of about nineteen small-time hoods that I had bought narcotics from while trying to work up to the big guys.

After copping a sample of cocaine from him, and turning the evidence to Ortiz Reyes, I'd been propositioned by Gonzalez about buying a collection of rare postage stamps he'd stolen. The loot was worth $100,000, he said, and I could have it for $1,500. He let me take eight of the stamps as samples.

Hell, I didn't know anything about stamps, it wasn't in my line. So I turned them over to Ortiz Reyes, who gave them to the San Juan police. And because the owner of the stamps was a big man in Puerto Rico the cops jumped the gun and made the arrest. And this left me standing in an alley holding a gun on three hoods who thought I had a part in it.

The question: what to do.

Should I run a bluff, or get the hell out of Puerto Rico and blow the assignment. I had about three seconds to make up my mind.

I decided to run a bluff.

"Hey," I said, "what's the matter with you bastards? You crazy or something? You have a bad dream last night? There's a hundred guys in town who could have fingered Gonzalez. How come you spell it Vince Vento?"

"But Vince—"

It was Blanco talking. His eyes were very much on the business end of my .38. The other two were beginning to sweat.

"Don't Vince me, you bastard. I come in here straight, shopping around, and you got the word out that I'm a stool. How long do you think I would last?"

"Just checking, Vince," said Blanco.

"Well, check this," I said, moving the gun a little closer to the end of his nose. From that distance, I knew that the muzzle looked like the entrance to the Holland Tunnel. I'd seen a few myself from that angle.

"Take a good look," I said. "And what's all this about killing me?"

Blanco Rodriguez Rosal didn't look very happy.

"I'm sorry, Vince," he said. "We just wanted to make sure."

I let the muzzle travel from nose to nose.

"You sure now?"

"We're sure," Blanco said, and the others nodded.

"OK," I said, like a man only half convinced. I put down the gun and told them to get back inside. Watching them disappear into the Ali Baba I wondered if I had done the right thing. Now I had four guys on the loose, very unstable and unfriendly guys. They would remember me. Well, I'd find out soon enough. I left by the alley and headed for the San Jeronimo Hilton.

At 5:30 I was waiting in the steam room for Ortiz Reyes. There were several other customers in the place, baking out the booze from the night before, and I found myself envying them their problem. Ortiz Reyes arrived, and we ignored each other until we were alone.

"We got problems," I said, trying to make it quick and to the point. I briefed him on what had happened earlier at my apartment and in the alley, and he was all for running in the whole bunch then and there.

"The situation has become very dangerous," he said. "If they should kill you, we will have nobody to testify in court when these cases come to trial."

I was touched by his solicitude about my safety. Sitting there in the 180° heat, watching beads of sweat form on my chest and dribble down toward the towel at my waist, I also knew that what he said made sense. Take what we could and get out. But I found myself shaking my head.

"No, lieutenant," I said. "All we'd be getting is trash. I didn't come to Puerto Rico to bust nickel-and-dime peddlers. I came here to get Caesar Vega and Luis Valdez. They're mine. If I have to change tactics, I'm ready to do that. But I'm going to need your help. I want the San Juan police to learn that Vincent Vento has a criminal record back in the States," I said. "I want this information passed on to the government examining board. This will get me fired from my croupier's job. I want to be harassed in public by the police. I want to be frisked and slapped around. I want to be treated like a garden variety hood that nobody wants and nobody protects. You think you can arrange it?"

"No problem," he said, "but is all this necessary?"

"It's necessary. It's also better than being found dead in an alley."

I said good-by to Ortiz Reyes and reported to the casino for what would be my last night of work as a croupier. The thought of abandoning my new trade, after all those hours of practice, made me sort of sad.

The next night Pagan called me into his office, closed the door and tossed a dossier on the desk. It was a rap-sheet showing that I'd been involved in swindles from Chicago to Vegas, with one assault charge in Wichita. He'd gotten it that day from the police.

"*Hasta la vista,* my friend," he said with a shrug. "There is nothing I can do."

I collected my back pay and turned in my colored jackets. The following afternoon, according to plan, I got some lumps from two plainclothes detectives outside the Farandula Club. They worked me over pretty good. They grabbed me on the sidewalk as I approached the club, pinned me up against the wall for a frisk and checked my I.D.

"We don't want your kind on this island, Vento," one of them said, giving me a backhand across the mouth. His partner let go with one to the gut, and I didn't have to fake it.

I went down on the bricks, gasping for breath. A shoe caught me on the bridge of the nose and I could feel the blood flow. Another kick got the side of my face. They gave me some advice about going back where I came from and left me lying there.

The underworld grapevine in any large city is a mysteriously efficient communications system, and I counted on the San Juan division being up to par. Anyone who saw the beating, or took a good look at my face, would tell three people and each of them in turn would tell three people and each of them in turn would tell three more. There was no better place for the word to start spreading than the Farandula Club.

I went inside, holding a handkerchief to my face, and put myself on display. The bartender reached for a bottle of Añejo and poured me a shot, compliments of the house. He seemed to know what had happened and mumbled something in Spanish about dirty pig bastards.

A local hooker named Carmelita, spit-curls and eyelashes in

place for the evening's work, left a customer and slid onto a stool beside me. She asked for some ice and a towel and applied a pack to my swollen face. Her touch was almost tender.

Through my unclosed eye I saw that Luis Valdez and Caesar Vega were among those present, seated at a table in the rear. After all, they owned the joint. I knew who they were, although they were never around in the early hours of the morning when I stopped off for my after-work drink.

Valdez got up and walked casually in my direction. He was slim, about forty, black unruly hair that needed cutting, sloppy in his dress but obviously pretty sharp in his thinking.

"You've had an accident, señor?" he said softly in Spanish as he approached.

"They beat hell out of me," I answered in English.

He paused a moment and then continued out the door.

These were the first words I had exchanged with either of the two men I had come to Puerto Rico to nail. I hoped that it would lead to more conversation. I could stand a few ups after all the downs I'd had on this assignment.

The break came two days later.

I was at a table in the Farandula, a mouse still showing under my right eye, when I got the message that Valdez would like to see me. I nodded and finished my drink. No use hurrying after all this waiting.

"Sit down, Señor Vento," he said, and after ordering me a drink got right to the point. "I hear that you've had trouble with Carlos Serra."

"He put the cops on me," I said, and left it there.

Valdez stared at me for a moment, then lowered his eyes and continued talking. "You come here as a croupier in a gambling casino. You have other dealings with people here in San Juan. You pass money orders that are supposed to be hot. What is your business, Mr. Vento?"

"My business is anything that makes a dollar—or a peso," I told him. Then I explained I was getting ready to set up a big-scale operation in Miami, that I needed a steady supply of top-grade stuff, and that I wanted a connection with reliable people who could keep their mouths shut.

"Who do you know in Miami?"

I looked at him. "I don't ask you who you know in San Juan. I don't ask you what your sources are. I don't ask damnfool questions. Let's keep it even."

"We've been suspicious of you, Señor Vento."

"Yeah," I said. "That's a good idea. I'm suspicious of everybody. That's why I'm still walking around."

He changed the subject, asked what kind of merchandise I wanted and how much of it. I gave him the big customer routine.

"I can always use cocaine but what I'm after is five kilos of H for starters. I'll need a lot more after that and I'll need it steady. But I'm not making any deals until I get a sample. I've laid out money around here and the stuff they bring me stinks."

"Ours is top grade," Valdez said.

"At what price?"

"Twenty thousand a kilo."

I turned away in disgust. "If you want to rob me put a gun in my stomach. But don't give me that kind of jazz."

We bargained for the next few minutes and finally agreed on an ounce for $750. Valdez told me to meet him at his home the next day. The address was 2167 Loiza Street in the Santurce section. By the time I left we were all pretty friendly.

I got to the house at 11 A.M. the next day, hoping that Caesar Vega would be there too. He was. I wanted to get them both on the same transaction. One ounce of cocaine was enough to incriminate both of them, no matter which one handed me the stuff, as long as I had conversation with both parties.

Valdez introduced me to Vega, who was chunkier than his sidekick and much better-dressed. He had a small mustache and dark glasses. Vega produced a plastic bag containing the sample and I peeled off seven hundreds and one fifty. I told them that this was the beginning of a big operation. Actually, it was the end of one.

Back at the steam room at the San Jeronimo, I gave Ortiz Reyes the sample I'd gotten from Valdez and Vega. He said he would have them in jail before the sun went down, along with Carlos Serra and all the others I'd collected evidence against.

As the undercover man on the case, my work was finished. I wasn't involved in the sweep that flushed out fourteen dope peddlers. They got Carlos Serra at the intersection of Del Carmen and Condado Streets. They got Blanco Rodriguez Rosal at the Dona Lola Restaurant. But when the sweep was over Vega and Valdez were missing.

I decided to see what I could do about finding them—still my prime targets. After all, as far as I knew, nobody had pegged me. My cover was still intact.

For the next two days I poked around my old haunts, putting out some feelers about Vega and Valdez. Nobody volunteered any information. The lid was on and I began to feel the chill.

The third night when I got back to my apartment I found it turned upside down. Everything had been searched but my refrigerator safe. Nobody had to write me a letter. They had to be on to me.

I didn't want to risk putting a call through the hotel switchboard. I left the hotel and headed for a phone in an all-night restaurant a few blocks away. It was very late and very dark.

Almost immediately I realized I wasn't alone. I stopped walking and the footsteps behind me stopped. Turning quickly, I spotted shadows in the darkness behind me. There were four of them, as near as I could make out, and it was no dream this time.

If one guy follows you, it could be a tail. If it's two, there's still room for doubt. But when four people are follwing you at 3:30 in the morning, on a dark and deserted street in San Juan. . . .

I began to look for a place to defend myself. I wanted a storefront that was boarded up, or equipped with a metal grill, so they couldn't put me through a plate-glass window. Backed up against this, at least nobody could take me from the rear. It shortened the odds a little.

I found the right place and uncoupled the chain from around my waist. Reaching down inside my pants I took my gun from inside an elastic thigh support. They came at me out of the darkness— just like I remembered it in my dream, two from one side of the street and two from the other.

The smallest of them was also the fastest. He got to me first, a knife in his hand. I lashed out at his arm with the chain and heard him yell. The next guy in had a gun.

It was too dark for accuracy, except at point-blank range. And besides, I had my gun in my left hand. We fired almost simultaneously. I was aiming low, at his belly, and must have got him because he sat down on the pavement holding himself. By now the other two were within range and I was swinging the chain.

The chain hit the side of one of their heads. He was dead before he crumpled. The second one swung a blackjack, numbing one shoulder. He hit me again as I turned on the little guy who had worked around behind me.

A knife cut me from wrist to elbow. The blackjack splintered a board at my head and then caught me solid across the forehead. I went down, roaring in my ears, and somebody dug a heel into my face.

I was blacking out, and I knew it, and I was being beaten to death, and I knew that too. I felt ribs and vertebra go as the blackjack worked on me. It was oddly painless and all of it seemed in slow motion.

Then I heard a siren. The two men working me over ran. They were carrying one of the others. I lay there looking into the sightless eyes of the dead man on the sidewalk. I knew I had to get away too; there would be too many questions.

Even then—habit I guess—I was worried about blowing my cover. I tried to get up and couldn't. As the siren came closer, I crawled into an alley, pulled myself up, and moved along by leaning on the wall. Somehow I made it to an all-night cab stand.

The driver looked at me. "Hit-run," I said. "A car hit me . . ."

He helped me into the cab and told me I should go to a hospital.

"First get me to a telephone."

I gave him Ortiz Reyes' private number and asked him to make the call. "Say Vincent Vento is in trouble, to come right away." The next thing I remembered was waking up in San Juan Hospital with a plainclothes policeman on guard in my room.

Well, at least I wasn't dead, but I wasn't far from it. And Ortiz Reyes was taking no chances of anybody coming back to finish the job. I had round-the-clock protection from then until I was taken to the airport in a wheelchair and put on a plane for Miami.

Luis Valdez and Caesar Vega had gotten out of the dragnet, he said, and had probably made their way back to Cuba. There was no doubt in his mind that they had put out a contract on me. The man found dead on the sidewalk was known to be a strong-arm boy for Jesus Rolon, alias the Sultan. So was the one I had shot in the stomach. He died later in the same hospital where I was taken.

Back in Miami, where I spent four months in South Miami Hospital, I had plenty of time to think how I would handle the case again—if I ever handled any case again.

They found that I had four broken ribs and that three discs in my lower lumbar were smashed. I was paralyzed in the left leg and part of the right. I couldn't open the fingers of my right hand. I would pick up a glass and it would fall out of my hand. I was practically out of my mind, being so helpless.

They wanted to operate but I said no. I wanted to try to work this out in my own way. After I got out of the hospital I spent part of every day in a swimming pool, sitting in an inner tube with weights on my legs. The doctor said swimming was good therapy.

Two years later I was still on a cane. Then gradually I could walk without one. The day would come soon when I would be pronounced healthy enough to assume routine jobs for the Bureau, and I had my decision ready.

On June 10, 1966, after thirteen years of being somebody else, I turned in my badge and got a new identity. I became Chief Sal Vizzini of the South Miami Police Department.

In my spare time, I train racing pigeons. In fact, I have one of the better lofts in southern Florida.

The house odds on living to a ripe old age are better training pigeons than being one.

Epilogue

THIS WAS not the end for Sal Vizzini. Far from it.

As this is written, he lives in South Miami, Florida, with his wife Marginelle and their son Samuel, a huge police dog named Champ and an aging friend from his operational days abroad, a Turkish retriever named Pierre which Vizzini trained in Istanbul to sniff out opium and marijuana.

But, as he says, the "retirement" couldn't stick, and contrary to what he says he really finds little leisure time for such hobbies as falconry, raising racing pigeons, fishing and scuba diving. In January of 1967 he discarded his cane and leg brace after 23 months of incapacitation. Two months later, when "the inactivity was driving me crazy," the City of South Miami learned of his availability and appointed him police adviser to reorganize the city's police department and write its new rules and regulations. In May of 1967 he was named acting chief of the department.

The legend of Sal Vizzini is widely known in police circles, and in August of 1967 law enforcement specialists recommended him to a large southern city seeking a new police chief. Instead, he accepted the City of South Miami's counteroffer to become their permanent Chief of Police.

At the end of 1967 Vizzini was drafted by then Florida Governor Claude Kirk to use his undercover talents to reinfiltrate the Mafia and expose its Florida connections. His revelations, after three trips to old stamping grounds in Italy, earned him the Governor's Medal.

Meanwhile, events have been far from dull in South Miami. Vizzini was shotgunned in the head, chest and left leg while personally apprehending an armed burglar. He successfully confronted political difficulties which arose because he stood behind his men in the performance of their duties. He was very much on the scene —or rather behind the scene—during the national political conventions of 1972 in Miami.

His abilities as a police administrator with a solid police background make him much sought after by other cities for aid in the reorganizaton of their departments and the training of personnel. The nationally recognized effectiveness of his own department permits such absences when they are considered vital.

Meanwhile, on occasion, Sal Vizzini tends to drop from sight. Usually after he reappears there is a news story about a heroin seizure in Marseilles, a counterfeit ring broken up in Rome or an opium haul in Turkey.

Coincidence? The old pro keeping his hand in? Draw your own conclusions.

In the line of duty the "infiltrator" was never one to put himself in the window.

—Oscar Fraley
—Marshall Smith